OPERATION FAMILY SECRETS

HOW A MOBSTER'S SON AND THE FBI BROUGHT DOWN CHICAGO'S MURDEROUS CRIME FAMILY

FRANK CALABRESE, JR.

WITH KEITH & KENT ZIMMERMAN AND PAUL POMPIAN

BROADWAY PAPERBACKS NEW YORK

Published in the United States by Broadway Paperbacks,
an imprint of the Crown Publishing Group,
a division of Random House, Inc., New York.
www.crownpublishing.com

Originally published in hardcover in the United States
by Broadway Books, an imprint of the Crown Publishing
Group, a division of Random House, Inc., New York, in 2011.

Library of Congress Cataloging-in-Publication Data
Operation family secrets : how a mobster's son and the FBI
brought down Chicago's murderous crime family /
Frank Calabrese, Jr. . . . [et al.]—1st ed.
p. cm.
1. Calabrese, Frank, 1937– 2. Gangsters—Illinois—
Chicago—Biography. 3. Murderers—United States—
Biography. I. Calabrese, Frank, Jr. II. Title.
HV6248.C126O64 2011
364.1092—dc22
[B] 2010028174

ISBN 978-0-307-71773-3
eISBN 978-0-307-71774-0

Printed in the United States of America

Cover design by Howard Grossman
Cover photograph courtesy of Frank Calabrese, Jr.

CONTENTS

CAST OF CHARACTERS

For easy reference, here are the major and minor characters who are mentioned in the book and figure into my story. It is by no means meant to be a complete list of family, Outfit members, crews, and associates.

Calabrese Family

Frank Calabrese, Sr.—*My father*
Nick W. Calabrese—*My uncle*
James and Sophie Calabrese—*My grandparents on my father's side*
Marie, James Jr., Christine, Joe, and Rosemary—*My aunts and uncles on my father's side*
Dolores Hanley Calabrese—*My mother*
Edward Hanley—*My uncle on my mother's side*
Kurt Calabrese—*My middle brother*
Nicky S. Calabrese—*My youngest brother*
Lisa Swan—*My ex-wife*
Kelly Calabrese—*My daughter*
Anthony Calabrese—*My son*
Angela Lascola—*Kurt's wife, granddaughter of Angelo "The Hook" LaPietra*
Diane Cimino—*My father's second wife*
Joy Calabrese—*Uncle Nick's first wife*
Michelle Calabrese—*My first cousin and Uncle Nick's oldest daughter*
Noreen Tenuta Calabrese—*Uncle Nick's current wife*
Franco Calabrese—*Noreen and Nick's son*
Christina Calabrese—*Noreen and Nick's oldest child*
Danny Alberga—*Longtime friend and owner and operator of Bella Luna*
Frank Coconate—*Longtime friend of both me and my father*

FBI and Federal Prosecutors

FBI Agent Michael Maseth
FBI Agent Michael Hartnett
FBI Agent John Mallul
FBI Agent Ted McNamara
FBI Agent Chris Mackey
FBI Agent Luigi Mondini
FBI Agent Tracy Balinao
Retired FBI Agent Tom Bourgeois
Retired FBI Agent Zack Shelton
Retired FBI Agent James Wagner
CPD Officer Bob Moon—*Organized Crime Task Force member*
Mitch Mars—*Assistant U.S. Attorney and Chief of the Organized Crime Section, Operation Family Secrets Prosecutor*
John Scully—*Assistant U.S. Attorney, Operation Family Secrets Prosecutor*
T. Markus Funk—*Assistant U.S. Attorney, Operation Family Secrets Prosecutor*
Patrick Fitzgerald—*U.S. Attorney for the Northern District of Illinois*

The Street

OUTFIT BOSSES

Tony "Joe Batters/Big Tuna" Accardo—*Consigliere*
Joey "Doves/Joe O'Brien" Aiuppa—*Boss*
Jackie "The Lackey" Cerrone—*Underboss*

CHINATOWN/26TH STREET CREW

Angelo "The Hook" LaPietra—*Capo and my father's mentor*
James "Brother Jimmy" LaPietra—*Angelo's brother*
John "Johnny Apes" Monteleone
James "Poker/Tires" DiForti

Joseph "Shorty" LaMantia
John "Big Stoop" Fecarotta
Frank "Toots" Caruso
Frank "Frankie C" Calabrese, Sr.—*My father*

THE CALABRESE CREW

Nick "Gus" Calabrese—*My uncle*
Ronnie "Little Guy" Jarrett—*My father's first lieutenant*
Mike Ricci—*Operation Family Secrets co-defendant*
Anthony "Twan" Doyle—*Operation Family Secrets co-defendant*
Nicholas "Nick" Ferriola—*Son of Joe Ferriola*
Larry Stubitsch—*My father's original partner*
Frank "Gumba" Saladino
Frank "Ciccio" Furio
Michael "Nef" Talarico
Phil "Philly Bean" Tolomeo
Phil "Pete" Fiore
Ralph "Curly" Peluso
Louis Bombacino

CICERO/BERWYN CREW

Sam "Wings" Carlisi—*Capo*
Joe "Joe Nagall" Ferriola
Ernest "Rocky" Infelise
William "Butch" Petrocelli
Harry Aleman
Tony "Tony Bors" Borsellino
James "Little Jimmy/Jimmy Light" Marcello—*Operation Family Secrets co-defendant*
Anthony "Tony the Hatch/The Hatchet" Chiaramonti
Salvatore "Solly D" DeLaurentis
Gerald "Gerry" Scarpelli
Michael "Mickey" Marcello—*Jimmy Marcello's stepbrother*
James "Jimmy I" Inendino
Louie Marino

GRAND AVENUE CREW

Joe "The Clown/Lumpy" Lombardo—*Capo and Operation Family Secrets co-defendant*
Anthony "Tony/The Ant" Spilotro
Michael Spilotro—*Tony's brother*
Frank "The German" Schweihs—*Operation Family Secrets co-defendant*
Paul "The Indian" Schiro—*Operation Family Secrets co-defendant*
Joseph "Joey" Hansen

CROWN HEIGHTS CREW

Dominick "Tootsie" Palermo
Nicky Guzzino

CHICAGO HEIGHTS CREW

Al Pilotto—*Capo*
Al "Little Caesar" Tocco
James "Jimmy the Bomber" Catuara

ELMWOOD/MELROSE PARK CREW

John "No Nose" DiFronzo—*Capo*
Joe "The Builder/Joey A" Andriacchi
Louie "The Mooch" Eboli

OPERATION FAMILY SECRETS

1.

FAMILY SECRETS

I set myself up in the corner of the prison library at the Federal Correctional Institution in Milan, Michigan, and banged out the letter to FBI Special Agent Thomas Bourgeois on a cranky old Smith-Corona manual typewriter. My mobster father, Frank Calabrese, Sr.—who was serving time with me in FCI Milan—had taught me to be decisive. So when I typed the letter, my mind was made up.

I didn't touch the paper directly. I used my winter gloves to handle the sheet and held the envelope with a Kleenex so as not to leave any fingerprints. The moment I mailed the letter on July 27, 1998, I knew I had crossed the line. Cooperating with the FBI meant not only that I would give up my father, but that I would have to implicate my uncle Nick for the murder of a Chicago Outfit mobster named John "Big Stoop" Fecarotta. Giving up my uncle was the hardest part.

When I reread the letter one last time, I asked myself, What kind of son puts his father away for life? The Federal Bureau of Prisons had dealt me a cruel blow by sticking me in the same prison as my dad. It had become increasingly clear that his vow to "step away" from the Outfit after we both served our time was an empty promise.

"I feel I have to help you keep this sick man locked up forever," I wrote in my letter.

Due to legal and safety concerns, it was five months before Agent Thomas Bourgeois arranged a visit to meet with me at FCI Milan. He came alone in the early winter of 1998. In 1997 the FBI and Chicago federal prosecutors had convicted the Calabrese crew, netting my father, Uncle Nick, my younger brother Kurt, and me on juice loans. Bourgeois seemed confused and wanted to know what I wanted.

I'm sure Bourgeois also wondered the same thing I had: What kind of son wants to put his father away for life? Maybe he thought I was lying. Perhaps I had gotten into an argument and, like most cons, was looking to get my sentence reduced. Yet in our ensuing conversation, I told Tom that I wasn't asking for much in return. I just didn't want to lose any of my time served, and I wanted a transfer out of FCI Milan once my mission was accomplished.

By imprisoning us on racketeering charges, the Feds thought that they had broken up the notorious Calabrese South Side crew. In reality they had barely scratched the surface. I alerted Bourgeois that I was not looking to break up the mob. I had one purpose: to help the FBI keep my father locked up forever so that he could get the psychological help he needed. The FBI didn't know the half of his issues or his other crimes.

When asked by Bourgeois if I would wear a wire out on the prison yard, I promptly replied no. I would work with the FBI, but I would only give them intelligence, useful information they could use, and with the understanding that nobody would know I was cooperating, and I would not testify in open court. Outfit guys like my dad called that "dry beefing." Frank Calabrese, Sr., was one of the Outfit's most cunning criminals and had been a successful crew chief and solid earner for the Chicago mob for thirty years. He could smell an FBI informant a mile away. If he hadn't talked about his criminal life in the past, why would he do so now?

I searched my soul to make sure I wasn't doing this out of spite or because Dad had reneged on taking care of me and Kurt financially in exchange for doing time. This *couldn't* be about money!

After Agent Bourgeois's first interview with me at Milan, he reported back to Mitch Mars, an Assistant U.S. Attorney and Chief of the Chicago Organized Crime Section. Mars wanted to know if there was enough to present the case to a grand jury and gather a bigger, more inclusive case against "the Outfit," Chicago's multitentacled organized crime syndicate, which dated back to the days of "Big Jim" Colosimo and Al Capone.

As I lay in my cell bunk, I thought about my refusal to wear a wire. Suppose I gave the Feds information, but my father got lucky and walked? I'd be screwed, Uncle Nick would be stuck on death row, and after my dad's sentence ran out he would bounce right back out on the streets to continue his juice loan business and murderous ways.

What if what I was doing was wrong? How could I live with myself? I loved my dad dearly, and I love him to this day. But I was repulsed by the violence and his controlling ways. I had to decide between doing nothing and cooperating with the Feds, two choices I hated.

I knew that if I did nothing, my father and I would have to

erences out on the street. One of us would end up other would rot in prison. I would be incriminat- I didn't want an immunity deal. If I needed to ime to keep my dad locked up forever, so be it. After I sent the letter, I was determined to finish what I started. I contacted Agent Bourgeois one more time to tell him I had changed my mind. I would wear the wire after all. All the deception my father had taught me I was now going to use on *him*.

My father's own words would become his worst enemy.

2.

THE PATCH, AND GRAND AND OGDEN

My father, Frank Calabrese, Sr., the boss of the Calabrese (pronounced Cala-BREESE) family and street crew, was born on the West Side of Chicago in a working-class Italian area known as "the Patch." This legendary neighborhood is bordered by Grand, Western, and Chicago avenues and the Kennedy Expressway. The Patch at Grand Avenue and Ogden was home to other famous Outfit gangster bosses like Tony "Joe Batters" Accardo and

' Lombardo. Tony and Michael Spilotro's parents, ntoinette, ran Patsy's Restaurant in the Patch, es such as Salvatore "Sam" Giancana, Jackie Cerone, Gus "Slim" Alex, and Frank "the Enforcer" often dined.

Another Italian neighborhood, Little Italy, ran along Taylor Street from Halsted Street to Ashland Avenue. Cicero, Melrose Park, and Elmwood Park became primary suburban fiefdoms of the Chicago Outfit. Taylor Street was in the First Ward, headed by former Alderman John D'Arco; his successor, Fred Roti; and First Ward "secretary" Pasquale "Pat" Marcy. Since the thirties, the First Ward had controlled a large bloc of city jobs and had a stranglehold on the Department of Streets and Sanitation.

Frank Calabrese, Sr., was born March 17, 1937, to James and Sophie Calabrese in the urban pocket of Grand and Ogden. Their family lineage was Barese and Sicilian, and both my grandfather's and my grandmother's parents immigrated to Chicago directly from the old country. James's family originally settled in the Taylor Street area (Little Italy), while Sophie barely left Grand and Ogden (the Patch).

Frank was the oldest of seven brothers and sisters. From oldest to youngest, his siblings were Marie, Nick, James junior (now deceased), Christine, Joe, and Roseanne. Although the family was raised Catholic, the Calabreses were not active in the church. With so many children, Grandma Sophie ran the family like a drill sergeant. If the kids didn't come home at the appointed time, they often slept in a doghouse outside, even in the dead of winter. For poor working-class Italians, money was tight throughout the 1940s and 1950s. My dad claimed the family was so impoverished they would eat "poor man's oatmeal," or polenta, for dinner.

At the age of five my father was stricken with scarlet fever and sent to Children's Memorial Hospital. Despite his youth, through a combination of intimidation and charisma, he took over the entire children's ward and became the de facto leader. Because of his illness, he started Otis Elementary School late. Big and stocky for his age, he ruled the playground. He was known to detest bullies and stand up for the underdog. As he got older, he became fast with his hands and would fight at the slightest provocation. After he was kicked out of Otis Elementary, he hit the mean streets of Grand and Ogden.

At age thirteen, he ran a newspaper stand with his younger brother Nick on the busy corner of Grand and State. Although my grandparents worked hard, the Calabrese sons wore hand-me-downs, stuffing cardboard into their shoes once the soles of their feet felt the pavement. By age fifteen, he generated enough cash from his newsstand so that his parents relied on him to help support the entire Calabrese brood. No matter how slim their coffers got, Grandma and Grandpa could look to their eldest son to help pull the family through.

During the Christmas season of 1949, my grandparents found they had no money to buy holiday food or gifts. Still a youngster, Frank had set aside one hundred dollars from his thriving newspaper stand. He handed it over to his mother and father to spend on food and gifts for his brothers and sisters, but with one stipulation: they buy him a fishing pole. Come Christmas Day, there was no fishing pole. The slight bothered him deeply, and he hasn't forgotten the incident, often retelling the story to me and my brothers.

To this day, my dad is self-conscious about his lack of formal education and has difficulty writing a simple letter. Though he didn't believe in running with organized street gangs, he emerged as a tough guy. By age sixteen, he began accumulating arrests for thievery and assault. He was a hothead, unable to control his temper. Before embracing the Outfit, he built a reputation around Grand and Ogden for being his own man.

In 1953, Grandpa Calabrese decided that he could no longer control his sixteen-year-old son's unruly behavior, so he brought him down to the recruiting center and signed him up for a hitch in the United States Army. Grandpa lied, claiming that his son was of age and eligible to serve. Against my dad's wishes, he was sent off to basic training.

He didn't like the Army and went AWOL almost as soon as he was inducted. While the military police tried to locate him, he returned to the Patch and secretly lived inside the rooftop pigeon coop of his parents' four-flat apartment building. Nobody found him for weeks, but once he was sent back to the Army, he got into a fight with one of his commanders in the mess hall and was locked up in the stockade. He went AWOL a second time. The authorities chased him through the fields of rural Illinois until a posse of farmers with bloodhounds tracked him down. After he was apprehended, the state police charged him with stealing a car. Rather than return to the military, he did his first stretch in federal prison, in Ashland in eastern Kentucky. Stocky and tough, he took up weight lifting in prison. Once he was released, he spent a short time in the ring as a semipro boxer and won a few weight-lifting trophies.

After serving his sentence, my dad worked at a series of grueling manual labor jobs. He and my grandpa shoveled coal out of the back of a truck and hoisted and unloaded blocks of ice into nearby boxcars for the Jefferson Ice Company. He was soon promoted to driving a truck for Jefferson Ice, which paid decent money. Yet his violent side simmered. He and a co-worker, a large black man, got into arguments on the job. The two men didn't like each other. He forged a phony truce with the guy, and after a night of drinking the man was never seen or heard from again. My dad didn't admit that he killed the guy, though he told me once that "after that night, nobody seen the guy again."

By the mid-1950s, Frank Calabrese, Sr., now in his late teens, was back roaming the streets, pulling off a string of gas station stickups, burglaries, and auto thefts. He decided to get into the "wedding business." He would scout out ceremonies and rob the guests as they left. At other times, he and a partner would stick up partygoers, lining everybody up and relieving them of their wallets, watches, and other valuables. Every Calabrese street heist was well planned, and he was careful to strike neighborhoods outside the Patch. As a calculating burglar, his number one rule was simple: Never steal from any of the Italian neighborhoods—especially where the bosses live.

In between robbing weddings and pulling stickups, at twenty-four he married my mother, Dolores Hanley, an Irish American girl. In 1960, with me on the way, Dad moved his budding family into a small two-bedroom apartment on Grand and Menard Avenues on Chicago's West Side. After my dad lost his day job driving a dairy truck, my grandpa on my mother's side came to the couple's rescue. He had ties to the notorious O'Donnell gang inside the Irish mob. Through his Irish connection at city hall, he got my dad a job. My dad also moonlighted with his new brother-in-law Edward Hanley at Hanley's, a bar in Chicago located on the corner of Laramie and Madison and owned by his father-in-law. At the time, Uncle Ed was an up-and-coming union officer. He later became one of the most powerful union bosses in the country as president of HEREUI (Hotel Employees and Restaurant Employees Union International) with 350,000 members.

My dad scored his first "ghost payroll" job with the city of Chicago as a member of Local 150 of the Heavy Equipment Operators. He reported to work as an "operating engineer" for the Department of Sewers. He would arrive at work in dress pants and a shirt to pick up his paycheck. As a "no-show," he'd cash it and dutifully kick back a share to the union rep that got him the job.

Leaving the apartment on Grand and Menard, he moved my mother and me farther west to his recently deceased grandmother's house on West Grand near Natchez Avenue, where his grandfather converted the unfinished basement into a den and the attic into two additional bedrooms. Throughout the early 1960s, my mother and father shared the house and the converted space with my grandparents and the rest of the Calabrese siblings.

Between 1961 and 1964, my dad worked as a thief and burglar. After he accumulated more than ten thousand dollars, he invested it around Chinatown and the 26th Street area by providing juice loans to desperate customers who were charged usurious interest rates. By catering to customers who couldn't secure credit with their local banks and needed short-term money, no questions asked, he soon had a thriving business. My father's ready-made customer base included the neighborhood gamblers, many of whom were in over their head and desperate.

As an independent loan shark, the Calabrese juice loan business increased rapidly in the 26th Street Chinatown area. This was before America was flush with easy money from legitimate credit cards and banks. Before MasterCard and Visa, usury was exclusively associated with organized crime. Today the banks have virtually taken over the usury business.

Juice loans work in the following manner: A "lender" like my dad will assign a percentage on top of the principal that a customer borrows. Depending on how much influence a gambler or a businessman has, the borrower might pay anywhere from 2.5 percent to 5 percent per week, also known as points. The juice loan business is a highly profitable enterprise. If somebody borrows $10,000 at three points, he is now on the hook to pay 3 percent, or $300 per week. This is called "the vig" (short for "vigorish" or Yiddish slang for "winnings") or, in my father's line of work, "the juice." In addition, the borrower still owes the principal amount of the original debt. For instance, if the borrower paid Calabrese $300 a week for the next twenty weeks, that would amount to $6,000 in juice. But the client would still owe the $10,000 principal. If the borrower was fortunate enough to pay his loan down by $5,000 (which would include the $300 juice payment for the original $10,000 that week), he would end up owing $5,000 on the principal, and the juice would be reduced to $150 per week.

Juice loans became big business for the Outfit, serving both white- and blue-collar borrowers. A clever and opportunistic street lender found that he could accumulate gradual wealth in the juice loan business, and my father's business flourished unimpeded by the Outfit. But that would soon change.

In early 1964, my dad caught the attention of the Outfit bosses when he was "whistled in" by Angelo "the Hook" LaPietra, an influential and feared underboss who had his own extensive juice loan operation in the Chinatown/Bridgeport area. LaPietra earned his nickname by his manner of murdering his victims. If someone couldn't pay or was a suspected rat, "Ang" would have his crew hang his victim on a meat hook, and torture him with a cattle prod or a blowtorch. When the coroner determined the cause of death, most often it was suffocation from screaming. In the early 1960s LaPietra and Jackie "the Lackey" Cerone were overheard by the FBI bragging how they had hung a three-hundred-fifty-pound enforcer, William "Action" Jackson, from a hook. LaPietra and his assistants tortured him for days, keeping him alive on drugs.

My father, twenty-four years old at the time, was driven to a nightclub near Harlem Avenue by an Outfit soldier, Steve Annerino, to meet with the Hook. LaPietra told him that the only way he could continue his loan operation was under the guiding eye of the Outfit. As an incentive, he was given an additional $60,000 to lend. Later he was given another $80,000.

My dad had teamed up with a gangster hustler named Larry Stubitsch, who was raised in Chinatown and knew the neighborhood well. He and my dad worked long hours together, and soon spread $350,000 across a few dozen borrowers. Stubitsch was ambitious. He wanted to become an Outfit big shot, while Dad recommended that it would be wise to keep a low profile.

Once my father became an Outfit earner, he was under tremendous pressure to produce. Failure was not an option, and those who mishandled Outfit money or did not live up to the bosses' expectations would pay with their lives. He understood the advantages of blending into the streets, choosing to become a solid earner instead of a loud and ambitious wise guy.

Frank James Calabrese, Sr., portrait of a gangster.

He stands five feet nine inches, is stocky, with hazel green eyes and a friendly "warm-up-the-room" smile, and doesn't appear to be a threat. That's what he wants people to think. But the real Frank senior has the strength of an ox and an explosive temper. His dress code is basic and unassuming, favoring neutral colors, never flashy. During the frigid Chicago winters he prefers a baseball cap, sweatshirts, jeans, and ski jackets to more stylish attire. Wanting to "blend in," he rarely frequents Outfit hangouts or get-togethers.

His cheap plastic-framed glasses slide down his nose as he peers at you from over the top of the lenses. Removing his glasses is the cue that a heavy conversation is about to take place and your undivided attention is required. On the streets, Frank senior is concerned about surveillance and speaks in a monotone, a step above a mumble. His speech is clipped neighborhood Italian tough guy: "Dems are nice pants." "I'll kick the shit outta the boat a ewes."

He may show no emotion; instead, he takes off his glasses and looks directly into your eyes. He'll speak in a low firm voice and await your response. Instead of yelling, he tightens up with rage as his right hand shakes and his eyes turn glassy. *Then* he'll start swinging and screaming.

Whenever "Senior" talks business he covers his mouth with his hand and speaks in code. Deceptive and unpredictable, he interjects into conversations an unexpected smile and a laugh to throw off anybody listening. Concerned about wiretaps, Senior's favorite place to talk is in the bathroom with the exhaust fan on and the water running. When it comes to certain incriminating words, he likes to make hand motions instead of actually saying them. He rarely uses words like "money," "guns," "knives," "killing."

Although my family lived in a cramped basement, it was a carefree time. As the eldest son, Frank Calabrese, Jr., I was called Frankie or Junior, to differentiate me from my dad. I recall my earliest memories of living on Grand and Natchez. I had a full family life surrounded by my parents, aunts, uncles, cousins, grandparents, and pets—all living in a single house. It was communal living, not unlike a dormitory, but more fun. I fondly remember spending time sitting under the stairs with my pet boxer, Duchess. The whole family would dress up for home movies. I have vivid memories of my dad performing silly skits for the camera. Every Fourth of July the entire family would crowd outside as Dad would bring home boxes and boxes of fireworks to set off in the street.

Of all of my uncles, my godfather, Uncle James, was the most easygoing. He and his girlfriend would often take me out driving until Uncle Junior, as he was called, died of cancer at twenty-one.

Dying so young, he became a patron saint for the Calabrese family. By 1965, the Calabrese family had its first new house in the suburbs, on the northwest side of Chicago in the village of Norridge, on Lawrence Avenue and Cumberland. We finally had a home of our own.

In September 1966 my father's juice business ran into its first real snag. Stubitsch was a brawler who loved to pick fights, including an ongoing beef he had with former Chicago policeman and Outfit associate Dickie DeAngelo.

Dickie DeAngelo was a friend of the much feared and soon to be boss "Milwaukee Phil" Alderisio. Plying his trade since the Al Capone days working for "Greasy Thumb" Jake Guzik, Alderisio was the consummate hit man, extortionist, juice loan operator, and schemer. Alderisio traveled extensively to Turkey, Greece, Lebanon, and Asia, brokering heroin deals.

Milwaukee Phil (who was actually from Yonkers and acquired the name because of his control of gambling, prostitution, and narcotics in Milwaukee) had contempt for both Stubitsch and my father because of their expanding juice operations. Phil was known for his huge ego and could be seen strolling down Chicago's Rush Street nightclub district like he owned it.

Although my dad tried his best to keep his partner in check, Stubitsch confronted DeAngelo. Once the shooting started, Dad took cover behind a car and watched as his trusted partner was gunned down by Dickie outside the Bistro A-Go-Go, a nightclub on Higgins Road. Stubitsch took two slugs to the midsection and was pronounced dead four hours later at Resurrection Hospital. DeAngelo told homicide investigators a curious story—the shooting occurred when four armed robbers approached him inside the club and the melee continued out on the sidewalk. The investigation stalled after no murder weapon was found, and the charges against Dickie were dropped. Another version of the story is that a fight occurred between my father and DeAngelo over a waitress. Dad put a beating on Dickie. DeAngelo grabbed a gun and started shooting at my father, but Stubitsch was the one who caught the rounds.

After the DeAngelo shooting, Angelo LaPietra took his young protégé aside and ordered him *not* to seek revenge for the murder of his partner. "These things happen, Frank. Sometimes we like it and sometimes we don't." My dad needed to let things go, or, as LaPietra went on to explain, "As long as you're with me, nuthin' is gonna happen."

Since my father was not a "made guy," he needed "a rabbi" or someone with enough clout to fend off any future hits on him. His status as an earner allowed LaPietra to intervene on his behalf.

With his success, Dad sold his house in Norridge in 1970 and made plans to move the entire Calabrese clan to Elmwood Park, a Chicago suburb. Until recently, it was the tradition in Chicago to buy what were known as three-flats, three-story buildings with an apartment on each floor, enabling extended families to live together. Many three-flats had remodeled basements, and their owners could add a half-story apartment upstairs or an additional room on top of the garage. In 1970, the Calabreses moved into their three-flat on 2515 North Seventy-fifth Court in Elmwood Park. Like others on their street, the property had a private alleyway next to the main road, enabling my dad to come and go at all hours. He and my family occupied the middle apartment, while my grandparents lived upstairs. Uncle Nick would later occupy the garden apartment.

The Calabrese three-flat was nicknamed "the Compound," with Dad acting as the family's patriarch. He took on a large responsibility by surrounding himself with family. He organized regular outings and holiday get-togethers, footing the bill. When his youngest brother, Joe Calabrese, married, and his wife gave birth to twins, it was agreed that Uncle Joe would move into the basement of the Compound, the converted two-bedroom garden apartment where my uncle Nick would later live. Instead of paying rent, he would help out around the house. Joe idolized his brother Frank. Uncle Joe worked two jobs, during the day at a bank and during the evening at a gas station across the street. Like my late uncle James, Joe and Nick treated me like a younger brother. The three of us would play football together, with Joe and Nick showing up at my games at school.

One day when my father suspected that Uncle Joe had been seeing one of the girls at the bank, he flew into a rage and left a note on his door ordering him to move out immediately. After reading the note, Joe stormed up the stairs. My brother Kurt and I could hear Uncle Joe banging loudly on the door, yelling, "FRANK! FRANK!"

Kurt and I ran into our bedroom expecting a huge row as my dad stomped to the door dressed only in his boxers. In a flash, he had Joe pinned up against the wall and was beating him with his fists and strangling him. Grandpa and Uncle Nick came rushing in to separate them. I had never seen two brothers fight so brutally. It was a traumatic altercation. The incident poisoned the relationship between dad and Uncle Joe for years. My grandfather became the only Calabrese who stood up to his oldest son. The two would have heated arguments and nearly come to blows. I would cringe as they would scream at each other. That's when I noticed a change in my father and that he was becoming more like Angelo.

As he spent more time with his mentor Angelo—or "Uncle Ang" as he was known around our house—he became increasingly short-tempered. Back when we lived in Norridge, the house was packed with family, friends, and relatives. After we moved into the Calabrese Compound, my father's disposition hardened. He became cautious of visitors, paranoid and moody. Worse, my mom noticed that Dad was explosive toward the children. The family chalked it up to Uncle Ang.

Angelo LaPietra was an irascible underboss who would yell to keep his crew on edge. Yet he was easier on my dad because he followed orders and did his job well. Angelo could rely on him to bring in more than his share of earnings every month. More important, he didn't cause problems by going "off the Outfit reservation." He was the kind of guy Angelo liked: a soldier and an earner who was low-key and content working his juice loans, gambling, and street tax operations. He wasn't looking to race up the Outfit ladder. If promoted, great. If not, he made it known to Angelo that he wasn't out to make waves.

After the death of Larry Stubitsch, business was booming, enabling Frank senior to put more money out on the street. Although he felt restricted having to report to so many layers of bosses, his stance was simple: "As an earner, you have value. If you follow the rules and turn in the dollars, nobody's going to bother you."

As his fortunes grew, in 1970 he enlisted Uncle Nick, whom he could trust and control. After a hitch in the navy, Nick was adrift, feeling restless and disconnected.

Born on November 30, 1942, Nicholas W. Calabrese had spent a large part of the 1960s in the military. After Nick did a tour of duty in Vietnam and returned to civilian life, my father convinced Uncle Ed Hanley to find my uncle a well-paying job as a union organizer. He worked on a few building projects for the city under the auspices of the Ironworkers' Union, including the construction of the McCormick Place Convention Center and the hundred-story John Hancock Building.

Nick viewed his older brother as a success, a local tough guy who worked for himself and kept a large bankroll in his pocket. By 1970, he felt the allure of my father's respect and expressed an interest in joining his crew. My father started him off as a driver making a few collections, a typical entry-level position. With hard work, my uncle established himself as a loyal soldier who wouldn't question authority. My father liked that.

3.

WHO WOULDN'T LOVE A GUY LIKE THAT?

At any given time, there were a dozen Calabrese family members living at the Compound, the three-flat near Grand Avenue and North Seventy-fifth Court in Elmwood Park. It was a typical Italian post-immigrant communal living arrangement. My parents and the three sons—Frank junior (me, born in 1960), Kurt (sixteen months younger than I), and Nicky (born in 1971)—occupied the main center apartment sandwiched between my uncles, aunts, and grandparents.

An upstairs addition included my father's personal office, a spare kitchen, a dining area with a large table for ten, a fireplace, and a couch. Our family used the room regularly, but it was open to anyone in the Compound. No one locked his or her apartment door. If I wanted to drop in on Uncle Nick or watch TV with my grandparents, I could just walk in. Grandma and Grandpa, Nick, and Dad spoke Italian and English, occasionally mixing the languages.

When my father came home in a pleasant mood, the dinner table was a haven where the Calabrese family could sit and talk about what was going on in their lives. The entire family sat down and had dinner every day at five o'clock with the TV off. Family time was extremely important to my father. Later, as he worked longer hours on weeknights, and as his three sons grew older, the mandatory family dinner took place every Sunday at three o'clock. Like many Italian households, eating together was a celebration.

Dad loved home-cooked meals: Italian "stick-to-your-ribs" fare. Eating was a big part of his day. There wasn't a car ride or an outing where he didn't stop for a meal. My mom was an excellent cook and baker. One of my father's favorite meals is lemon chicken with Vesuvio potatoes, homemade ravioli, stuffed pizza, crème puffs, and fresh-baked cookies.

Dad didn't use linen or a paper napkin at the table. He wiped his face on a dish towel that mom would dutifully place by his plate. He demanded that his sons observe basic table manners: Never take the last piece of food off a serving plate unless you offered it to everyone at the table. Don't lean in or reach over somebody's plate. Don't talk with food in your mouth, and don't smack your lips while chewing. He was strict about us washing our hands before eating, and we didn't wear a hat at the table!

The Compound was situated on the north side of the railroad tracks of Elmwood Park. The bosses lived on the south side of Elmwood Park, where the beautiful homes were. Other Italian neighborhoods in the area included Grand and Harlem, Riis Park, Amundsen Park, and Galewood.

Elmwood Park was predominantly Italian when the Calabreses first settled. Its population of twenty thousand lived in a close-knit set of neighborhoods. The village had more than its share of delicatessens, bakeries, and Italian restaurants. Immigrant Sicilians opened their small cozy cafés. In addition to the Italians (and some Greeks) living in Elmwood Park, there were Poles, Irish, Germans, and people of mixed European descent. I was half Irish and half Italian.

Melrose Park was only a couple of miles southwest of Elmwood Park. Both communities had close ties. The Cook County Forest Preserve divided the two areas, and most of the gangsters' children went to Holy Cross High School in River Grove. Working-class kids attended the public school at Elmwood Park High. The local newspapers would stoke crosstown rivalry between the Italians and the Irish whenever Holy Cross and Saint Pat's from Chicago's Belmont Avenue would play football under the Friday night lights.

Most of the residents knew who the gangsters were by reputation. To the residents of Elmwood Park, they were ordinary people. Everybody seemed to have connections. Despite its reputation, Elmwood Park was a safe and protected environment to grow up in. It was the kind of village where if help was needed, somebody would be there.

During the 1970s, the neighborhoods were overflowing with kids. There could be groups of two dozen or three dozen teenagers hanging out. They dressed in baggy pants, gym shoes, leather jackets, and dago T's and would congregate on the side of the street or by the city parks. There were fights among the boys as rival neighborhoods squared off. Other teens came from Berwyn, Cicero, Taylor Street, and my father's old stomping grounds, Grand and Ogden.

There were a number of Outfit bosses, underbosses, and capos that lived in the Chicago suburbs of Elmwood Park and Melrose Park. On the east side of Harlem Avenue was the Galewood/Montclare area; on the west side was River Forest. Some of the bosses who lived in River Forest included Tony "Joe Batters" Accardo, Paul "the Waiter" Ricca, and Joe "the Builder" Andriacchi. I grew up with the grandchildren of Mafia chief Sam Giancana, who lived in Oak Park, an upper-middle-class community. I attended school with Joey Aiuppa's nephew and Louie "the Mooch" Eboli's son. If someone's old man was away in prison and the question "What happened to Joey's dad?" was asked, the answer was, "He's away at college."

I was in grammar school when I first noticed FBI agents parked in their unmarked cars out in front of the Compound. I had a vague idea about what was going on with my father and the law. A lot of it was unspoken; I knew about mobsters. Once when I was very young, I approached my father. "They asked me today at school what you do for a living."

"Tell 'em I'm an engineer."

"Like a train engineer?"

"No, like a hoisting engineer." Dad showed me his union card. "I worked for the city as a crane operator. Local 150."

The Calabrese sons knew that Dad wasn't exactly a nine-to-five working stiff. Like a lot of other Italian guys, he was strict with his boys. If Kurt or I stepped out of line, we got the belt. We had our chores to do before and after dinner. We were taught about manners. Open the door for your elders. Don't talk back or swear around ladies.

One day I got into a scrape with a boy who lived a few doors down the street. I was playing in the alley with the other kids my age, and an older boy got into my face. He was a sophomore in high school, and while I was only thirteen and in the seventh grade, the two of us mixed it up. When the older boy had his legs scissored around my neck and began punching me, I bit him hard in the leg and wouldn't let go.

As the opposing kid screamed in pain, I jumped up and punched him a few times. Then I ran home. A little while later, the older kid's mother rang the doorbell at the Calabrese Compound. She was extremely upset over what I had done to her son. My bite would leave an indelible scar. My father shrugged his shoulders and reached for his money roll and offered her compensation if she needed to take her son down to the hospital.

"Good job," he later told me as I was expecting the back of his hand instead of a reassuring pat on the back. "Don't worry about it. At least you defended yourself."

After Uncle Junior died young, I was a tagalong with Uncle Nick and Uncle Joe and their madcap group of friends, up for a little bit of reckless fun. Once we went down to the amusement park in Melrose Park, Kiddie Land, and liberated the bumper car ride. While everyone was instructed to drive in one direction, we circled back the other way, smashing into the other cars until the operator ran out screaming at Nick and Joe. "Fuck you!" they yelled at the guy. In the summer they took me to Riis Park to go swimming in the municipal pool. Grabbing me by the shorts, they'd throw me into the deep end, like older brothers would do. "Now swim!"

I was twelve years old in 1972 when I first saw *The Godfather* at the Mercury Theater on North Avenue and Harlem Avenue. It created quite a stir among me and my friends. Suddenly "organized crime" became popular culture fare among a community quietly versed in the ways of the Outfit. The popular fascination with the mob sparked controversy in Elmwood Park when an article on the Outfit appeared in the *Chicago Daily News*, mentioning Frank Calabrese, Sr., with a picture of the Compound plus a photo of him with his mentor, Angelo the Hook.

The legend of the Outfit was well known in Chicago. In April 1973 a good friend of mine was out with his father at Sears and Roebuck in Galewood when they heard on the in-store radio that the psychotic mobster "Mad Sam" DeStefano had been found murdered in his garage. My friend and his father knew that DeStefano lived only two blocks from the Sears store. They drove over to the "death house." It was like a celebrity sighting, with a small crowd milling around the sidewalk. Inside the garage was the bloody body of "Mad Sam" with two shotgun blasts in his chest and one in the torso that severed his left arm. The FBI and the Chicago

Police Department homicide detectives determined that Tony Spilotro had visited Mad Sam.

One day while Kurt and I were playing in the alley next to our three-flat, we looked over at the nearby parking lot and saw two plainclothes detectives sitting in an unmarked car. As we walked toward the car, the detectives, having been spotted, didn't know what to do next. Suddenly they slumped down and pretended to be asleep. The police were often staked out across the street next to the pay phone at the Kentucky Fried Chicken. During the winter months a car would be parked with the motor running. Inside, two plainclothes detectives trying to stay warm. The Compound phone would ring.

"Hey, little buddy, is your dad home?"

"Hold on and let me check."

I knew whether or not to say if he was home.

When my father got a call from one of his Outfit friends, it was the classic ring-once-then-hang-up-then-start-ringing-again code. If this was someone he needed to speak to, then he would know. If the phone rang *twice,* stopped, then started ringing again, it was a different mob connection. Because of my dad's occupation, it was a matter of habit among the Calabrese family to let the phone ring many times before answering. It was a given that the line was tapped.

I reveled in both my Italian and my Irish roots. On long holidays it was one day of Italian celebration and the next day Irish. As I got older, I noticed that whenever the family went to an Italian event on my dad's side, it was organized and festive with a lot of food. There was a seating protocol according to "rank." When I went to the Irish affairs on my mother's side, they were much looser, with little food but a great deal of liquor. The atmosphere was loud and everyone had a great time.

For the Calabreses, the mix of Italian and Irish culture was a positive experience. On my father's side, I was the oldest of my cousins. Yet on my mother's side, Kurt and I were the youngest.

Dad had an overwhelming personality that appealed to both sides of the family. The Irish relatives especially liked him, and he was deft at winning over a room. Other than Uncle Ed, the Hanley Irish side of the family had little money. They were cops or city workers. Their kids attended Catholic schools and lived in modest houses. Whenever there was a funeral there would be a couple bottles of whiskey on the table and a case of beer in the fridge. My father would then go to the store and come back with boxes of liquor, cases of beer, and a large spread of food. He'd throw it out on the table with a huge smile. To his Irish relatives, Frank Calabrese, Sr., was a kind and considerate gentleman who treated everyone with the utmost respect and equality. He appeared to have no motive other than providing for my mother's family.

Who wouldn't love a guy like that?

4.

LIKE FATHER, LIKE SON?

During the 1970s, when the Outfit controlled four casinos in Las Vegas, the Calabrese family would stay at the Stardust Hotel and be comped for nearly everything. My father and his friends would sit by the pool playing gin. The Stardust had a paging system in the hotel, so he would remind us that if he was needed, make sure

we paged him under his assumed name, Frank Mauro. At first I didn't understand, but soon I realized it was important to keep a low profile in case law enforcement was tracking him or members of the family.

By the time I was thirteen, Kurt and I and some of the other gangsters' children had our own scams running.

"Dad?" I would ask in earshot of my dad's mob pals. "Can I have some money to play the arcade games at Circus Circus?"

He would hand over twenty dollars, and as I turned to leave, each of his friends would call me over.

"Here, kid." Voilà! I scored over a hundred dollars. The same trick worked for the other kids. One of Tony Centracchio's daughters would take her money over to the slot machines, while the casino hosts and security guards looked the other way.

Another time Grandma Sophie and I went to see Wayne Newton at the Aladdin Hotel. My father and Frankie Bella, head of the pit bosses at the Stardust, walked us over to the show early, taking a shortcut through a lounge that wasn't yet open. On our way back to the Stardust after the show, Grandma and I cut through the same lounge, now packed with customers and topless dancers. Grandma had to drag me out.

Mob buddies like Tony Centracchio checked into the biggest suites closest to the pool. One time I came back to the room early. "Dad, I'm back!"

Up the spiral staircase leading up to the bedroom, I heard the shuffling sound of someone running into the bathroom. I started up the stairs, when he yelled, "Stay there! I'll be right down."

My father hustled down the stairs. "Me and Tony were upstairs watching TV in our shorts. He got embarrassed and ran into the bathroom."

My mother had stayed behind, and although I was only in the seventh grade, I knew that he was up to something, and it wasn't with Tony in his underwear. I felt uncomfortable but kept quiet about the incident.

My father's personal tastes in music reflected his love for Las Vegas. He enjoyed singer Jimmy Roselli, a middle-of-the-road crooner who lived in the shadow of Frank Sinatra. His favorites included Dean Martin, Louis Prima, Nat King Cole, Billie Holiday, Barbra Streisand, and Connie Stevens. He was an acquaintance of comedian Pat Cooper, who opened for Sinatra and Roselli.

Dad was a friend of Gianni Russo, the actor who portrayed Carlo Rizzi in *The Godfather*, who, in the movie, married Don Vito Corleone's daughter Connie. Russo came by our house a couple of times to eat. Appearing on a late-night television talk show, he showed off a knife that he said had been given to him by a "real mobster."

Dad laughed at the TV. "I gave him that knife."

My father was not prejudiced. He spoke highly of the black gangsters in Chicago who ran numbers in their neighborhoods—known as "the policy"—impressed with the amount of money they squeezed out of their communities. Yet he despised *all* drug dealers, black or white. He was impressed by how the Jews, like the Italians, stuck together. He saw them as smart businessmen, citing how the Outfit and their Jewish counterparts had worked well together, and how, historically, they respected each other.

Like many sons who try to imitate their fathers, at age fourteen I committed my first burglary.

Breaking into a neighbor's house while the occupants were away on vacation, I made off with about fifty dollars in change plus a stash of worthless costume jewelry. Not knowing what to do with my haul, I took it down to the basement of the Compound and stashed it inside an old unplugged clothes dryer. Inside the dryer was a black clothing-store bag containing paperwork. I put my stash underneath the black bag and went to bed.

A few hours later, Uncle Nick woke me and summoned me to the big room, where my father was waiting with the lights on. My father sat me down.

"You wanna tell me where you got that stuff downstairs?"

I knew I was found out and wasted no time confessing. "I broke into a house down the street."

"Why?"

"I don't know. I guess I did it for the thrill of it."

"Son, you don't do stuff like that. Do you know what they do in this town if you steal?"

I had an idea who "they" were. I waited for the cupped-hand smack across my temple. But it never came.

"Do not steal from anybody in the neighborhood. I don't want you to do it again. People lose their fingers for breaking into other people's houses. You're grounded for a week."

It was the first time he had grounded me.

"I want you to go to bed and think about what you've done." He motioned to my uncle. "You know what to do with this stuff."

There was an understanding between Outfit guys not to steal in certain neighborhoods, especially Elmwood Park, River Forest, and Taylor Street, where the bosses lived. If you were a known thief and they discovered your identity, you were a dead man.

I couldn't figure out how my father found the stash so quickly. It turned out that the black bag contained his and Uncle Nick's juice loan reports and football betting slips. I had selected the identical hiding place as my father.

While I didn't like getting busted, I was gratified that he had spoken to me like a real father. Strangely, it felt good seeing him act the traditional role of the caring dad. I had experienced an important rite of passage, even if I had picked the wrong neighborhood.

A few months later, a similar but more confusing rite between him and me wouldn't end so warm and fuzzy.

Sitting in the den watching TV, my father asked me if the shirt I was wearing was new. Yes, in fact it was. Except that, on a dare, I had shoplifted the shirt at a teen clothing store on Grand and Harlem. Again, I was amazed. How had he found out, and was he testing me?

"How much did you pay for the shirt?"

"Twenty dollars," I lied.

In a sudden moment of rage, he slapped me down hard and tore the shirt off my back. I fell to the ground and hunkered down, expecting a beating for stealing the shirt. Instead, he screamed at me.

"Who the hell are you? Some fucking big shot who pays twenty dollars for a T-shirt? From now on you buy your shirts at Sears like I do!"

Years later, while browsing in a hardware store, Dad suddenly instructed me, "Block me."

To my horror, I watched him pocket a handful of screws and nails. Once we got outside, I handed him a couple of bucks.

"What's this for, Frankie?"

"Next time, I'll pay. Why would you risk everything you've got for a few lousy screws?"

Embarrassed, he laughed and shrugged. "I don't know. I guess I did it for the thrill of it."

5.

FAST WITH HIS HANDS

One day while washing my father's Buick Park Avenue Limited, I lifted the floor mat to vacuum on the passenger side, and there it was—three thousand dollars in loose bills. I ran upstairs to tell him what I had found.

"Did you take any of it?" he asked matter-of-factly.

"No."

He had known that I would find the money. What he hadn't known was whether I could be trusted handling large sums of cash.

There were many people on the streets of Chicago's South Side who played by my dad's rules. But if you crossed Frank Calabrese, he was fast and furious. My father had multiple personalities, and what made it hard was that I never knew which one I might be dealing with at any given time. He was a chameleon and could change in an instant. A lot of people knew about his dual personality, but only a tight core knew about his third, the deadly one.

The first was the caring and loving provider, the patriarch. The second was the controlling and abusive father, demanding and strict, the streetwise Outfit member who ran a vicious and profitable crew. And the third was the killer, whose method of murder was strangulation, followed by a knife to the throat.

Only his victims and Outfit associates saw number three firsthand. Those who were close to him sensed it. The Outfit bosses—they knew. He sat at the feet of the master, Angelo the Hook. My dad was treacherous and a hothead. He was intense even by Outfit standards. It wouldn't take much for him to get that glassy-eyed stare.

We would be having a nice time, laughing, talking and jiving, when something in the conversation would flick a switch.

My father was a gale force to be around. He was a savvy businessman and didn't like to back a customer into a corner unless it was necessary. He tried not to bully but he was scary. If someone got cracked in the face, it probably wasn't his first infraction. In my dad's eyes, you had it coming or else you had ignored the warnings that had preceded his taking physical action. He had an anger problem—he would resort to violence quickly and was fast with his hands. Many felt that it was his temper that kept him from obtaining an Outfit leadership position.

Dad wasn't one to yell. He didn't puff his chest out or point his finger or bellow accusations. But he was a heartbeat away from erupting. Then his hands did the talking. Not a punch to the face, but a calculated smack to the side of the head with a cupped hand placed strategically around the eye, the temple, and the ear. It came quickly and unexpectedly, like a Tyson left hook, first knocking you off balance, jamming your equilibrium, and down you'd go. With the second personality, if you were habitually late with your payment or street tax, or if you crossed him by ignoring the various warnings, things could get ugly fast. After a few minutes in an empty room with the door locked, many wondered if they would come out alive.

Frankie "Ciccio" Furio, a longtime associate now deceased, worked closely with my father after Larry Stubitsch was murdered. He was one of the guys who saw the early signs of multiple personalities. Ciccio put it best, giving my dad, his boss, the best advice a guy in his position could offer: "Never bring the street into your home." It was an unspoken Outfit code not to be broken. Yet, to me, Dad was the family mentor and savior, and a "temple of knowledge." Both Uncle Nick and I looked up to him, admiring his strength and talent as a provider and a leader.

I had spent my final high school days in Elmwood Park. The neighborhood was about 60 percent Italian. I went to school with kids whose fathers worked for the Outfit. We knew what our fathers did, but it was unspoken.

To me and my classmates, going to school in the neighborhood was about getting an education and staying out of trouble. I was taught (and so were a lot of my friends) that you never acted the big shot, never implied, "Do you know who my father is?" If we did get into trouble, the people we feared most *were* our fathers. They pushed us to stay away from trouble, to study hard and make something of ourselves. Go to college. Land a respectable job.

Both Kurt and I attended Holy Cross, the local Catholic high school. In high school I was generally trouble-free, a talented athlete in football and basketball, and an average student. In New York City, mob power is traditionally handed down from father to son, but the Outfit viewed its family legacy differently. With few exceptions, the offspring of Outfit members were pushed to be "legit." As a result, many became lawyers, doctors, and professionals, as if the majority of Outfit families took Frankie Furio's advice seriously: Don't pass the Outfit lifestyle on to your sons. While there were a few brothers out there working the streets together, there weren't too many sons getting involved in the mob business.

My father continued to test me. One day he had an altercation with the next-door neighbor, who had a habit of parking his car and blocking the Compound driveway. When Dad approached the man, the neighbor responded with an obscene retort. He was a huge man, standing a head taller than my dad. I ran into the garage and grabbed a baseball bat. As the two men exchanged words, I came out of the garage with my bat, ready to swing.

Seeing me out of the corner of his eye, my father stayed in the guy's face until he backed down.

"Just talk to me," he explained to his neighbor diplomatically, "and don't threaten me or swear at me. I'll talk to you like a man, you talk to me like a man, and we got no problem."

After the guy walked away, I put down the bat. My father smiled, seeing the potential in me, knowing there was a sense of loyalty that he could nurture and control.

One of my first part-time jobs was making pizza at Armand's on Grand Avenue, where a lot of the locals hung out. It has now relocated after fifty years in business, but there was a time when, if somebody walked into Armand's, chances are he would see prominent Outfit gangsters dining in the corner tables. During its heyday, Armand's paid street tax to boss man Jackie Cerone.

In 1975, about three months shy of my sixteenth birthday, I was completing my driver education class to get my learner permit. At the time Uncle Nick was living in the three-flat, and he would take me out driving without my permit.

One day after school, Dad called me down to the garage. He handed me a letter from Holy Cross that needed to be signed and returned. He confronted me in a mob sit-down style.

"What is dis?"

It was a deficiency notice alerting my parents that I was behind in my math studies, and that I still had time to raise my grade before the semester ended. In quick response, my angry father vowed to pull me out of my driver education class; without passing driver's ed, I would have to wait until I turned eighteen to get my license. My heart sank and I pleaded with him, promising that if he would only let me finish driver's ed, I would get my grade up by the end of the semester.

He was adamant. The answer was no. School was more important. But with his next breath, he had an odd request.

He handed me a greeting card "to Frank" and told me that if Mom asked me if this was my card, I should say yes. I looked at the card, and it was an "I love you" message from his goomah. It was bizarre. One minute, he's punishing me for my grades, and the next he wants me to lie to my mother about a card from his mistress that he thinks she may have seen.

When it came time to take the driving test, he took me down to one of his friends who worked for the DMV, who gave me the answers. Whenever possible, he would show me how best to cheat the system.

By the time I left high school in 1978, my father was dating Diane Cimino, his longtime goomah, behind my mother's back.

He began mixing business with family. He would stash stuff at home and have me running small errands. While I didn't have any designs to join the Outfit, I wanted to work with my father and enjoy his same independence. My father did not sit me down and ask what I wanted to do with my life. Nor was joining the Outfit encouraged as a possibility. Instead, he slowly groomed me.

I bought into what he was doing. I was to be his secret weapon, his behind-the-scenes guy, low-key like him. Out of father-son loyalty, I stood ready to do whatever he asked of me.

I never actually saw him kill anybody, but one night he came home with his adrenaline pumping. He would talk in the bathroom with the exhaust fan on and the water running in the sink. I could see the high in his eyes as he rambled on about a murder he'd just committed. He was almost breathless as he spilled his guts.

"We just got 'im . . . and this is how we did it. . . . Our guy wasn't listening to the rules . . . so we shotgunned him."

To which I thought, I wonder what my friends' fathers are telling *them* right now about their day at work.

One day in 1976 Dad arrived home carrying some heavy duffel bags. We went into the back room where we worked out together with weights, next to the washer and dryer, and he told me, "I want you to set up the folding table, count these quarters, and put them in bags." I gladly followed his order.

After counting the quarters came the late-night rides and waiting in the car, going to restaurants, dropping in at different people's homes, and meeting guys on the street. I rarely listened to what was said or what business was transacted. At first I didn't know why I was going along, or what he was doing. It was just, "C'mon, son, take a ride with me." Growing up, I was my dad's favorite, and he took me out with him a lot.

I learned that the quarters came from a string of adult bookstores that Uncle Joe was running for my dad. When Uncle Joe tired of the job and my father's inflexible rules, Uncle Nick and I took over as collectors. Once a week we'd drive around, emptying quarters from peep show machines, counting the money and coins before stashing them in another garage. The take came from six stores in downtown Chicago and a seventh just over the border in Indiana.

In a bookstore operation a patron would pay two dollars to enter the store (refundable upon making a purchase). He might wander into the back room, lit by black light, to feed the machine quarters to watch a short porno movie. Years ago, peep show machines were cash cows and adult bookstores were the places where sexual deviants could go. It was a rough atmosphere that neither my uncle nor I took pleasure in. Perverts would urinate on the machines or, worse, defecate on the floors.

We found that seven or eight o'clock on Monday nights was the slowest time of the week, the best time to collect. I knew that when we went into a shop, my uncle was "carrying." We'd flip the lights on and there would be some guy blowing another guy on the floor.

As a nineteen-year-old collecting quarters and ordering Triple-X inventory like dildos, blow-up dolls, and magazines, shadowed by my heat-packing gangster uncle, I got a firsthand look at life in the seamy underworld.

My father had slowly been running the businesses into the ground. He constantly expected more money to come in. If we were bringing in eight thousand dollars a week, he wanted to know why it wasn't nine thousand dollars. Whenever we'd take money out to buy new films and inventory, he'd get agitated. "Why does it cost so much?"

We had a store in Mishawaka, Indiana, right next to South Bend, that featured nude shoeshine girls. They had a room with two large benches where the patrons would sit down and a naked girl would come in and shine their shoes. It cost seven dollars at the desk. Whatever the girl did extra for the customer, we didn't want to know, as long as we got our seven bucks for the nude shoeshine.

What happened to the string of bookstores was symptomatic of how the Outfit operated businesses once they took over. What the Outfit did was bleed a business until there was nothing left. Had we taken care of those stores, they could have generated a lot of passive income. When my father first approached the owner to pay a street tax, I think he was paying three thousand dollars a week for the whole chain. After a while we took over counting his quarters and keeping track because my father wanted more. It was the classic Outfit greed. They were making three thousand dollars while the owner was bringing in, say, twenty thousand. But the guy was a natural at running his business and he worked hard. He had contacts inside the city who helped him obtain the necessary licenses. Had we kept him in place, my father could have made thousands per week by not bothering him, and could have been paid a tidy sum for little effort.

But once Dad gets involved in an enterprise, he wants to see the books. Next he's sending his guys in—like us—to count his quarters. We were stealing a fortune in quarters at each store for my father, and the owner knew it. Then my father cracked the guy in the face. That's what he was about, more control and sucking out more cash.

He tightened the grip until one night the owner filled up a couple of grocery bags full of cash, threw them in the trunk of his car, and fled to California to take a job with the government. Such was my official entry into my father's crew. I kept my work at the porn shops a secret from my friends in the neighborhood.

He was slowly grooming me, and from that point on, I was ready to lead two lives: mine and the life my father had mapped out for me.

6.

THE ART OF BLENDING IN

Before Nicholas Calabrese was honorably discharged from the U.S. Navy in the late 1960s, he had followed orders without question. One night, during an ocean storm, the young sailor was ordered to straddle the missile destroyer USS *Bainbridge* and the aircraft carrier USS *Enterprise* to repair communication between the two vessels. Encased in a small wire cage that spanned the two ships, with the waves crashing at heights of twenty feet, he could easily have been swept away and drowned. Uncle Nick later told family and

friends that it was the scariest moment of his life. But he obediently carried out the order without a flaw. Such was the loyalty of Nick Calabrese.

When my uncle joined my father's crew in the summer of 1970, many figured him to be just a lackey for his brother. He was a pleasant-looking guy, dark-haired with a smaller build than his older brother—and he wasn't as intimidating on the juice-collection trail. Some likened Nick to the mild-mannered Fredo in *The Godfather*.

If Uncle Nick spoke, it was in a low, respectful tone. He read constantly, and liked to sit on the couch doing the *New York Times* crossword puzzle. He was the guy who picked up Dad's dry cleaning. He was the accident-prone klutz who would trip and fall, jamming his fingers, when he moved furniture for his brother. When he had a few too many drinks he was goofy, and occasionally, in fun, he would throw a punch or two to show how tough he was. He raised a daughter, Michelle, with Joy, his first wife, and a son and a daughter, Franco and Christina, with his second wife, Noreen.

Nick's July 1970 initiation into my dad's Chinatown crew was a chilling affair. When he first joined as a driver and gofer, Dad was dodging a subpoena issued by the Illinois Crime Investigating Commission, which was probing juice loan rackets and mob activity on the streets of Chicago. Michael "Bones" or "Hambone" Albergo, a former running buddy with the late Larry Stubitsch, was tagged as a collector for the Calabrese crew. But Albergo was viewed as a weak link who could roll over and cooperate with law enforcement. When the order came down from Tony Accardo and Angelo LaPietra to "retire" Albergo, my father told Uncle Nick they needed to find a suitable site to dig a four-foot-deep hole.

At first my uncle thought he was giving him the business, but after casing the South Side, it became apparent that he wasn't joking. After passing on a site or two, the pair settled on a site at Thirty-fifth and Shields across from Comiskey Park. Packing a shovel, the two took turns digging the hole in an obscured area, covering the finished dig with a large sheet of plywood.

In August of 1970, Ronnie Jarrett, a Calabrese crew member,

stole a Chevy (as a work car) and arranged to pick up Albergo on the pretext that he was going to "a short meeting." After one failed attempt, Jarrett snagged his soon-to-be victim. With Albergo in the front passenger seat, Jarrett pulled up to where Nick and my father were waiting. My father climbed in behind Jarrett on the driver's side while Uncle Nick sat behind Albergo. Both men surreptitiously slipped on their gloves as Jarrett pulled up near the Thirty-fifth and Shields grave. Ronnie shut off the ignition, and Nick, as ordered, grabbed a stunned Albergo's right arm and held it tightly behind him while Jarrett grabbed Hambone's left arm. My father, as executioner, slipped a rope over Albergo's head and tugged hard until his body went limp. Albergo was dragged out of the car, then undressed down to his underwear. His clothes were thrown onto some railroad tracks, and to make sure the hit was complete, my father cut the dead man's throat. In the cover of darkness, he, Ronnie, and Uncle Nick pushed Albergo into a deep hole and smothered the body with lye.

Uncle Nick later admitted to peeing on himself during his first hit, and hiding the fact for fear that my father would mercilessly mock him. With a gangland murder under his belt, in one short month he was "all in," both with his brother's crew and the Outfit.

Many years later, while driving near the Chicago White Sox ballpark, Dad pointed out to me an area near Thirty-fifth and Shields by the elevated train tracks.

"There's one over there," he told me, making the sign of death, a finger across his throat, like a knife.

Like during his navy days in the steel cage, Nick performed without question. He got the job done. True to his brother's wishes, he mastered the art of blending in, and for the next thirty years, Nick would operate under the law enforcement radar.

Unlike Uncle Nick's swift transition from driver to hit man, my ascent into my father's street crew was a gradual process. When your father asks you to do something, you assume that what he's telling you is best for you and the family. He was the master at using people for what they were good at. He was a quick read.

He could sense their strengths and their weaknesses. My uncle's strength was dependability and commitment. But under pressure, there were times my uncle didn't think as clearly as my dad would have liked. Dad knew that I thought like he did and that I could handle myself.

Like my uncle, I was taught the art of blending in through a series of street-smart, day-to-day rules. Very few of the street crews would be as careful and deliberate as my father's. His rules ranged from the use of common sense to subtle tactics that kept law enforcement confused and at bay. He set the example of his prime rule: Remain low-key.

I was instructed, Never flash a roll of cash in public. Don't be a hot shot—*spaccone*—and if you are handling or exchanging a large sum of money, conduct the transaction under the table. I learned to talk with my hands in front of my mouth, a habit I still practice. While talking at a phone booth, I made sure my back was to the phone box, with a 180-degree view of the street. I would carry a small .22 five-shot pistol in my pocket that I could toss away should the cops arrive unexpectedly. If I suspected I was being followed, I drove slowly and made a lot of turns with the signal on. If a car pulled up next to me, I was taught to stare back intently. If the driver didn't look back, he was probably tailing me.

When my father was followed by undercover agents, to throw them off, he would visit places where he wouldn't normally go. Once he ended up in a Greek restaurant and took a seat at the counter and ordered a meal. He asked to speak with the owner, and when the owner came out, he shook his hand.

"I gotta tell ya, this is the best restaurant I ever ate in, and I thank you very much."

After he left the restaurant, the cops stormed in and grilled the owner.

"We know you were paying him money. What did he say to you?"

"He told me I had good food."

Because of my dad, whenever I leave a hotel room, I keep the lights on, turn up the television, and on my way out of my room, I always say, "See you guys later."

Although he loved and owned a lot of automobiles, my father drove Fords and Chevys instead of Mercedeses, and he expected the same of his associates. In his eyes, a top-of-the-line Chevy, Ford, or Buick was preferable to a Mercedes or Cadillac. It was a matter of perception.

His other rules included mixing up the meeting and collection locations on a week-to-week basis, even if the sites were only a block or two apart. Crew members would meet their clients on side streets that contained lots of bushes and trees. They avoided the clichéd gangster scenario of two guys loitering on a corner and looking around with their hands in their pockets.

While walking the streets, I would leave my hands *outside* of my pockets. When hooking up with fellow crew members or clients, there were two things you had to have. The first was the cash and the second was the paperwork. The cash was folded into a standard-sized envelope unless it was an extraordinarily large amount. We would walk side by side as we made the exchange. After it was transferred we would shake hands, then give each other a hug.

Juice loan amounts were entered into the books in code. A check mark would be $50, a circle, $10, and a slash, $5. Three check marks, a circle, and a slash would mean a payment of $165 in cash. If a client wanted money, how much? If a client was late, why? I would keep track of the information and pass it on to my father at weekly sit-downs.

Because it was preferable to work under the cover of darkness, most of my monetary exchanges were done at night. In the summer months, we would meet later, and in the winter months, earlier. A great deal of business was conducted walking outside. Another of my dad's rules was never to stand in the same spot, in case somebody was nearby with a listening device. After meeting on a corner and taking a short walk, we would separate and go off in opposite directions. If a member of the crew was under surveillance, the FBI would have to decide who was to be followed, since agents commonly worked in pairs.

Another of his rules was that too much conversation with a customer was fatal. That is what brought feared hit man Frankie Schweihs down. He couldn't help himself and was recorded bragging at length to porn operator William "Red" Wemette, whom he was extorting.

Collecting a street tax at the front counter in the presence of an establishment's clientele was unacceptable. Payments were collected in a discreet spot with only the principal present. The hug was an important gesture. It would conclude the transaction or collection, and serve to confuse law enforcement by giving the appearance that the huggers were friends. It might tell the "hugger" whether his victim, the "huggee," was wearing a wire or carrying a weapon. My father was concerned about wiretaps, one of the reasons he preferred to talk with the television blasting, or to walk outside where there was a great deal of ambient noise.

Like most of the bosses, my father forbade members of his crew to deal drugs, which he felt were a magnet for law enforcement. If a drug dealer was caught operating with money from a Calabrese juice loan, the crew could face serious conspiracy charges, which carried stiff prison sentences.

An associate of ours once brought in a bunch of new customers at two hundred to seven hundred dollars each per week. Thirty guys on the juice. But when Dad found out that they were dealing or doing drugs, rather than confronting them on the issue, our associate ate the money, wiped their debts clean, and sent them on their way with a message: Don't come around again.

People on juice were either businessmen or blue-collar guys who gambled and had suffered a few bad weeks. But most of the clients were businessmen who made a decent living and needed quick financing. To avoid the difficulty of dealing with a bank and the loan application process, they would come to the Calabrese crew, which would charge twenty-five dollars per thousand per week, or 2.5 percent.

The crew might loan out ten thousand or even twenty thousand, knowing that repayment was more than likely. As a backup, we kept titles (and keys) to cars and houses. Customers signed promissory notes, which was more the standard. At the height of the juice loan business, the crew had upwards of a million dollars on the street. My dad was reported to be one of the biggest loan sharks in Chicago. And he was.

The Calabrese crew had a simple business model. My father was on the top with final word, followed by Ronnie Jarrett (when he wasn't locked up). Uncle Nick and I gathered and organized the collections. Later, when the family "went away," Ronnie Jarrett oversaw the crew's street operations. Approximately fifteen guys—or agents—saw to loan, gambling, and extortion collections. During pro football season and during various playoffs and tournaments, the crew added more agents to collect more action. Bookmaking for college and pro football, long a staple in the gambling world, was highly profitable.

The Calabrese crew compensated the Outfit with a predetermined share and became partners with bookie networks and their subagents, laying claim to guys operating in certain territories in the Chicago area. The Calabrese crew would split the action fifty-fifty with the head of the bookmaking ring, or else the ring could pay a street tax or bankroll their bookmakers with Calabrese juice loans.

By lending money, my father built a network of influential acquaintances—politicians, celebrities, and businessmen—who were only a phone call away. Family members, cousins, aunts, and uncles might stash his money in an account for him under their name. While it was my dad's money, they'd keep the interest. If he needed the principal back, it was there waiting because nobody would consider stealing from him.

If a businessman took out a juice loan of forty thousand to sixty thousand dollars every few weeks and paid it back, that raised a red flag. My father needed to know more about that person. Could he be a future target of opportunity? What amount of money was he making? What was his net worth? What was his Achilles' heel?

If he liked girls, ply him with hookers. If it was gambling, offer him a credit line. The idea was to corrupt the legitimate, and open the door to possible extortion.

In addition to juice loans, gambling, and the collection of street taxes, extortion was another of the Chinatown crew's moneymakers. One example was how the crew extorted the Connie's Pizza chain by adding Frank Calabrese, Sr., to the company payroll for many years as a "delivery consultant." The owner of Connie's Pizza, Jimmy Stolfe, was the brother-in-law of my father's first partner, Larry Stubitsch.

Setting up a successful extortion racket was time-consuming and relied on a crew member's psychological prowess and the ability to present it as a business proposition. I was instructed to hang out with the sons of debtors who owed my father money, so he could stay on top of their family situation. A typical extortion technique begins by planting fear in the mind of the victim. Unbeknownst to the victim, the crew member plays the dual role of predator and protector. Here's a typical extortion scheme:

Let's say you and I are hanging out together. I'm going to get close to you and take you out to a few places. I'll introduce you to the guys who own the restaurants, people whom we might already have the "arm" on. By now I've already profiled you and I know that you have a lot of money or that your business is doing well. While we're out drinking, you'll confide in me, and I'll give you some background on myself.

You'll feel like you know me; then a couple of guys will come around to your business and say, "You have to pay us two hundred thousand dollars, or we're going to shut you down." Based on the way these guys dress and talk, you know who they are. You're going to run to me: "I've got a problem." I'll ask you, "What have you been doing? Were you bragging? Have you done anything wrong? Did you get somebody angry? Let me snoop around and see what I can find out. I'll get back to you." Most people are easy marks. Everybody has secrets and skeletons in his closet, things that are shady.

The entire time I'm working both sides of the scam.

The whole time it's me. I'll report back and say, "Look, I don't know what you did, but somebody is pissed off. They want money, but because you're a friend of mine, I can get it knocked down to a hundred thousand, and if you pay me two hundred a month, nobody will bother you again. These are rough guys. You make the call. I don't care what you decide. You asked me to help you, so I'm just telling you."

It wasn't long before I picked up the tricks of the collecting trade from my father and uncle: raising your voice a notch or two for emphasis, or getting in somebody's face. They felt that if you hurt your debtor, you damaged his ability to pay. They also believed that it wasn't necessary to hurt someone unless you were ordered to do so by a boss. If you're going to hurt a customer, how are you going to gain access to his money? The rule was: People deserve a chance as long as they're trying to pay. Sometimes all it takes is an adjustment of the terms, in my dad's favor, of course. For instance, pay only ten dollars a week and essentially make the loan two thousand dollars instead of one thousand. Make sure you don't miss a week or else the principal is going to go up an extra thousand.

And that was my father's genius, coming off as scary but reasonable. Today, the banks and the credit card companies have adopted a similar method. It's called the "minimum payment."

7.

OUTFIT REIGN OF TERROR

I remember the Sunday morning in the fall of 1983 when my father and Uncle Nick were going to get made. I was washing the car in the driveway and they were both standing there with suits on. I rarely saw them wear suits, but I do remember my dad saying, "We're in now. We're part of the group and we're going for dinner. It's like a ceremony."

Street crews have made millions of dollars for the Outfit. They are the lifeblood of the syndicate. Although the dominant mob crews are named for key areas around Chicago, they do not necessarily operate by strict geographic boundaries. The key Outfit crews—Elmwood Park, Melrose Park, Rush Street, Chinatown/26th Street (the Calabrese domain), Cicero, Chicago Heights, and Grand Avenue—handled their rackets, which included juice loans, gambling, vice, protection, street tax, extortion, stolen goods, and chop shops.

There were many fearsome gangsters working alongside my father who were part of the 26th Street/Chinatown crew. They included South Side lieutenant Johnny "Apes" Monteleone, hit man disguised as union organizer John Fecarotta, Jimmy LaPietra (the Hook's younger brother), street soldier Frank Santucci, and dreaded hit man and collector Ronnie Jarrett. When Chinatown capo Angelo LaPietra received an order from the bosses, Joseph "Joey Doves" Aiuppa and West Side underboss James "Turk" Torello, that somebody needed to be killed, he had an impressive array of talent to draw from.

After the murder of juice collector Michael "Hambone" Albergo, the Calabrese street crew went from loan sharking and extortion to murder incorporated. Starting in the 1970s, the Calabrese brothers became blood-in-blood-out members of LaPietra and Aiuppa's elite hit squad fraternity. The other favorite hit team was Butchie Petrocelli's Wild Bunch. With fastidious planning and stalking skills, and aided by loyal henchmen like Johnny "Apes" Monteleone, John "Big Stoop" Fecarotta, Ronnie Jarrett, Frankie Furio, and four-hundred-pound thug Frank "Gumba" Saladino, my father's crew became Angelo's favorite go-to guys. As far as Angelo was concerned, the more low-key a hitter was, the better, and the Hook relished that neither my dad nor my uncle dressed the part or talked trash like Fecarotta and Petrocelli did. While both Dad and Nick were ambitious and organized, they weren't climbing over the backs of their underbosses for a rapid rise. Petrocelli was audacious and publicly claimed that one day *he* would lead the Outfit. He was marked for death because he had been skimming from collections and extorting victims without approval. Petrocelli also violated Outfit protocol by hosting hooker parties at the Ambassador East Hotel and becoming too visible.

In June 1976, Paul Haggerty, a twenty-seven-year-old thief, was suspected of robbing a Chicago suburban jewelry store that was tied to the Outfit. After Turk Torello and Angelo met with my father regarding the situation, a plan was put into motion. My dad warned Uncle Nick that the two of them would be busy for a while. They staked out the South Loop halfway house on Indiana Avenue where Haggerty lived after his stretch in the penitentiary. He and my uncle monitored Haggerty's routine. They watched his habits, where he worked, what buses he took, and where he hung out. Then the Calabrese crew made their move. Gumba Saladino grabbed Haggerty outside his halfway house, threw a few punches, and stuffed him into the backseat of a Ford Mustang with Ronnie Jarrett at the wheel. They brought the stunned Haggerty to Jarrett's mother-in-law's garage in Bridgeport.

After a particularly rough session, Uncle Nick was assigned to keep watch on Haggerty while Jarrett and my father returned with Angelo and Turk, who asked Haggerty a few questions. When my father and Jarrett left again with Angelo and Turk, Uncle Nick was put back in charge of Haggerty, who was handcuffed, with his eyes and mouth taped. My uncle brought Haggerty water and helped him to the bathroom.

"I guess only Batman and Robin can save me now," Haggerty told Nick.

By the time my dad and Jarrett returned with a car they had stolen from a nearby movie theater parking lot, Haggerty's time had run out. As Nick and Ronnie held Haggerty down, my father slipped a rope around his neck and strangled him to death. As was Michael Albergo's fate, he slit Haggerty's throat, making certain he was gone. On June 24, 1976, a week after Haggerty's disappearance, the stolen auto was discovered with the jewel thief's body stuffed in the trunk. His murder would not be solved anytime soon.

Angelo LaPietra's dark sense of humor (as well as his admiration for my father) surfaced during the 1977 hit on gangster Sam Annerino. Annerino was suspected of being an informant, and his demise was assigned to two hit teams, Butch Petrocelli's Wild Bunch and a group that consisted of my father, my uncle, Ronnie Jarrett, and Gumba Saladino. Shorty LaMantia's job was to lure Annerino to a predetermined spot, which happened to be an empty building that would later become the Old Neighborhood Italian American Club on 26th Street. When Shorty wasn't able to get Sam to the site, he showed up with Angelo LaPietra. Once Shorty and Angelo walked through the door, one of the hit crew grabbed Shorty by the neck. Shorty turned milk white, thinking *he* was the one slated to be bumped off. But Angelo laughed, and assured him that everything was okay, they were just "practicing" on him.

But pointing to my father's lineup, Angelo remarked to Shorty, "Take a look at these guys and remember; these are real men."

After a few hours spent waiting for Sam to arrive, my dad's crew gave up and retired to Ronnie's mother-in-law's house on South Lowe to await their next order. A short while later, my father received a message: Sam Annerino had been shotgunned by three masked gunmen, Butch's boys, on the corner of 106th and Cicero Avenue, in front of Mirabelli's Furniture in the suburb of Oak Lawn in broad daylight. The town motto of Oak Lawn was "Be Prudent, Be Safe." Annerino was neither.

On the Saturday night before Christmas of 1977, a highly skilled crew of jewel thieves threw a tarpaulin over the alley side of Levinson's Jewelers on North Clark Street. Using an acetylene torch, they cut through the bars on a second-floor bathroom window and broke open five vaults. The crew worked all day Sunday and into the early hours of Monday, leaving behind in the alley a foot of water used to cool the torches. They walked away with over a million-dollar haul of jewels, furs, and cash, but they neglected the largest safe, which held the coveted seventy-carat Idol's Eye diamond.

After contacting the police, Levinson made a phone call to Tony "Big Tuna" Accardo. The following day, over lunch at Chez

Paul with Accardo, Levinson asked for help. The Levinsons and the Accardos were close family friends, so close that when the Levinsons' son was born, Tony presented the child with a T-shirt emblazoned with the moniker "Little Tuna" on the front.

It was clear that the only guy who had the capability for a heist of this magnitude was John Mendell, an alarm expert and electronics whiz. The FBI and mob insiders knew that he had the expertise and chutzpah to pull off such a caper. Accardo, after checking with his underbosses and Tony "the Ant" Spilotro, came to the same conclusion. The Levinson heist had Johnny Mendell's fingerprints all over it.

Accardo sent word that the Levinson job was not Outfit-sanctioned and wouldn't be tolerated and that the score was to be returned to him personally. A panicked Mendell went on the lam to consider his next move, stashing the loot in the rafters of his business. When Mendell and his crew complied with Accardo's demand by returning the merchandise, there was discontent among the group of burglars that they had nothing to show for their work. Deluding himself that he had "power in numbers," Mendell and his gang planned a sequel far more daring than the original heist.

On a cold January morning in 1978, Michael Volpe opened the door to 1407 Ashland in River Forest. Volpe, Tony Accardo's personal caretaker, would periodically check on the house to make certain everything was in order while the Accardos wintered in Palm Springs, California. With his first glimpse, Volpe knew that this was not the immaculate and fastidious Accardo residence he was used to. As Volpe gazed into the mirrored foyer, he could see something was amiss. Drawers were overturned. Furniture was askew. A pair of pants lay in the middle of the floor, with pockets turned inside out. As it turned out, Mendell and fellow burglar Steven Garcia had struck again. The other members of the gang were too frightened to take on "the Boss."

Volpe, a stately Italian immigrant in his late seventies with white hair and a slim build who spoke in broken English, knew enough not to call the cops. Instead, he dialed his employer in

Palm Springs. The next morning, a livid Accardo boarded a flight back to Chicago to deal with this shocking intrusion.

No one burglarized the Boss and lived to tell the tale. At the time, the Outfit had many sources within the Chicago Police Department to help track down the perpetrators. William Hanhardt, for one, was the mobbed-up former Chief of Detectives for the CPD and after retirement a convicted jewel thief himself. He alone could provide the Outfit with enough information to round up the usual suspects.

The first suspect to "go missing" was Bernard Ryan, thirty-four, found with four bullets lodged in the back of his head. With a police scanner at his side, used to monitor street action, Ryan was a well-established jewel thief and convicted burglar. Next was Steven Garcia, stabbed with an ice pick numerous times, his throat slit ear to ear.

My father, Uncle Nick, Gumba, and Jarrett were assigned to grab Mendell. Jarrett, an experienced burglar himself, located Mendell and brought him in. It was a classic lure-your-friend-to-his-murder scenario. Jarrett had previously worked with Mendell and wanted to show him the fruits of a recent heist stored in his mother-in-law's garage—the same place where Haggerty was killed. It was a trap. There was no score, only my father, Uncle Nick, and Gumba lying in wait. On January 16, 1978, Mendell was severely beaten by Saladino and strangled by my dad, and his throat was slit by Nick. Afterward, his body was unceremoniously dumped into the trunk of his car.

The Outfit wanted to send a message from Accardo that no one was exempt; all the participants were to be killed. The Outfit's revenge campaign continued. Vincent Moretti and the innocent Donald Renno were rounded up. Moretti was suspected of being part of Mendell's crew and was known for stealing and fencing items without giving the mob its cut. Moretti, like Hanhardt, was a CPD cop gone bad.

Moretti and Renno were ambushed by two Chinatown crews after John Fecarotta lured them to Cicero on January 31, 1978, on the pretext of arranging a meeting for a deal to manufacture pizza boxes. Fecarotta was joined by Outfit hit man Tony Borsellino, Johnny "Apes" Monteleone, and Butch Petrocelli, who shared a hand in executing Renno, while Jarrett, Gumba, my father, and Uncle Nick allegedly took care of Moretti. This time it was my uncle who applied the rope around Moretti's neck while the four-hundred-pound Gumba joined in by mercilessly bouncing up and down on him. My father called the murder the "Strangers in the Night" killing because Sinatra's song was playing in the background.

Both Moretti's and Renno's bodies were found in the backseat of a parked car in Cicero with multiple stab wounds to the head and neck, a clear message that they had been tortured. Renno had nothing to do with the burglary but had the misfortune of being Moretti's friend. They were together when Moretti was grabbed. A coroner's autopsy indicated that Moretti had been stomped on and worked over. His face was unrecognizable. His ribs were broken and his kidneys were ruptured.

In February of 1978, John Mendell's body turned up on the South Side on a subzero day in an Oldsmobile sporting numerous parking tickets flapping in the Chicago breeze. Police opened the trunk and found him frozen stiff, icicles caking his eyes and mouth. His throat had been slit and a rope was wrapped around his neck. Mendell wore only a brown sweater and his underwear. His hands and feet were tied behind his back.

The entire Levinson's Jewelers affair was proof positive not only that the Outfit enjoyed free rein over Chicago to conduct its business, but that its style of vengeance had gone over the top. The hits ordered by the Boss had every burglar in town on the run. Bobby "the Beak" Siegel, a six-foot-two, 220-pound convicted murderer and jewel thief who claimed to be related to Bugsy Siegel, became concerned that he was next on the hit list. He went to his lawyer and asked for a polygraph test to show the bosses he wasn't involved in the Accardo break-in. The test saved his life. He was later also able to testify against the mobsters because of the test.

Just as the body count was subsiding, Michael Volpe, Accardo's caretaker, was called before a grand jury. Speculation was rife that before Carl Walsh, Accardo's attorney, could arrive, Volpe told more than he should have. Five days later, the seventy-five-year-old inexplicably vanished, never to be seen again.

The Calabrese crew had become an Outfit secret weapon. While my father carried out his orders, he felt that Accardo had taken the Levinson heist a little too personal. Leaving a trail of corpses in parked cars around town created a firestorm, and the press had a field day with screaming headlines about tortured bodies. Such was my father's concern, and it was warranted. Guys like him didn't need the heat.

But the Calabrese crew didn't refrain from imposing their own treachery on any customer who crossed them. Before the Levinson murders, on March 15, 1977, the smelly, decomposed body of Henry Cosentino, a two-bit hood, was found in a police auto impound, his head resting on a box of hamburger patties in an abandoned car on West Division Street. According to testimony, Cosentino was killed as a result of a juice loan gone horribly wrong. After Cosentino's brother took out a loan from Gumba and my father, an argument ensued, during which Henry shot Gumba in the leg. My father and Jarrett grabbed Cosentino and, in trademark fashion, strangled him and slashed his throat.

Uncle Nick was not present for the Cosentino slaying. He was out on a date, which didn't stop his older brother from berating him later for failing to show up for the assignment.

Throughout the 1970s, criminals operating in Chicago, be they burglars, bookmakers, or thieves, paid a "street tax" to the most ominous quartet of Outfit strongmen: Tony Borsellino, Harry Aleman, Jerry Scarpelli, and Butch Petrocelli. In return for his tribute, a bookmaker would get a phoned warning to clear out his office to avoid an upcoming police raid. The information came directly from corrupt cops throughout most of the police districts that the Outfit had on its payroll. Guys like Petrocelli, Borsellino, Scarpelli, and Aleman survived off their ability to intimidate.

My father had particular disdain for Petrocelli, whom he dismissed as a blowhard and bully. On the other hand, Dad showed enormous respect for Tony "Bors," whom he saw as a stand-up guy. "Tough Tony" reportedly whacked thirteen guys for the mob. Butch and Tony were continually at odds. Butch had more clout with the upper ranks, and he bent the ear of Rocky Infelise, boss of the West Side crew, that Borsellino was not to be trusted and that he was cooperating with law enforcement. There was no indication that Borsellino was a snitch. After discrepancies arose over the amount of money the Wild Bunch was supposed to turn in to the Outfit, with Butch stealing the cash, the blame was placed on Tough Tony.

Borsellino approached my dad, wanting to jump crews and come work for him in Chinatown. They spoke about Tony's problems with Butch, and how Petrocelli was holding back money and spreading rumors. Dad was sympathetic to Borsellino's situation. He welcomed having Tony as a member of his crew. At the same time, he couldn't risk rocking the boat by bringing him on without an okay. It was decided that he would speak to Angelo on Tony's behalf.

My father sat with Angelo to explain that Tony was being railroaded by Butch and that the hit should be stopped. But the Hook was in no mood for mercy and wouldn't intervene. According to Angelo, the only way my father could save his friend would be to step in and take his place. Not long after their sit-down, Borsellino was found in a Frankfort, Illinois, farm field with five bullet holes in the back of his head.

By the end of 1980, Butchie Petrocelli's act was getting tiresome to the Outfit hierarchy. He was suspected of skimming his collection money while shaking down street thieves and robbers without Outfit clearance. Worse, Petrocelli crossed the line by coming on to the wives of Outfit members who were away in prison. As his flamboyant behavior on the street drew more heat, the shoe dropped when Angelo discovered that a hundred thousand dollars of the cash Butch had raised one Christmas at a Gold Coast hotel to benefit his imprisoned friend Harry Aleman's family had ended up in Butch's pocket. LaPietra and Joe Ferriola, the boss of the Cicero crew (and Aleman's uncle), bristled at the thought of Petrocelli charging each guest a thousand bucks and dipping into the proceeds.

On December 30, Petrocelli was whistled in to meet with LaPietra at a Cicero social club. A block from their social club meeting spot, he was grabbed and dragged into a storefront office as Frankie Furio and Johnny Apes waited outside in their cars. Evidence at trial concluded that Uncle Nick, along with Frank Santucci and Jimmy LaPietra, held Petrocelli down while my father gave him the Calabrese necktie.

According to my uncle, Petrocelli's body was thrown into the backseat of Butch's red four-door 1977 Ford LTD and abandoned by my dad and Furio in an alleyway. When the pair returned, Jerry Scarpelli, who had accompanied Butch, now needed to search the car to retrieve his keys.

After my father, my uncle, and Scarpelli returned, LaPietra ordered Nick and my dad to go back a *third* time, this time to burn the body and the LTD. After emptying two large cans of Zippo lighter fluid, my uncle tossed a lit book of matches into the car. Butch's car windows were blackened, but the automobile didn't properly incinerate. Nick forgot to crack a window open to oxygenate the fire. His failure to understand a basic tenet of physics led to some concern that Butch had survived. (He hadn't.)

Petrocelli's car was ditched just before a heavy snowfall. Three months later, in March of 1981, Petrocelli's vehicle was found, his body thawed after the winter snows had melted.

8.

FRANKIE & JOHNNY'S

Some families eat to live. The Calabrese family lived to eat. Eating was an event and a daily celebration. My father loved food, restaurants, and cooking so much that eating could supersede business and his fervent love of money. There were rules attached: Do not talk business at the dinner table or in the car or in the house unless it was in his office with the television on. Information was doled out on a need-to-know basis. As a clever precaution, if Dad told a story, he'd tell a slightly different version to each person. If something got back to him, he would know who in his family or crew was the leak.

Dad loved to eat in the neighborhood restaurants and ma-and-pa joints (sitting facing the front door). His taste for food spanned the globe. When his family visited San Francisco, he scoured Chinatown, asking not where the tourists ate, but where the Chinese locals dined. Our family wound up eating a great Chinese meal in a small place, the only non-Asians in the dining room. In Chicago, he loved the lamb dishes in one of his favorite haunts in Greektown.

One day I came home from school to find five dead lambs, heads and all, hanging from hooks in the garage. "Your father is having Uncle Ang over to barbecue the lambs in the yard this weekend," my mother said.

Uncle Ang had a reputation for cooking the best lamb dishes. When asked if he ate the heads, he replied, "That's the best part, especially the eyes."

Once I graduated from high school, my father landed me a job with the city. After working the summer of my senior year on the curb and gutter crew, I graduated to the sewers as a full-time city employee. While I attended junior college for a few classes, I worked for the Department of Sewers.

When I was working curbs and gutters, there were two crews. One was the finishing crew, whose work included putting in new sidewalks and curbs. The guys from Chinatown and Taylor Street were assigned to that crew, where Dad had the most pull. We'd ride in big dump trucks into the worst neighborhoods, the projects. For the Department of Sewers, I started out as a laborer and worked my way up to crew foreman. Our responsibilities included cleaning, maintaining, and "rodding" the city sewers. Our city crew would hand-clean sewers and turn on hydrants to flush them out. Nobody works too hard for the city, but I got into it. The work ethic I was taught was when you did something, you took pride, whether it was laying sidewalk, cleaning sewers, or collecting money.

I spent much of 1978 and 1979 working on a "hand crew."

Workdays weren't too hard until I was transferred to the airport, where I worked on a vector, a large truck that sucked the dirt and leaves out of the sewers, starting at six o'clock in the morning. An old-timer Italian took a liking to me and brought me onto his crew, where I learned about operating heavy equipment. This old-timer was formerly a bookie for the Outfit who went legit.

Dating back to his days as a no-show, my dad was a legend with the city crews, as were the bookies and gangsters who pulled strings to "work" a city job. But I rarely used my status as Frank senior's son to become a no-show or skip work.

A lot of the bookies and gangsters who worked for the city were ghost payrollers. But I figured I didn't want to sit in a chair all day and watch other people work. I was on a crew with a black guy and an old Italian and became the subforeman who handled the paperwork.

Once I joined the city crew, I learned how to operate the Orange Peel Grapple, a special crane with a bucket that went into the catch basins, fetched the dirt and leaves, and deposited the stuff into a truck. You pulled the lever, the arm moved. You let the lever go, the arm stopped. I was intrigued by it. I got good at it. Plus, I could make twice the money running equipment emptying out the catch basins on the curbs. We'd work all over town.

Running the Orange Peel was a skill that would later come in handy while working with the crew.

I rode the political waves working for the city. Depending on who won the Chicago mayoral seat, I'd watch workers come and go as the city jobs changed hands based on who was allied with whom politically. One time a new guy who didn't know how to run the Orange Peel was breaking car and store windows while the rest of the crew workers ducked for cover, getting nothing done. I was the one who sat in the cab for him and worked the machine while he collected his paycheck.

Throughout my time working for the city, my father controlled all of my finances. Twice a month, I would dutifully hand over my paycheck to him and he would dole out a small portion back to me for pocket money.

When I worked at Armand's making pizza as a kid, I didn't have my own bank account. I'd bring my check to him and he would urge me to save my money. Out of the forty or fifty dollars, I'd get ten or fifteen. Here I was in my early twenties, handing over my checks while he deposited them into accounts under my name. That's how he controlled my brother and me. When I made twenty-six thousand dollars a year, twice a month he'd ask me how much out of an eight-hundred-dollar check I needed. Then he'd bust my balls: "What do you need two hundred dollars for?" He'd put the rest in the bank and enter the amount on a balance sheet. He never stole the money. It was about control. At the same time, he was laundering his own money while paying me in cash.

Like a lot of city workers, I did weekend jobs on the side, mostly sidewalks and driveways, to supplement my income, which was how I made pocket money without my dad knowing it. While working for the city, I had a lot of friends who were doing well fighting on the boxing circuit. There was a park in a nearby black neighborhood filled with Italian boxers. I began sparring with my friends, and in 1979 I entered in the Golden Gloves.

When I first started boxing, I couldn't tell my dad. Finally I had to let him know because my friends and I began making names for ourselves as fighters. A few of my friends ended up being ranked. When I came home one night from a fight, I showed him the trophy I had won, and he went nuts. I told him I just wanted to try it. It was odd that he would get upset, since he boxed amateur for a while and went undefeated. He was critical even though he had done the same things.

"No son of mine is gonna be no fuckin' boxer."

In 1980, I fought my Golden Gloves championship fight at the International Amphitheater in the old Chicago stockyards, in front of eight thousand spectators. Televised on WGN, it was the one fight he attended. He asked that I dedicate the fight to his dying father, who would be watching the bout from his hospital bed. Rated as the underdog, I won the fight by unanimous decision.

He was proud of me because I walked through the tournament and beat all my opponents. Like him, I was undefeated. At the time things were good. I was making money working for the city. I had a job and a girlfriend. But my heart wasn't into boxing. I didn't want to fight for a career. I did it mainly because I liked the jackets you received when you won. Yet, when I won the jacket I never wore it, because I thought it would look like I was bragging and calling attention to myself.

While working with the city, I was at my father's beck and call. I'd take off early some days from my city job to make time for my father's assignments—like a trip to Melrose Park as Uncle Nick's backup, when, under Joey Aiuppa's orders, Nick had to slap a guy around for selling fireworks without permission and not paying a street tax.

On Saturdays I'd go to Philly Tolomeo's apartment, while my father would go over the bookkeeping and have me sit next to him and watch. He'd have me check the figures or recount the money. It was very subtle. At no point did he ask me, or say that he wanted me to start working with him full-time. He would tell me that Philly was a moneymaker but a fuckup, and that we needed to get the money from him every week.

After I spent more time on the streets with the crew, my responsibilities expanded. There was this guy we knew, a friend, who operated a parking garage. My father found out he was selling drugs. He was working with us as a bookie, but he made the mistake of asking my uncle if he was interested in getting into the cocaine business. It was the 1980s. Everybody was doing it. He was a nice guy who was just being honest with my uncle. A lot of guys were selling, including Tony and Michael Spilotro.

My father wanted to send him a message. So we put a box together. He showed me how to mix kerosene with just the right amount of gasoline, putting it in gallon milk jugs. Then we drove out to the guy's garage, stuffed the jugs in a box with a lot of paper, lit a flare, and put the box up against the garage. That was the warning we sent out. At the time, the Chicago Outfit was adamantly opposed to drugs. When a guy's garage gets burned down, he knows something isn't right, that somebody knows he's doing something wrong. He got the message to stop.

In addition to working for the city, I hit the local nightclub scene, developing an interest in running my own joint.

I was spending a lot of time with my dad and my uncle, helping out a lot. I had ideas. For instance, why not take over a spot on Grand Avenue and put in an arcade? At the time, arcades were making a ton of legal money. Video games were just coming out. But my father would shoot down my ideas, so I kept them to myself. One day he said, "I don't understand what the fuck's going on with you. You had these great ideas. Now you've got no ideas or ambition."

I wanted to say, "It's not me, it's you!" If my kid came to me, especially when he was nineteen years old, and wanted to start a business, I'd work with him and maybe put up the money. I'd want to see my son succeed. But it was always about him. So I backed off.

Back in the neighborhoods, the young Italians were still fighting one another. Different neighborhoods would hang out in the nightclubs where there would be matchups. Elmwood Park against Melrose Park, or Riis Park versus Taylor Street.

One club was the 1-2-3 on Diversey and Central in Chicago. In 1993, it became a Polish nightclub called the Jedynka Club. But back in early 1980s, when you walked in the door, the 1-2-3 was a cross between *GoodFellas* and *Saturday Night Fever*. The crowd was predominantly Italian, and every neighborhood had its section inside. The club owner would take a guy from each neighborhood and designate him as a bouncer. The guy would stand around with the people in his section, drink, and keep order.

The rule at 1-2-3 was that you couldn't fight inside. When a section was ready to fight another group, everybody piled out into the street. Most Fridays, Diversey Avenue and Central Avenue traffic was blocked off because so many guys were hanging out and street fighting. Occasionally the Italians clashed with other races, especially when the North Austin district turned black. Sometimes it was the disco guys wearing leather jackets versus the rock guys with the long hair and biker look. Usually it was guys from different Italian neighborhoods fighting over a girl.

I wound up getting a weekend job at the 1-2-3 bouncing the Elmwood Park section. I was perfect for the job: tall and good at handling myself, and well respected in the neighborhood. The pay was fifty dollars a night, plus drinks. I didn't tell my dad until one night when he asked me what I was up to. Then he told me, "Whattaya mean you're fuckin' workin' security? I don't want you to be no fuckin' goon bouncer at some crazy place." But eventually he agreed to let me earn the extra hundred dollars a week.

I got along with the guys from the club, and one day I was talking to my friend Johnny Galioto, who was James "Little Jimmy" Marcello's nephew. Johnny was working the 1-2-3 as a bartender when he and I talked about starting our own club.

We had a lot of ideas about opening up a champagne room. There was a guy from the Patch who had a place called Sassafras and was looking for someone to reopen and run it. Johnny and I had a following. The guy came to us and asked if we'd be interested. We sat down and worked out a handshake deal. He gave us ten thousand dollars to fix up the club. We ordered drink inventory and had about four thousand or five thousand dollars left in the till. We got our friends together, glass etchers, electricians, builders, and carpenters. We fixed up the club and it was absolutely beautiful. We called it Frankie & Johnny's. It was on Irving Park, just west of Harlem. This was 1984 and I was twenty-four years old. We were the first place in the city to feature a VIP champagne room. We had waitresses in sexy outfits. People loved it.

At first my dad gave me a hard time.

"Who the fuck are you, owning a nightclub?" To him, a nightclub was way too high-profile. Plus, if I began making money, he would feel that he had lost control of his son.

As much fun as I had running my own joint, it took its toll. I was working during the day for the city, running the club at night, and going out with my father and uncle on the crew. I was running around all the time, but I loved the idea of having a legit business. Not only was there prestige, but I had a feeling of accomplishment. And there were the beautiful girls. It was a business Johnny and I both enjoyed. We hired the best bartenders in the area.

After about a year, the owner, a guy nicknamed Poopsy, started getting uneasy. Poopsy ran a concession at city hall, which made lots of money. He wore black combat boots, a toupee, and a little hat. When he found out who Frankie and Johnny were related to, he feared the worst. But I was determined to keep the place afloat by being straight, since there was no paperwork verifying our arrangement with Poopsy.

One weekend, Johnny and I arrived at the club to find the locks changed and the doors padlocked. Somebody must have bent Poopsy's ear, because he got scared. We sat down and pleaded with him.

"We're running a legit business. We put in our time and haven't taken a dime out of the business."

But we knew the club was history. Poopsy wound up giving us the keys back. As soon as we got them back, we stole everything out of the joint. We carried out the liquor and sold it. We sold whatever we put into the place. Later we locked the doors behind us and never went back. Poopsy called, tossing around Joey Lombardo's name to try and scare us into returning everything.

We told him, "Do what you have to, but are you sure Joey knows you're using his name like that?"

My ace was that Lombardo senior was in jail at the time, and we knew that my dad and Johnny's uncle, Little Jimmy Marcello, would back us.

Still in my early twenties, I returned to work at the 1-2-3 part-time, while Johnny opened a bar with his father on North Avenue. Then I left my job with the city and felt ready to work with the crew full-time. My dad was more than happy to expand my role in the family business.

9.

A WHITE FLASH AND A BURST OF HEAT

Throughout the 1980s, under the noses of federal and local law enforcement, my father and his Chinatown crew ran wild. It was the climax of an era during which my father survived the Outfit's changing leadership, starting in 1969 with hit man Milwaukee Phil Alderisio.

Next was the bloody decade-and-a-half (1971–86) reign of Joey "Doves" Aiuppa. Then came Sam "Wings" Carlisi in 1989. Throughout the 1980s, my father weathered numerous power plays between Angelo LaPietra and Turk Torello. My dad complained that Torello repeatedly snubbed the 26th Street/Chinatown crew because of Angelo when legit money opportunities—like owning legal OTB (off-track betting) parlors—became available to Outfit crews.

One constant remained. Whenever the boys on top needed someone eliminated, my father got his share of calls. He was respected and feared as an accomplished killer.

The June 1981 assassination of Michael Cagnoni in ritzy Hinsdale in DuPage County, twenty miles from downtown Chicago, is a case in point. Cagnoni was a successful entrepreneur in the refrigerated-trucking business who made sure his trucks crisscrossed the country fully loaded. As a result of his load efficiency, Cagnoni's firm retained satisfied customers including the mob's produce-hauling concerns. By maintaining high profitability in a tough business, Cagnoni offered lower rates, which caused competitors such as Flash Interstate, one of Cagnoni's local subcontractors, to lower theirs.

Flash Interstate Trucking in Cicero was co-owned by mob bosses Joe Ferriola and Turk Torello. Located on South Laramie Avenue, Flash conveniently served as a clubhouse and rendezvous spot for organized crime figures like Rocky Infelise. According to one Flash insider, there was always one hundred thousand dollars in cash waiting in the safe to bankroll mob bookmaking or juice loan operations.

In the tradition of gangsters hiding "in plain sight," Ferriola and Infelise often held their meetings both in the Flash parking lot and in an adjoining garage, out of earshot of FBI surveillance agents parked nearby. For over thirteen months, the FBI listened in via phone taps and monitored visitors. By mid-1981, the FBI was convinced that Flash was the site where many Outfit schemes and hits were hatched, during visits by Ferriola, Infelise, and a lineup of other gangsters and jewel thieves.

Cagnoni religiously paid his weekly street tax of two thousand dollars in cash. He was often seen entering the Hyatt Hotel in Rosemont, where Joey Aiuppa would lunch. Cagnoni would go to the Flash office to drop off money. In return for his cash payments, Cagnoni's operations ran free from labor problems.

When he realized that he could no longer justify the weekly cash outlay in case of an IRS audit, Cagnoni tried negotiating to make the payments some other way. He was willing to draw up contracts and continue making the payments by check. Ferriola and Infelise were inflexible and demanded cash. Ferriola had eyes to take over Cagnoni's business, so when an exasperated Cagnoni stopped making payments, he hired a bodyguard, donned a flak jacket, and hoped for the best. While the FBI kept a watch on Flash Trucking, another surveillance unit placed John Fecarotta, Frank Santucci, and my father meeting together in a parking lot about a block from Cagnoni's business.

Once Aiuppa pushed the button on Cagnoni it was up to my father and the crew to carry out the hit. For almost a year, Cagnoni was shadowed in and around his affluent west suburban Hinsdale home. Once the crew determined his daily routine, they elected to firebomb him. My dad tested different combinations of explosives, blasting caps, and remote firing devices to determine how close they needed to be to set off the fatal explosion in or around Cagnoni's automobile. During the preparation stage, there were mishaps, including one ill-fated test that nearly took off my father's hand.

After months of stalking, my father and Fecarotta settled on a plan. They inserted a brick-sized portion of malleable C-4 underneath Cagnoni's silver 1978 Mercedes. Then they placed a transmitter inside an unattended car left in a restaurant parking lot next to the Ogden Avenue on-ramp, which Cagnoni habitually used to drive onto I-294. A remote car starter receiver was attached to the explosives under Cagnoni's car either the night before or early in the morning. Inside the parked car, a K-40 antenna and the transmitter, modified to increase its range, emitted a continuous signal. The button on the transmitter was taped down under a block of wood. Once Cagnoni drove by, the receiver and the explosives in his car would set off a lethal blast.

Michael Cagnoni's pending murder became a turning point for my uncle, as he harbored doubts about his role as the dependable cold-blooded killer. He was a family man with kids, and while staking out the Cagnoni residence one day, he watched in horror as Cagnoni's wife, Margaret, started up the family Mercedes to take their young son, Michael junior, to school.

"This poor woman," Uncle Nick later said, "got in the car. If she had come east and not west . . . I don't know what . . ."

Had she driven by the engaged remote-control detonator, the device would have set off the C-4, instantly killing Cagnoni's wife and child. After the close call, my uncle confronted my dad. Killing gangsters and shaking down businesses for Outfit money was one thing, but murdering innocent women and children was another.

My father responded angrily by smacking my uncle with his hand, fracturing his face, his psyche, and his allegiance to his older brother. This incident would prove to be the beginning of the end of their relationship.

Cagnoni later drove into the trap alone. One witness, James Mammina, testified that on June 24, 1981, while driving his Ford van, he saw Cagnoni's Mercedes pull up in front of him and head toward the Tri-State Tollway at Ogden Avenue and I-294. He heard a loud explosion, saw a white flash, and felt a burst of heat through his windshield.

"The smoke cleared and I was able to see his vehicle, or what was left of it."

In a grisly FBI photograph that no jury would see, human remains, mostly head and shoulders, are plopped in the middle of the I-294 on-ramp. Pieces of the luxury Mercedes-Benz were strewn everywhere, and from as far away as a quarter mile, birds came to feast on Cagnoni's scattered body parts.

In the months that followed, more bodies were strewn in my father's wake. Barely three months after the Cagnoni bombing, Nicholas D'Andrea, a lieutenant of Chicago Heights boss Al "Caesar" Tocco, was found in the trunk of a burning car in Crete,

Illinois. D'Andrea was suspected of participating in the botched hit of Al Pilotto, whose day job was president of Local 5 of the Laborers' International Union of North America. At night Al ran the gambling, prostitution, extortion, and juice business in the southern suburb Chicago Heights. As Pilotto was playing a round of golf, out of the bushes came a surprise visitor with a .22-caliber pistol. After a couple of misses and a nonfatal hit, the assailant ran off, missing his hole in one.

D'Andrea was quite the ladies' man at age forty-two. He was courting his fifteen-year-old girlfriend, Terry. D'Andrea eventually married Terry and left her behind when he was dispatched by the mob's trunk stuffers.

With the bombing death of Cagnoni accomplished, restaurant owner Nick Sarillo was the next victim when his blue Econoline cargo van suddenly exploded in April of 1982. According to court testimony, the blast "had something to do with gambling," and it was alleged that Sarillo, a tough guy in his own right, refused to pay off Joe Amato, the designated leader of Outfit gambling interests in the northern suburbs. When the explosion occurred, Sarillo was driving in the village of Wauconda in Lake County, located on the far northeastern tip of Illinois. Sarillo was seriously injured and very sooty, but he miraculously survived Wile E. Coyote–style and remained silent. Since there was no room for the explosives under the driver's seat, they were placed instead under the passenger's side. The engine area between the driver and passenger sides deflected the blast, and the blowout backfired to the cargo portion of the van.

"He looked like a cartoon face, all in black," recalled Chuck Fagan, a deputy for the Lake County Sheriff's Office. "But when you try to talk to these fellas, it's like talking to a wall. Even in all that pain and agony, they've got nothing to say."

Years later, despite Sarillo's silence, the Bureau of Alcohol, Tobacco, and Firearms would link the characteristics of his bombing to Cagnoni's, thanks to the identical brand of motherboard connected to the electronics and the modus operandi used to detonate the chunk of C-4 strategically placed under the seat of the van.

But it was the deaths of Richard Ortiz and Arthur Morawski in the summer of 1983, dubbed the "Half and Half Murders," that would propel my father's reputation as hit man du jour. Ortiz had drawn the ire of Johnny Apes, who was irritated by Ortiz's drug deals and that Ortiz owed him money—whether from street tax or juice—and was ducking him. The Outfit also suspected that Ortiz had killed one of their own, Leo Manfredi, in a Cicero pizza parlor without authorization. This meant Ortiz had to go.

My father served as the maestro of Ortiz's demise. On July 23, 1983, after pulling up in front of the His 'N' Mine Lounge on Twenty-second Street in Cicero, he dispatched Uncle Nick and Jimmy DiForti, both carrying shotguns, to do the dirty work while he strategically parked his car diagonally, blocking any chance of escape. Arthur Morawski, it was later revealed, was an innocent victim who was in the wrong place at the wrong time. He had just hitched a ride home from the racetrack. A prime piece of evidence collected on the scene, a live shotgun shell, was found on the back passenger-side window of Ortiz's car.

10.

KEEP THINGS IN THE FAMILY

By the mid-1980s, the domestic landscape of the Calabrese home was dramatically changing. After nearly a dozen years with his mistress, Diane Cimino, on the side, my dad separated from and divorced my mom, or more accurately she divorced him. Dad married Diane at an intimate family gathering at Tony Spavone's restaurant in Bloomington, Illinois, in early 1986.

I believe that my father manipulated my mom into divorcing him. He wore her down with his ways. Living in the Compound with his whole family, she'd had enough. Moving to a brand-new house in the affluent suburban village of Oak Brook with Diane, he found that transitioning his goomah-turned-wife into his sons' stepmother wasn't easy.

None of us wanted to meet her, but we were never comfortable telling my dad no. My youngest brother, Nicky, was just a teenager at the time, and he took the divorce badly. Dad called Nicky and me upstairs to talk about meeting Diane. Nicky wouldn't answer. My dad kept pushing, but Nicky wouldn't say anything. His eyes were full of tears. I wanted to butt in and tell my father to lay off him, that he was having a hard time with it.

Nicky yelled, "I don't wanna meet Diane because I hate your fucking guts for what you did!"

My father lost it. He jumped up and whaled on Nicky, both hands flying, swinging and cracking him in the face. "You don't fucking talk to me like that. I will kick your ass."

It kills me that I didn't protect my little brother.

After my dad moved out of the Elmwood Park Compound, he would occasionally show up for one of Mom's home-cooked holiday meals. I would take my mother out every Christmas in my pickup truck to buy a Christmas tree. One year, with me in bed with the flu, my father happened by in a cheerful mood and volunteered to take Mom to get a tree if she agreed to make one of his favorite Italian chicken dishes. Kurt was enlisted to come along, although he had plans. My mother took a long time selecting the tree, and by the time they got back to the house, Dad was in a foul mood.

Kurt was pouting "with a puss on his face," and as my father tried to straighten the tree in the stand, he erupted. He cracked Kurt in the head, knocking him and the tree to the floor, and stomped out, yelling, "Look what you made me do, asshole!"

After his honeymoon, he felt threatened by Diane's close relationship with her father. Dominic Cimino was a retired police chief of Melrose Park and a war hero, and was well-liked around town. I was with my dad one night in Diane's father's garage. I could see that something was eating him and that he was hatching a plan—to lure Dominic into the garage and whack him.

I was speechless. I couldn't believe it. Suddenly murder became the best way to solve a family problem. I no longer knew where he drew the line and whom he would or wouldn't kill. He never whacked Dominic Cimino. In time, their relationship improved, and Cimino died from natural causes in 2008.

Gunning for a family member wasn't an entirely new concept to my dad. According to a story captured on tape, my uncle Ed was once heard bad-mouthing Italians and the Outfit during a drunken tirade at a downtown bar. After confronting Hanley, Joey Aiuppa set up an ambush at a local steam room with my father and Angelo parked outside. On Aiuppa's signal, when Uncle Ed walked out of the bathhouse, the two were to spring into action. But the signal to kill did not come. My father's original plan was to spirit Uncle Ed into the car by telling him that something had happened to my mother, his sister.

I asked Dad if he was okay with that, and he said, "An order is an order, and the Outfit comes before your family."

Angelo became part of the family when Kurt became romantically involved with his granddaughter, Angela Lascola. Kurt and Angela were young when they began dating. At first, Angelo took a shine to Kurt. He was "Frankie C's" son, and Kurt and Angela's impending marriage "would keep things in the family." But the couple's relationship soured.

A few years later Kurt and Angela reunited, which didn't sit well with Angelo, who was in jail at the time. Kurt and Angela continued to see each other secretly, and when Kurt confided his renewed love for Angela to my father, he blew a gasket. Kurt and Angela reacted by eloping at city hall.

When my father found out, he nearly killed Kurt. He chased him in his car at speeds over ninety miles per hour, trying to run him off the road. When he caught up with Kurt, he gave him a beating and threatened to disown him.

In 1986, not long after his marriage to Diane, my father suffered intense migraine headaches and had problems with his eyesight. He wasn't keen on doctors, dating back to his childhood, when he spent months recovering from scarlet fever. Diane persuaded him to get a checkup, and after the results of the tests came back, I met with him at his Oak Brook home. The news wasn't good. He had problems with his pituitary gland. His white blood count was minuscule, and it was feared that he might have a tumor in the middle of his brain.

After further tests confirmed the tumor, my dad required immediate brain surgery. Assembling his family for a sit-down, he sugarcoated his condition, laughing it off. But privately with me, he was very worried. His orders were precise.

He told me I needed to step up and run things with Uncle Nick because there was a good chance that he would die from the surgery or else go blind. I was to stay in the background with the bosses and let them think my uncle was running everything.

As my dad's health problems worsened, my devotion to my ailing father increased. We spent "quality time" together going over specific scenarios and rules: Never completely trust or confide in anybody. Any direct questions about his businesses, plead ignorance. Take care of my mother, and don't fight with my brothers over anything material. He wanted me to be cautious and work closely with Uncle Nick. He knew that people on the street could take advantage of Nick's kindness whenever they came up short on collections.

My father sat down with me and Kurt and pulled out a large case of expensive jewelry. He urged us to divide everything in half. Kurt and I looked at each other.

"We don't care about your jewelry. We only want you to get well." We knew how hard it was for him to give up control.

On the day of the operation, my father insisted that both families be present in the waiting room. My dad's will was strong. At the same time, he looked vulnerable as they wheeled him away. For the first time in my life, my big strong dad looked helpless.

An awkward air hovered over the waiting room as my father's two families occupied opposite ends. On one side was Diane and her family; on the other was my mother and my two brothers and Uncle Nick. After Dad had been under the knife for hours, the doctors pulled a golf-ball-sized tumor out of his skull. But the prognosis was good. He would be in pain for a while, but the surgery had gone smoothly. I was encouraged.

Wow! Things were going to change for the best. With a second chance at life, my father would be more humble. He would see the light and maybe walk away from his life with the crew. Maybe the tumor was the reason for his multiple personalities and abusive behavior, and after the surgery the "good dad" would return permanently.

I spent most of my time with Uncle Nick while my dad convalesced. We both hit the streets and collected loan payments and street taxes and set up a temporary office in the basement of my father's Oak Brook home. While he was getting stronger, I hatched a bold plan. I painted an overly grim picture of his health to Dad's mob friends and associates. Every time I ran into a friend of my dad's or an Outfit associate, I'd sadly hang my head. Soon word spread on the street that my dad was very sick and possibly wouldn't make it. I asked him, "Why not play the sick card and step back from the crew so that you won't be obligated to the Outfit anymore?"

He seriously considered the idea, but the stronger he got, the more remote the possibility of "stepping back" became. All my hopes of his retirement fizzled after he told me he was itching to get back into action and reaffirm his presence on the street. "I'm gonna be back out on the street and get everybody back in line! And the first place I'm gonna start is in the neighborhood. I will get everybody's asses twitching again."

While recovering on the sidelines, my father missed out on a pair of plum Outfit assignments: the killing of Emil Vaci in Arizona and the murders of Tony and Michael Spilotro.

11.

PHILLY BEANS

With its sprawling green industrial parks and grand highways, Oak Brook in DuPage County was a long way from the Patch. It was home to the world corporate headquarters of the McDonald's fast-food chain. One intersection in Oak Brook could be as large as a city block in Grand and Ogden. Although it was out of his comfort zone to build a large dream home and be

ostentatious, my father hired an architect to design his very own McMansion.

He didn't set out to build the biggest house in the neighborhood, as he now lived among the Outfit brass. Joe "Nagall" Ferriola had a home one block away, while Joey Aiuppa's compound was just down the street. My father's finished house featured a grand wood staircase cascading into a large open foyer. The bedrooms were spacious and jumbo-sized compared to the salad days of the Elmwood Park three-flat. The home's interior was similar to television gangster Tony Soprano's. Years later, whenever my mother and I watched the TV series, we would laughingly associate the Soprano dwelling and its fancy appliances with my dad's house in Oak Brook.

Unlike today's Chicago Outfit bosses, who have converted much of their Outfit fortunes into legitimate business enterprises, it was difficult for my father to make the same transition. He was often too stern and unyielding to be a lawful, let alone silent, business partner. Just like with the adult-bookstore owner, he would wear people down and drive them away with his demands. As a result, his foray into legitimate business was limited to co-owning hot-dog stands and other eateries with his mob buddies.

My father, Uncle Nick, Kurt, and I launched a general contracting company, hiring a few of my Elmwood Park buddies. Together we would remodel income properties to resell at a tidy profit. After I gave up my coveted city job, the fledgling Calabrese contractors won the bid for the masonry work and drywall for an addition at North Central College in Naperville. The partnership proved tense from the start. With my father in total control, the shortest tasks might take hours to complete.

Outfit business on the streets of Chicago flourished. Father controlled his empire like Genghis Khan. It would take the smoothest of the smooth to bilk a Calabrese out of his hard-earned cash—that is, until he hooked up with journeyman Outfit juice collector Philip "Philly Beans" Tolomeo.

Philly Beans started out as a Chicago policeman who grew up with another Chicago cop gone bad, Mike Ricci. They worked side by side until Philly got kicked off the force. In fact, Philly ran the Bistro A-Go-Go the night Larry Stubitsch was shot and killed by Dickie DeAngelo. As a young man Philly had that *Saturday Night Fever* Italian pretty-boy look that women ate up.

Philly had a weakness for underage girls, and loved to con older women out of their fortunes. Yet Philly the hustler could effectively lay out a ton of new juice money on the streets. He had a load of connections and was especially well liked. My father was confident he could manage Philly Beans and let him join his crew. Joe Ferriola felt that if anybody could rein him in, it was Frankie C.

I first met Tolomeo at a hot-dog stand in Melrose Park that my dad co-owned with Mike Ricci, Nick, Johnny DiFronzo, and Ronnie Jarrett. I recall seeing Philly Beans talking on the pay phone, dressed in a loud sport coat with matching slacks, and a garish yellow-and-rust-colored fedora.

By 1987, Philly Beans had juice all over town. He was one of the crew's biggest earners. Although Philly was a moneymaker, he was "a fuckup" whom my father and I needed to stay on top of. Every Saturday night my father and I would meet next door to Armand's Pizza, inside an antique car storefront after closing hours. I would wait for my father to pull into the back. Philly would arrive through the back door, and later Ronnie Jarrett would follow. Tolomeo would turn in his loan paperwork for us to review. A typical Calabrese "loan application" was handwritten on an index card, complete with a customer's vital information, including driver's license, date of birth, job and salary information, what jewelry and titles he owned, and whatever he could put up for collateral. My father and I would go through the same routine with Philly every week.

When my father returned to working with the crew after his convalescence, he put two and two together and figured that Philly was loaning my father's juice to himself. Apparently Philly Beans had attended the Bernie Madoff/Charles Ponzi School of Banking. My father sent my uncle around to check up on a few of Philly's delinquent customers, and it turned out that he had a long list of ghost debtors. Philly wasn't distributing Calabrese loan money to new accounts after all; he was pocketing the money for himself. To make up for the deficit in payments, Philly Beans rotated different customers as late. On the days he came up short or the numbers didn't add up, he repeatedly took Uncle Nick's kindness for weakness, and my uncle would often make up the shortfall out of his own pocket.

My father confronted Philly with the damaging evidence at M&R Auto, a repair shop in Elmwood Park owned by a mechanic friend, Matt Russo. Dad beat Philly badly, breaking his cheekbone. Philly Beans wound up owing my father over three hundred thousand dollars.

My father and uncle paid a visit to Elmwood Park to sort out Philly's problem with his mother. My dad explained to her that Philly had stolen a large sum of money from "certain people" and that her son could be in deep trouble. While he didn't threaten her, he gave her an out to use the house as collateral for the loan. He promised not to kick her out and gave her the option to sign over the hundred-thousand-dollar house to him or place it in the name of one of Nick's in-laws.

Once the house was taken over, he rode Philly Beans pretty hard, slapping him across the back of the head and giving him barely enough money every week to live on. Philly knew that if he ran wild again, he would get more than a broken cheekbone. This time his life was on the line. The only reason he was kept alive was to work in the crew and make restitution for the rest of the three hundred grand he had stolen. Yet Philly understood that once he paid the money back he would become disposable.

Philip Tolomeo disappeared from the Chicago area. It turned out that the Calabrese crew was not the only organized crime group Philly Beans had scammed. In addition to embezzling my father's money, he had taken cash from another Outfit crew. Tolomeo fled to California, where he set up more con jobs on unsuspecting ladies and widows. When his luck ran out on the West Coast, Philly Beans turned himself in to the FBI. Before entering the Witness Security Program, he handed over to the Bureau detailed records of the juice collections he had made on behalf of the Calabrese family 26th Street/Chinatown crew.

Now it was the government's turn to babysit Philly Beans until they could build a case against my family. This proved to be highly problematic for the FBI and the WITSEC Program because Philly was up to his old grifter ways. He was arrested for soliciting an underage prostitute and had to be re-relocated. A short time later, the FBI discovered he was back in the juice loan business, working with the South Philly mob. He was arrested again, and had to sit in WITSEC isolation until his case came up.

Despite his flamboyance, Philly was a problem for my father and the crew if they went to trial. His smooth style, personal panache, and firsthand knowledge of the inner workings of the crew could help the government win over any jury.

12.

THE BOYS OUT WEST

If Uncle Nick's involvement in the murder of Emil "Mal" Vaci wasn't so gruesome, it might be right out of *The Gang That Couldn't Shoot Straight*. My uncle, Big Stoop, and Frank Schweihs were sent by the bosses to Arizona and Las Vegas to settle a couple of troubling problems. Everything that could go wrong did, and for Nick, it ranked as a very surreal road trip.

The sad fate of Emil Vaci started at the Stardust Hotel and Casino in Vegas during the 1970s. The Stardust was

run by Al Sachs, Bobby Stella, and the Outfit's gambling ace, Frank "Lefty" Rosenthal, portrayed by Robert De Niro in the film *Casino.* Lefty worked under a variety of job titles to get around the gaming license requirements. Rosenthal had previously pleaded no contest to charges of conspiring to fix a New York University basketball game by approaching the star point guard, Ray Paprocky. The Stardust's owner of record, Allan Glick, and his company, Argent, operated three other Vegas properties, the Hacienda, the Fremont, and the Marina. But the Stardust was Glick's flagship hotel.

By 1979, the FBI had begun investigating the Vegas money trail. In what later became known as Operation Strawman, quarterbacked out of the FBI's Kansas City office, a series of FBI wiretaps uncovered the infamous Las Vegas "skim." A skim is cash income being skimmed off the top, uncounted, pocketed, and hidden from government tax returns. During the 1970s, this cash was diverted to Chicago and Kansas City mob headquarters. Part of Rosenthal's job was to make sure the Stardust kept up its skim numbers.

Operating at the nearby Fremont was a clever slot manager, George Jay Vandermark, who was a six-foot-two, 190-pound, older version of Alfred E. Neuman. Vandermark was easy to spot with his trademark black horn-rimmed glasses and dual hearing aids. Long a mastermind with the slots, Vandermark set up a system at the Fremont where a group of phantom change booths stood in the middle of the casino floor, right under the nose of the gaming commission inspectors, generating pure mob revenue by miscalibrating the scales that counted the coins by weight. While the Fremont's "legitimate" change booths were only "counting" nine hundred dollars per thousand brought in, "extra" booths generated 100 percent unaccounted, unreported skimmed funds to the tune of millions of dollars a year. The exact amount that was actually sent back to Chicago was another story.

It wasn't long before Lefty Rosenthal moved Vandermark from the Fremont to the Stardust. It was then that Dennis Gomes of the Nevada Gaming Control Board figured out the skim. Only he couldn't prove it, because, time after time, a leak inside Las Vegas law enforcement warned the gangsters of any pending raids on the casino counting rooms. Gomes, tired of the tip-offs, acted independently and staged his own impromptu raid on the Stardust.

Gomes's spontaneous raid uncovered a seven-million-dollar Vandermark skim. The trouble was that the Outfit had received only four million of it. Realizing that he had just opened a can of worms for Vandermark, Gomes set out to warn him, only to be informed by Jay's son that his father had gone "on vacation" to Mexico in mid-May 1976.

A few days later, Vandermark's son was found dead, apparently of a drug overdose. Vandermark returned to the U.S. after his son was murdered. Instead of coming back to Vegas, he relocated to Phoenix and checked into the Arizona Manor, an Arizona hot spot for celebrities, under the name of George Skinner. The Manor was managed by Emil Vaci—who had run junkets from Phoenix to Las Vegas, and was tied in with the Outfit. Vaci tipped off John Fecarotta and Jimmy LaPietra. They paid Vandermark a visit at the Manor and took him for a walk. After Vandermark was killed on the premises, his body was taken out in a wheelchair, driven to the desert, and buried.

Almost five years later, in 1981, a grand jury in Kansas City indicted a handful of mob bosses, including Joe Agosto and KC mob boss Nick Civella, for skimming and redirecting gambling funds from Vegas hotels into mob accounts. But after seven convictions in 1983, the government still wanted to know about Vandermark's disappearance.

On January 21, 1986, Emil Vaci was questioned by a grand jury on the disappearance of Jay Vandermark. Outfit bosses were concerned that his testimony would not only expose them, but affect their entire skimming operation.

Vaci's grand jury appearance was problematic. Ordinarily gangsters taking the fifth in front of a grand jury spend only a short time behind closed doors. Vaci spent over three hours pleading the fifth. Though he revealed nothing, the Outfit had grave doubts, and since it was better to be safe than sorry, it was decided back in Chicago that Emil Vaci had to go.

It was decided that a group of elite hit men would be dispatched west from Chicago not only to deal with Vaci's worrisome grand jury appearance, but to also take care of Tony Spilotro in Las Vegas. Spilotro and his crew were out of control, pulling heists and drawing attention, irritating Tony Accardo and Joey Aiuppa. Spilotro had become one of the most celebrated Outfit crime figures since Capone. His high-profile crime spree plagued the Outfit and continued to garner unwanted publicity as the Vegas news media regularly reported burglaries and home invasions, unauthorized by the boys back home.

The hierarchy in the Outfit was fed up with the trouble out West, and the frustration peaked when Joey Aiuppa and Jackie Cerone were sentenced to prison because Spilotro was out of control in Vegas. Stories were getting back to Aiuppa that Spilotro was involved with Rosenthal's wife, Geri (played by Sharon Stone in *Casino*). The old mustaches, as they were referred to, frowned on violating the long-held taboo of sleeping with the wife of a high-ranking mobster. The icing on the cake was the unauthorized murders and heists, which were only drawing more attention to Spilotro and his so-called Hole in the Wall crew.

In March 1986, Uncle Nick got the call from "Big Stoop" Fecarotta to come west to Arizona. Because he was toting explosives (supplied by Little Jimmy Marcello) inside his carry-on bag, my uncle opted to take a train rather than a plane. Once he arrived at the Phoenix train station, he was met by Big Stoop and Frank "the German" Schweihs. The three men drove to Las Vegas together to spend a couple of weeks "laying on" Tony and Michael. The initial plan was to take out the Spilotros first, then go to Arizona and complete the Vaci assignment.

The trio floated a few ideas on how to kill the Spilotros. Frank the German suggested gunning them down with an Uzi in the basement offices of a local lawyer. Or how about killing them on the courthouse steps after an upcoming court appearance? Death by explosives was discussed. My uncle, not a risk taker, wasn't convinced. No use "cowboying" it Wild Bunch–style, like Butch Petrocelli might have done.

"If we kill these guys with an Uzi in broad daylight," my uncle reasoned, "they'll lock the whole city down. There's only a couple of ways in and out of Vegas. We'll never make it out alive."

As the crew found out, it proved extremely difficult to get both Spilotro brothers together and vulnerable. Arriving back in Arizona from Vegas, Uncle Nick met Paul "the Indian" Schiro for the first time. The Indian, a career burglar, served as the Outfit's point man in the Southwest. He was an old friend of Emil Vaci's, a fact that didn't seem to deter him from helping to plot his death.

As the days and weeks passed, back home in Chicago, imprisoned boss Aiuppa was getting impatient with the boys out West. They had already spent close to a hundred G's, sent via Federal Express by Sam "Wings" Carlisi, hidden inside a shipment of cigars. After weeks of stalking the Spilotros with zero results, my uncle was getting concerned about having squandered so much Outfit dough with nothing to show for it. Fearing an impatient Outfit might push the button on *them*, they decided that Emil Vaci had to be killed next, and pronto. But how?

One proposal: my uncle would dress up as a FedEx man, walk into the back of Vaci's wife's dress shop, and shoot him, a plan that was foiled when a telephone man was in the back, up on a pole installing wire for new phone lines. Was he a fed?

Another option: murder Vaci outside Ernesto's, the restaurant where he worked as maître d'.

After suddenly being called back to Chicago and redispatched, the hit team, now consisting of Nick, Paul Schiro, Jimmy DiForti, John Fecarotta, and Joey Hansen (leaving Frank the German behind in Chicago), returned to Arizona with a new plan. The four mobsters quickly went back to work. They dug three holes forty-five minutes outside of town. They parked a stolen 1986 Pontiac Grand Prix (grifted earlier by Frank the German) to hold a place next to Vaci's regular parking space. According to a report and citation written on March 26, 1986, all four of the Pontiac's tires were slashed by vandals, which raised concerns among the hit squad that someone was possibly wise to the hit.

Prior to the murder, my uncle and Big Stoop drove from Phoenix to Las Vegas, possibly to pick up weapons. On their way back to Phoenix, they stopped at an Arizona casino in Bullhead City, where Fecarotta hit a $2,100 jackpot. Curiously, it was my uncle who signed the tax form using his own name, which again, decades later, placed him in the vicinity of the Vaci murder.

Fecarotta would leave Phoenix again for Vegas prior to Vaci's murder. After being forced to testify in a Washington, D.C., hearing investigating Outfit links with labor unions, Big Stoop felt that he was drawing law enforcement heat. Capo Jimmy LaPietra would later equate Fecarotta's departure to Vegas with abandoning his Outfit obligations in Phoenix.

The final plan was simplified. Uncle Nick and Hansen would grab Vaci one night after work, throw him into an Econoline "pleasure" van parked directly next to his car, shoot and strangle him, and then deposit his corpse into one of the three holes outside of town.

Each team member's role was assigned the night of the Vaci hit: Nick was the shooter, Joey Hansen was the van driver, and Paul Schiro and Jimmy DiForti were lookouts. After closing time on Saturday night, June 7, 1986, Vaci, who had just bought a new suit to wear to a ceremony to renew his wedding vows, walked out to his car. Suddenly Uncle Nick slid open the Econoline door and grabbed him. A struggle ensued. Together, Hansen and my uncle dragged Vaci into the van. At first, Vaci thought he was being robbed. But as Hansen drove off, and my uncle pulled the .22-caliber pistol with a silencer, Vaci knew exactly what was going down, especially when he noticed the blue plastic tarp on the van floor.

Vaci pleaded, "I didn't say anything, guys. You don't need to do this. I didn't say anything."

My uncle held the .22 to Vaci's head and squeezed the trigger. Nothing happened. The gun jammed. But not for long. He shot Vaci multiple times in the head with the .22. The body was wrapped inside the blue plastic tarp. On the drive to one of the graves, Hansen wondered aloud, Was Vaci dead? To make certain, Uncle Nick shot him in the head once more. Nervous about a forty-five-minute drive with a dead body in the van, Nick and Joey decided to forgo the holes and pull off to the side of the road and dump the tarp-wrapped body into a dry canal embankment. As they sped off, my uncle noticed his spare gun, a .38, missing. It later turned up—wrapped inside the blue tarp with Emil Vaci's body.

13.

KILLING OF THE ZHIVAGOS

The fate of Tony and Michael Spilotro on Saturday, June 14, 1986, a week after Emil Vaci's death, is well known through the motion picture *Casino* and the national interest the story garnered. Tony and my father (Dad being one year older) grew up in the same neighborhood, the Patch. The Calabrese family's first connection with the

Spilotros was when my father's family rented an apartment on the third floor next to the building that housed Patsy's, the Spilotro family eatery.

Named after father Pasquale Spilotro, Sr., an immigrant from the Italian province of Bari, Patsy's was a cozy Italian joint located right at Grand Avenue and Ogden. Patsy's old-country cuisine (and its adjacent parking lot used for mob meetings) was a magnet for major Outfit figures Tony Accardo, Sam Giancana, Jackie Cerone, and Gussie Alex. At one point, six Spilotro brothers worked at their father's restaurant before striking out on their own.

I remember standing on the corner of Grand Avenue and Ogden with my dad as he told me about Patsy's and that Pasquale junior, whom we knew as Dr. Pat Spilotro, was the toughest and most levelheaded of the Spilotro brothers. He said it was ironic because Dr. Pat was the one brother who steered away from trouble and became a great dentist and family man. He was our family dentist for years.

Like my father, Tony took to the streets after dropping out of school. His first arrest was in 1955 for shoplifting and purse snatching. By 1962 he began his association with Lefty Rosenthal by trying to fix college basketball and football games. As Tony's notoriety burgeoned, he ascended quickly up the Outfit ladder, rubbing shoulders with Joey Aiuppa, Turk Torello, Angelo and Jimmy LaPietra, and later Joey Lombardo.

My father often told me that he and Tony butted heads when they were younger at Grand and Ogden. Tony didn't scare my father. One night they were at a nightclub and Tony was giving my father the evil eye from the other end of the bar. Here's how tough my father was. When he saw Tony go into the bathroom alone, he followed him in, locked the door, and turned and asked him if he had something on his mind. Tony said no, so they went back out into the lounge, sat for a couple of hours, talked things over, and worked everything out. They understood each other. Tony respected my father because he wouldn't back down, unlike most people on the street.

While Tony may have respected my father, there was a time

when my dad seriously considered inviting Michael Spilotro to join his Chinatown crew. Of the two brothers, Michael was the most personable, and later his rugged good looks earned him television acting roles (once portraying an FBI agent) with Robert Conrad and with Larry Manetti on *Magnum, P.I.* Both Conrad and Manetti are Chicago-born actors.

The one thing that Tony and my father had in common was that they were born leaders, but what the bosses didn't like was that both were fast with their hands and too violent.

By the early 1970s, Tony was shipped off to Las Vegas to succeed Marshall Caifano as the Outfit's eyes and ears in Fun City, a job for which my father was in the running. It came down to the two of them because what the bosses wanted in Vegas was somebody who was feared and who could keep everybody in line. I think my dad would have done better because he was more low-key and listened to the bosses.

With Michael in Chicago in 1971, Tony moved to Las Vegas and quickly reunited with his pal Lefty Rosenthal. He soon exceeded his responsibilities of overseeing the Outfit's casino skim by organizing the burglars, pimps, call girls, and stickup artists, demanding that they pay a street tax—and they paid.

He set up the Gold Rush Jewelry Store on West Sahara Avenue with the help of another childhood friend, Frank Cullotta. The Gold Rush served as a gathering place for criminals who came west. In a short time they became known as the Hole in the Wall Gang. They got the name by gaining entry with holes cut through walls, doors, or rooftops. Included in this all-star cast were Tony's brother Michael Spilotro, Sal Romano, and their leader, Frank Cullotta. As Nicky Santoro's sidekick, actor Frank Vincent portrayed Cullotta in the 1995 motion picture *Casino*. Cullotta served as a "technical consultant" for the film.

By 1978, the Hole in the Wall Gang had graduated from burglaries, strong-arm robberies, and extortion to ordering hits on key FBI agents. By 1979, the Spilotro name was entered into the Black Book, barring him from entering any casino in Nevada. This served to accelerate Hole in the Wall Gang's capers.

On the first floor of the Gold Rush was the jewelry section, where rings, bracelets, and necklaces were sold at unusually high discounts. Upstairs was off limits to the public; there, Tony sold police radio scanners and surveillance equipment to burglars.

The more reckless Tony got with his victims, his crew, and his visibility, the stickier his situation got back home in Chicago. While Tony was the dominant criminal mind of the two, Michael was ambitious and wanted to rise through the ranks and taste his brother's status. It was evident to everyone that Michael was riding on his brother's fearsome reputation. Both were involved in extortion schemes, robbery, call girls on the Strip, and bookmaking. Things started changing quickly for Tony when Angelo LaPietra and Joey Aiuppa were sentenced for their convictions in the Operation Strawman Las Vegas skim case.

Tony and Michael's demise a week after Emil Vaci's is the stuff from which crime legends are made. Once the hit squad of Uncle Nick, John Fecarotta, Jimmy DiForti, and Frank the German came up empty, the imprisoned Joey Aiuppa and Angelo LaPietra gave word to Sam Carlisi, the boss. Tony had to go, and Michael was to be included. The Spilotro act in Las Vegas had worn thin.

When Tony got a severance from their racketeering trial because of his "heart condition," it was one more nail in his coffin. Aiuppa was enraged that he was spending his golden years in federal prison, and felt that it was because of Spilotro's high-profile and out-of-control behavior that he was behind bars. The coup de grâce was Spilotro's affair with Geri Rosenthal, Lefty's wife.

As the clock was ticking on Tony and Michael Spilotro, the two brothers were whistled back to Chicago, ostensibly for an important meeting under the assumption that Michael would be "made" and Tony would be promoted to capo.

It was Big Stoop Fecarotta who, a week prior, gave Uncle Nick the heads-up that the Spilotros were slated to be killed. When he reported back to my father, with me in the room, my uncle told us of the plan to kill both Tony and Michael. My father wasn't happy. He was disappointed that the bosses hadn't involved him in planning the hit.

I saw concern on my father's face about Michael's having to go. He thought things were getting out of hand with the bosses and wondered what would stop him and Uncle Nick from being on the hit list someday. We talked for a while about how things were changing.

Saturday afternoon, June 14, 1986, Nick drove alone to the Oak Brook Shopping Center on Route 83, just south of Bensenville. There, in the parking lot of Venture, a department store chain in the area, he met Big Stoop and Jimmy LaPietra. They were picked up later by Jimmy Marcello, who drove them to a Bensenville address.

According to my uncle, when they entered the house, they were met by John DiFronzo, Sam Carlisi, and Joe Ferriola. After exchanging greetings, Uncle Nick and the group made their way into the basement, where he saw Louis "the Mooch" Eboli, Louis Marino, and three other "gentlemen" whom he didn't recognize or know. Since it was a "formal murder party," everyone was wearing gloves.

With everything in place, Marcello left the house to pick up the Spilotro brothers. He returned with them about thirty minutes later. They were heard exchanging greetings with people upstairs. Nick was in the basement. He didn't know exactly who was upstairs, other than Marcello, Michael, and Tony.

According to Nick's testimony, Michael entered the basement first and was grabbed by Eboli, Marino, and my uncle. Nick testified that Marino and Nick held him down while Eboli quickly threw a rope around his neck and strangled him. While my uncle was distracted with the killing of Michael, he did hear Tony say, "You guys are going to get in trouble." Then, realizing it was the end, he asked to say a prayer. Request denied. (DiFronzo and Marino have never been charged.)

After the murders, Marcello drove my uncle, Fecarotta, and Jimmy LaPietra back to the shopping center. Uncle Nick accompanied Fecarotta and LaPietra to dump Tony's car at a hotel, where it was later found. Nick doesn't know how the Spilotros got to their "funeral home" in Indiana, but he concluded that each crew had a specific responsibility and had no knowledge of what the other crews were doing.

Ann Spilotro, Michael's wife, later testified that Michael told her he was meeting with Marcello on Saturday afternoon with Tony, and they were moving up in the organization. The night before, Friday, June 13, Michael told Ann that if he wasn't at the graduation party they were planning to attend the next evening by nine o'clock, something had gone wrong. They left their rings and jewelry behind in a plastic bag. Michael's daughter Michelle testified that she answered a call at their home on that Saturday morning from a man she knew as Jim, who asked to speak with her father. (It was Michelle who identified Jimmy Marcello, voice number 6, as "Jim" in a voice "lineup" conducted by the FBI. According to FBI tapes, Jimmy Marcello's code name for the Spilotros was "the Zhivagos.")

My dad told me numerous times it was Aiuppa who ordered Tony killed and that he wanted it done before he and Angelo reported to prison. Aiuppa didn't care how; he just wanted it done. While it was Tony who had incurred the wrath of the Outfit bosses, killing Michael was deemed a necessary precaution. Had he remained alive, there was concern that he might exact revenge, or worse, flip with enough information to bring down the entire Outfit.

Frank Cullotta has his theory that both Spilotro brothers knew it was the end of the line. "I knew he was going to get killed," said Cullotta, "and when he disappeared, I was asked, 'Do you think he ran?' 'No, he's dead.' 'How do you know?' 'Oh c'mon, Tony ain't gonna run. He knows he can't go anywhere.' "

There was a rumor that Tony had his own skim going, and that shortly after his death, when authorities went to his Las Vegas home, they found millions stashed in a hollowed-out section of floor under a waterbed. Had Spilotro been skimming the skim for years and not giving the bosses a straight count?

It was first thought by the FBI that Tony and Michael were buried in an Illinois junkyard. This was based on a tip and a search that turned out to be fruitless. Gangster and chop shop king Al "Caesar" Tocco and Nicholas "Nicky" Guzzino were among those who botched the burial, leading to the discovery of the Spilotros' bodies by a local Indiana farmer alongside Highway 41.

Betty Tocco, Al's wife, subsequently testified that on Sunday morning, June 15—Father's Day—Tocco called at six o'clock screaming that she was to leave the house immediately to pick him up at a gas station on Route 41 near Enos, Indiana. Betty made the twenty-minute drive and found Tocco disheveled and filthy in blue work clothes. The gas station was approximately one mile from the burial site.

According to Betty's testimony, Al was angry that he got split up from Nicky, Tootsie, and Chickie; Nicky Guzzino, a member of the executive board for Local 5 of the Laborers' International Union of North America and pension board trustee; Dominick "Tootsie" Palermo; and Albert "Chickie" Roviero. Tocco and his three "undertakers" were given burial detail.

In reconstructing the murders of the Spilotros, Ross Rice of the FBI concluded that it was a highly compartmentalized operation. There were guys at the Bensenville house murder scene that didn't know each other, and this was purposeful. It was apparent that members of various crews were given their respective assignments from the top. Tocco, as the Chicago Heights boss, was in charge of burying the brothers.

Betty Tocco continued her testimony by recalling that Al was irate that Chickie, Nicky, and Tootsie had gone off with one of the walkie-talkies. While they were digging they became spooked when a car came down the road too close to the burial site. After they became separated and Tocco had no way to communicate, he walked all night, and finally at around 6:00 a.m. found his way to the gas station on Route 41, where Betty picked him up. After driving her husband to Chickie's house and finding he wasn't there, they went to Al's sanitation company, the Chicago Heights Disposal Company, with him still wearing the same dirty clothes.

According to retired FBI agent James Wagner, the former president of the Chicago Crime Commission, Tony Spilotro was "a killer and a very dangerous individual with a 'little man syndrome' " and a "quick temper," and was "very arrogant and antagonistic." Since his death, Tony Spilotro has become an immortalized mob legend.

Retired FBI agent Zack Shelton recounts a 1978 dinner he had with fellow FBI agent and tough guy Bud Hall in Tony's restaurant. They were in Las Vegas to serve Spilotro as part of the Operation Strawman case. As Shelton and Hall were eating, they heard loud comments coming from a table in the far corner of the restaurant.

"The motherfuckers from the FBI are here . . . those chicken-shit FBI agents . . ."

At that point Hall walked over to the table to find Tony Spilotro and his associates with their girlfriends.

"We're trying to enjoy a meal and don't appreciate hearing your foulmouthed comments from our table. If you have anything else to say, let's go outside right now."

Hall returned to his table, and the agents finished their meal without a problem. Later during the trip, agents were booking and fingerprinting Tony at the Las Vegas FBI office when Ron Elder, Zack's fellow agent, stood in the doorway and peered in.

"Ron gave Tony an up-and-down look," Shelton recalled, "and said, 'You really are a little fuck, aren't you?' "

While it is common knowledge that Tony was the template for the Nicky Santoro role played by Joe Pesci in the 1995 Martin Scorsese and Nicholas Pileggi motion picture *Casino*, there are chilling similarities between Tony Spilotro and another fictional Pesci/Scorsese/Pileggi movie character, Tommy DeVito in the 1990 *GoodFellas*. In addition to Pesci's remarkable resemblance to Tony as the Santoro character in *Casino*, the Tommy character of *GoodFellas* meets a fate similar to Tony and Michael's after being whistled in by mob hierarchy on the pretext of being made. When he arrives, he is efficiently executed in a residential basement that's part Spilotro, part Sam Giancana.

In *Casino*, there's another famous scene in which the Spilotro-inspired Nicky character gouges a man to death with a fountain pen in a bar. I remember my father telling a similar Tony Spilotro tale, except with a much different setting.

When *Casino* first came out, my dad talked about that scene. Only his experience didn't happen in a bar. It happened at a car wash on Harlem Avenue, just down the street from where Tony and Michael lived in Oak Park. My father just happened to be driving by and saw Tony fighting in the car wash lot, stabbing a guy with a pen. He ran over to see if Tony needed any help. Tony was fine, but my father told him to get the hell out of there.

I'd see Michael at his restaurant, Hoagies Pub. He and Tony ran pot and cocaine out of the place. Later, I told my dad what I thought was going on with Tony and Michael. At first my dad thought I was wrong, as I had to be careful because I didn't want my father to find out how *I* knew where cocaine was being sold. Michael, my father, and West Side underboss Tony Centracchio hung around a lot socially and did some business together.

Centracchio, who passed away in 2002, oversaw the west suburban video gambling network while legitimately funneling his money into a jewelry store, a retail carpet outlet, and, strangely, an abortion clinic. An FBI wiretap placed in the clinic revealed that Centracchio was having sex with a considerably younger female employee.

While my father was recuperating from brain surgery, he discussed the killing of the Spilotro brothers with my uncle and me as we did our bookwork in the Oak Brook basement.

After Tony and Michael turned up dead, my father told me to stop going to Dr. Pat. He was afraid that Pat might try something because his brothers had been killed. So we found new dentists.

My father had a hard-and-fast rule that harkened back to Tony Spilotro's affair with Rosenthal's wife, Geri. My father never intentionally went to the home of an Outfit guy if the wife was home alone. Instead, he would send Kurt and me. When Ronnie Jarrett was in prison, my dad sent Kurt and me to drop off the monthly money for Ronnie's wife and kids.

My father was concerned that he could be compromised by going to the house of a friend who was in jail. The wife was lonely, and might be looking for a shoulder to cry on. This could create problems. What if she made a move on my father and he said no? Or what if the woman went to her husband and said that my father made a move on her? In my father's mind that could present a huge problem within the Outfit, especially in light of Butch Petrocelli and Tony Spilotro getting involved with other Outfit guys' wives.

The deaths of the Spilotros sent ripples of fear not only throughout the streets, but through the ranks of the Outfit. Things *had* changed. Everybody needed to be smarter, to be more careful, and to trust *nobody*. The new rule became, if my father and uncle were whistled in by the bosses, they wouldn't go together. Instead, they would make excuses about the other being sick. My dad and uncle speculated about who in the Outfit might want *them* dead.

I was instructed by my father and uncle that in the event they were killed like Tony and Michael, I would have a mental list of whom I needed to go after to avenge their deaths.

14.

OH NO, NOT YOU!

I was supposed to be in the backseat of the stolen Buick work car the night my uncle Nick killed John "Big Stoop" Fecarotta. By September of 1986, I was twenty-six and fully signed on to my father's crew and his way of life. After taking a larger role in the day-to-day operations, I was ready to take a massive step forward by planning and assisting in my first gangland murder.

It was decided that John Fecarotta had to go. He was

quickly losing face with my father and his bosses, Johnny Apes and Jimmy LaPietra. Jimmy "Tires" DiForti knew it, too. Big Stoop's days were numbered.

Once Jimmy LaPietra handed down the order, my father, uncle, and I carefully planned Fecarotta's murder in the basement of Grandma Sophie's duplex. Because there had been bad blood between them, it was agreed that my father shouldn't be in the car; otherwise Fecarotta would catch the play. My father reluctantly agreed that I would take the backseat of the stolen Buick and that Big John would be more at ease seeing me there than him. While my father had reservations about my going ahead with the hit, my uncle was 100 percent against it, so much so that he insisted on doing it alone. Although hitting Fecarotta solo from the front seat would be extremely risky, he wanted to proceed without me.

"Look, I can do this by myself," he said to my dad.

I believe my father let my uncle talk him out of my going because he was torn about me doing it in the first place. The compromise was that although my uncle would go it alone, instead of packing just one gun, he would carry a backup . . . just in case.

My father was the master of the "sit-down." Earlier he had arranged Fecarotta's demise by drawing up a list of grievances he presented to Jimmy LaPietra, successor to his brother Angelo, who was in federal prison. The list of Big Stoop's indiscretions was long and convincing. It detailed how he didn't pay back the money he owed Johnny DiFronzo for cars, and how his girlfriend accompanied him out west for the hit. It recounted when he spent over a hundred grand of Outfit cash stalking Tony and Michael Spilotro in Las Vegas and Emil Vaci in Phoenix, and when he won the taxable—and IRS traceable—$2,100 jackpot at a casino and conned Uncle Nick into signing the payout form. This displeased the bosses in Chicago, especially since the members of the hit squad were to be traveling under fake identities and no one was to know they were anywhere near Las Vegas.

The relationship between the Calabrese brothers and Big Stoop soured after Uncle Nick was cajoled into signing for Fecarotta's winnings amid the growing sentiment that Big Stoop was a major fuckup. But what annoyed my father the most was the poaching of a Calabrese juice loan customer, Richie Urso, a degenerate gambler who was ordered by Fecarotta to pay the mortgage on his house at 268 Gage Road in the Illinois suburb of Riverside. Fecarotta was months behind on his mortgage (even mobsters make house payments) and went too far by drafting *paperwork* outlining Urso's financial obligations to him, completely cutting out my father. Big John undoubtedly knew that Urso was heavily in debt to our crew.

"I want my fucking money," my father demanded, holding a blade to Urso's genitals.

"But I'm paying Fecarotta."

"You fuckin' pay me. It's my loan."

"What about my payments to Fecarotta?"

A heated meeting between my father and Fecarotta proved unproductive. When my father arranged a sit-down with Jimmy LaPietra, my uncle was on hand to recap Fecarotta's shenanigans. Through capo Jimmy LaPietra, they got their wish, the green light from Outfit boss Sam "Wings" Carlisi to eliminate Big John. My father and the crew wasted little time plotting Fecarotta's murder.

At sundown on September 14, 1986, three months to the day after Tony and Michael Spilotro were murdered, Uncle Nick picked up Big Stoop in the Buick on the pretext of planting a bomb on a deadbeat union dentist who had betrayed the Outfit. Although it was unseasonably warm, both men wore thin dark leather gloves. At first my uncle wanted to wear construction-type work gloves, which would draw less attention in Chicago on a warm September evening. When he could not find them, he grabbed a pair of black dress gloves instead.

Fecarotta never suspected that the bomb that Nick produced from a paper sack was a fake, constructed of flares taped up and decorated with "det" cord, disguised to look like a bundle of explosives. Nor did Fecarotta notice that the .38 pistol that my uncle had stashed for him in the glove compartment had its firing pin filed down and was rendered completely useless.

With Fecarotta the experienced wheelman doing the driving

and Uncle Nick sitting in the passenger seat, they pulled up to an alley across the street from Brown's Banquets on West Belmont Avenue. Brown's was the parlor where Grandma Sophie played bingo. Although it was early Sunday evening, one of my father's concerns was that none of the ladies from the neighborhood recognize my uncle walking on West Belmont.

The plan called for Nick to get out of the car, pull the gun out of the bag containing the bomb, and kill Big Stoop. Instead, Fecarotta caught the play inside the car and shouted, "Oh no, not you!"

As Uncle Nick struggled with Fecarotta inside the car, he pulled his left arm into the line of fire and shot both himself and Fecarotta. A struggle for the weapon ensued, and Big John held the hammer on the revolver so that it could not fire another round. He popped open the chamber, spilling .38 cartridges all over the Buick's floorboards. Then Fecarotta jumped out of the car and made a run for it. Nick dashed out of the car in pursuit, pulling his second gun. Fecarotta ran for his life, crossing West Belmont Avenue toward the bingo parlor. Nick shot him two more times before catching up and firing point-blank into his head.

Prior to the shooting, Uncle Nick was supposed to call my father and Johnny Apes, who were on backup in separate cars with hand-held radios, to let them know that he and Fecarotta were in position. That would be the signal that my uncle was exiting the car and that he was ready to whack Big Stoop. But amid the confusion, he didn't have the opportunity to make the call, so neither my father nor Johnny Apes showed up at the alleyway to pick him up.

Not seeing my father or Johnny, my uncle composed himself and decided to walk the three-quarters of a mile to where he had originally stashed his car. On the way, he tossed the gun into a sewer on the curb. So as not to look suspicious, he slipped off the dark (and now bloody) gloves. As he tried to shove them into his pants pocket, he inadvertently dropped both gloves on the street, only yards from the crime scene.

Bleeding as he walked past a lawn sprinkler, my uncle leaned down to rinse the blood off his arm. Then he made it to his car unnoticed and drove home. When my father hooked up with his brother at his house, he was fit to be tied.

"Where the fuck were you?" my father asked Nick. "Why didn't you call? I was running around like a fucking donkey."

Just before Johnny Apes arrived, my father instructed Nick to embellish his story. ("So you'll look like a hero instead of a fuckup.") As my dad opened the door, he announced to Johnny with a smile, "Fecarotta caught the play. He pulled on Nick and shot him."

That night I was supposed to receive a page from my father by nine o'clock, signaling the all-clear, that Fecarotta was *morto*. If not, my orders were to empty the house and the office of anything incriminating should the cops arrive with a search warrant. The page never came. I waited until my father called. We spoke in code. Apparently things hadn't gone as smoothly as when the three of us had rehearsed things back in Grandma's basement. As was typical of my father, information was sparse. He would volunteer only that he had things under control.

My father then drove my uncle to an apartment in Cicero for meatball surgery. The surgeon wasn't Dr. Kildare but a veterinarian sent over by Jimmy Marcello. He patched Nick up, dressed the bullet wound, and handed him a few painkillers. Later that night the vet returned to finish the job, removing a couple of stray bone fragments from Uncle Nick's arm.

While my father cursed his brother, I looked at my uncle with admiration. After being shot, he managed to carry out my father's order alone, unconcerned about who was there to pick him up. When I met up with my uncle, he pulled me aside and whispered, "Frankie. I threw the gun in the sewer. You need to go get it."

I still had my connections with the city and the Department of Sewers, so I went over with a truck and an Orange Peel and cleaned out the sewer where he told me he'd tossed the gun. I found it and gave it back to him before my father found out. He didn't know until later that I had retrieved the gun.

At the time Fecarotta was killed, I was willing to make the crew and the Outfit my life. But rather than become a made guy and meet the same fate as Fecarotta, I wanted to stick close to my father. I wanted to be like him. I was okay with the killing of Fecarotta because he had set up my uncle in Vegas. Had it been over something like Outfit cash, I wouldn't have volunteered. But my family was another matter. Fecarotta jeopardized my uncle's freedom. I was ready to climb into the backseat.

What I didn't realize was that by edging me out, my uncle was trying to tell me that the crew and the Outfit weren't what they were cracked up to be. Uncle Nick knew that my father and his controlling ways would be my undoing. By keeping me out of the backseat, it was as if my uncle was telling me, "This isn't the life for you. You need to back away." September 14, 1986, was the night that my uncle saved my life.

When he later appeared back on the streets with his arm bandaged and in a sling, my uncle joked with his friends that he had clumsily fallen at home. Knowing Nick, nobody doubted his story. What he didn't tell anyone—and what he himself didn't realize—was that while he had remembered to tell me to recover the gun, he had forgotten about the bloody gloves he had inadvertently left behind on West Belmont Avenue.

15.

HOW BAD COULD IT BE?

One evening during the fall of 1987, Lisa Ann Swan, a pretty blonde of Italian and Norwegian lineage, was out with friends at Eric & Me, a local bar in Elmwood Park. Lisa had grown up in Galewood, which was one neighborhood east of Elmwood Park. Everybody at Eric & Me knew one another. If you weren't a local, you stood out like a sore thumb.

Lisa saw me from across the bar. She knew who I was, but we hadn't been formally introduced. When she asked her friend if I was dating anybody, her friend looked back at her like she had two heads. "He's a nice guy, but his dad is another story. He's one very scary man. I would *never* get involved with that family."

Lisa uttered those famous last words, "How bad could it be?"

When Lisa and I first met, she'd heard that I was a boxer. Once we were introduced, after a few conversations we found that we both wanted the same things out of life.

From the start, we had a peculiar dating pattern. We would meet at ten thirty or eleven at night. Lisa would sit in a running car behind a restaurant and wait for me. When I arrived I was usually carrying a fat envelope full of street crew business.

We went out three nights in a row when we first met. We went ice skating on a Friday. When we got to the rink downtown, it was closed for a private party. Lisa said, "Let's leave," but I insisted.

"Just watch," I told her.

I talked my way into the private party, and Lisa and I (plus two of her friends) ended up eating and skating on the private party's dime. I could tell she was impressed with my gift of gab. On Saturday I took her to the annual Christmas party for the Italian American Club for our second date. She found it strange the way the southern Italian guys in the neighborhood would hug and kiss each other.

Lisa called the Italian American Club "Frankie's Grease Ball Club." She was hanging out with a couple of her girlfriends while I went off, smoking cigars and drinking with my friends. I figured maybe she didn't like me because we didn't spend much time together that night. She wore a pretty red suede dress and crimson nail polish. The party was held in a banquet hall in the western suburbs. I introduced Lisa to Jimmy LaPietra. A lot of politicians were there. It was like a wedding reception with people paying tribute, an "informal" formal gathering.

By our third date, our relationship had already accelerated. I took Lisa to my father's house. Her friends were shocked. *"He's taking you to meet his dad? This must be serious."* She found my father delightful the first time they met. He wasn't what her friends had led her to believe. He was jovial. Funny. Her first impression was that she liked him, and while he seemed a little controlling over his sons, she figured he was just being a typical strict Italian father. Again, how bad could it be?

Like me, Lisa was half Italian and working-class. Her mother and grandmother were born in Trieste, not far from the Yugoslavian border, perched in the upper northeastern part of Italy. The Calabrese side of my family was full-blown southern Italian. Northern and southern Italians are like oil and water. People in northern Italy look down on Sicilians. Northerners often claim that only *they* speak true Italian, and that the slang of the Sicilians isn't the real language.

Lisa's neighborhood of Galewood was situated across the way from Elmwood Park, bordered by Harlem Avenue. Like Elmwood Park, Galewood was home to a lot of gangsters. You could easily tell an Outfit house by the wrought-iron fence and the statue in the front yard of a Roman soldier or the Madonna. The lawn was manicured with cropped spiraling bushes and motion detectors installed over the front porch. While Lisa's family loathed the gangster reputation of the Outfit and their ways, I guess I was such a nice guy, and so much fun, I was an easy sell.

I kept mum about the double life I led working on my father's crew. While out with my buddies and girlfriends, I would often abruptly say, at any time, "Gotta go."

I would disappear for hours, days, only to return to my friends as if nothing out of the ordinary had happened. Most of my friends assumed that I was fulfilling my family obligations while in reality I was secretly working for my father collecting gambling debts and street taxes, maintaining and collecting juice loan payments, keeping books, and helping Uncle Nick.

During the years my father groomed me, dating back to high school, we did our bookwork around town, places where we kept our guns and work cars hidden and money bundled and secretly coded. We would meet on a Saturday night; I couldn't drive directly to my father's house. We used other people's homes, basements, or garages as our "offices." We frequently met in my grandma's basement. I'd arrive in the middle of the night, park a few blocks away, and walk to a predetermined location at around two in the morning. There we'd do our weekly bookwork. Saturday night was specifically chosen by my father to keep his sons off guard and out of their social circles. How do you tell a girl you're out collecting gambling debts or scooping up quarters from the back room of an adult bookstore?

The cash collected for juice loans and gambling bets was stashed in drop sites throughout the city. My father stashed money in safe-deposit boxes around town. They were in my name, my brothers' names, and my uncle's name. Every so often we'd go in and "change it out," that is, rotate it for new money. I'd go with him. We'd go in, rotate the new cash in, and come out with the old. My father was very precise with money. He meticulously counted, stacked, bundled, and marked everything by the amount. He knew the exact count and where things were supposed to be. He kept a long list of the drop spots.

Some of the cash was stashed at the "Calabrese Cottage," our summer home in Wisconsin near Lake Geneva. There we'd fill garbage cans or sealed drums full of money. We'd put a quilt on the bottom with some mothballs, stash some money, layer in some more quilts and mothballs, and then more money, until we filled up the drum. We could stash a hell of a lot of cash in fifty-five-gallon drums. We'd put household objects around the drum to make it blend in. Then we'd set our alarm system, arming the garage. In addition to Lake Geneva, a stash of cash might be anywhere: in a garage full of my father's classic cars, or a garage in Stone Park.

Everything was accounted for. We even had a couple of hiding places in my grandma's house. I knew where things were, and although my grandmother didn't know what we were up to, she liked to snoop. We'd set traps to find out if she was snooping around. Once when an envelope was discovered left open, we knew that Grandma had struck. We would put the money on a higher shelf so that she couldn't reach it.

Whenever my father, uncle, and I would meet to tally up the

weekly accounts, there was the chance we were being watched by law enforcement. Whenever we had surveillance on us, we went into red alert. We had a code word that we used to let one another know if we were being followed. "My feet are bothering me" meant that I was being followed. For instance, if I said, "They're hurting me *real* bad," that meant there were a lot of FBI cars following me. The other code word for the FBI, *"Scarpe Grande,"* which in Italian means "big shoes," was a reference to the shoes FBI agents wore.

At three o'clock in the morning, I'd walk out the back door of my house, head down the alley, and cut through a gangway. I would walk two blocks to where my father would be parked with the lights and ignition off. He would drive us around to make sure we weren't being followed. We'd park the car two blocks from "the office" and walk through the gangways, alleys, and backyards.

To keep one step ahead of the law, my father maintained a series of aliases and IDs, backed up by phony driver's licenses, Social Security cards, credit cards, armed forces IDs, and a badge and picture ID from the "American Investigation Security Bureau." A few of the IDs he purchased from magazine ads. The Indiana driver's licenses he applied for in person.

The idea was that with over a million dollars stashed, and with a bevy of identities to choose from, my father could "disappear" within a matter of hours under the name of James L. Traviso, Shelley Morris, or Bruno Adams. Other aliases actually had roots in the Calabrese and Hanley family trees. Like Primo Massie, a cousin on my father's mother's side. Or Tony Cononi, an uncle on his mother's side. Or Eugene Vincent McLaughlin, an Irish cousin of my mother's.

The crew frequently changed offices. During the time I worked for the city, I split my remaining hours working for the crew. Because I was working two jobs and kept long hours, it was difficult to get on a normal sleep schedule. One time I overslept. And I panicked.

I knew my father was waiting at our designated spot. I figured he'd wait ten minutes, then go ahead on his own. So I got up, ran out the back door, and headed down the street. As I suspected, he wasn't there. I got into my car, drove around awhile to make sure I was clean, parked a few blocks away, and walked to my grandmother's basement.

As I reached the bottom of my grandmother's basement stairs, I turned the corner to find my father standing there.

"Dad, I'm sorry. I overslept."

To which he unleashed a volley of punches. Boom. Boom. Boom. Lefts and rights to the side of the head. Rather than hit back, I fell to the floor, trying to protect myself. I saw the glassy stare in his eyes.

Uncle Nick was sitting in a chair nearby. He couldn't believe what his brother was doing even though he wasn't immune to a beating now and then himself. Yet he didn't break it up. He simply shook his head. "You sick motherfucker," he muttered to his brother, then walked out and went upstairs.

A few moments later, my father stopped punching me and said, "Listen, motherfucker. Get here on time! Stop disobeying me. I can't believe . . ."

"Okay, okay, okay, okay."

"Get up, go upstairs, wash your face, and come back down here."

I went upstairs, washed my face, and came back down, and everything was fine, like nothing happened. For the rest of the morning, my father was the "business dad," going through the numbers. My uncle didn't return that night. Later, he and I talked. We agreed that we couldn't take it anymore. Not only did we worry about the FBI, but now we had to worry about taking a beating, the mood my father was in, or what personality mode he was in at the moment.

16.

SCARED COW

Lisa and I were married on September 4, 1988. Before we entered the courthouse to get our marriage license, Lisa was presented with a blank prenuptial agreement, compliments of my father. Either sign the document or we don't get a marriage license. As she signed the prenup, she could see that I was embarrassed.

An early red flag came up when she and I discussed wedding invitation responses

over the phone. As soon as Lisa began naming names—like LaPietra—I would nervously cut the conversation short. I later told her not to name names on the phone in case a third party was listening. Lisa figured that my dad was some loan shark or bookie; she had no idea that she was in the presence of something far worse.

We had a small wedding by gangster standards at Al's in Cicero. About two hundred guests were invited, compared with the five hundred or more who would attend a standard Outfit wedding. Consistent with his philosophy of blending in, my father wanted the wedding to be low-key, so we invited only a tight circle of friends. While not wanting to offend high-ranking Outfit members, it was important not to attract the press and law enforcement. My father's excuse for not inviting too many Outfit guys was that I wanted a small wedding, and there wasn't enough room at the hall.

Invariably the police camped outside to film and take photographs. There was a great deal of food and liquor. Lisa and I paid for the wedding, although my father gave our guests the impression that he had footed the bill. Later Uncle Nick told me that there was word on the street that a lot of guys felt offended, and it showed. No envelopes were given to me from those who weren't invited.

Lisa anticipated joining our colorful Calabrese clan with its herd of brothers, sisters, uncles, aunts, and a myriad of cousins. But later she learned that none of our family really liked one another, and there was constant sniping. My father complained about the clothes Lisa wore and that she didn't show enough respect.

After our marriage, Lisa became versed in the quirky gangster lifestyle of Melrose Park. Fur coats with the wrong monogrammed initials. Hot clothes sold out of the homes of gangsters' wives. When Rocky Infelise was arrested for racketeering, he was photographed wearing the same green Eddie Bauer hunting jacket that everybody else wore, swiped from a hijacked forty-footer.

Lisa liked going to the house of Ruth Aleman, wife of Harry Aleman, along with my mother. They found lots of good stuff. Lisa was exhilarated. Here was a girl scared to break the law, but she didn't think anything of going over to Ruth's house to buy hot clothes. Ruth had racks of clothes set up in a bedroom. She kept the price tags on her merchandise, and we paid 50 percent of what was printed on the tag. Ruth fenced a lot of merchandise, and she had runners going into stores doing special-order grab-and-runs.

Rather than buy our own home, Lisa and I rented houses owned by my father. My relationship with my father was often erratic and confusing, and especially embarrassing whenever he would treat outsiders better than his sons. When Johnny Marino, a neighborhood friend, bought one of my father's rentals, my old man arranged for the financing and a job promotion with the city.

"It's funny," Marino said to me. "I'm paying six hundred dollars a month for a mortgage and you're paying seven hundred dollars rent. I like your father, but it seems like he treats me better than he treats you and your brothers."

When Lisa and I hosted a party for our daughter Kelly's first birthday, we invited my father and Diane to Papa Milano's, a Near North Side restaurant. He was seated with one of his associates, ordering special Italian dishes while drinking a more expensive wine than the rest of the party. Afterward, he accused Lisa and me of being big shots for staging such an elaborate birthday party. The next week, he raised our rent two hundred dollars a month.

One day my father stopped by the house. He was angry because I wasn't available and was home babysitting my daughter. As I opened the door—boom!—I took the two shots to the face just as Kelly rushed up to give Dad a hug and a "Hi, Poppi."

My father saw the confusion on Kelly's face. "Laugh like we're joking around," he hissed to me.

One night I came home late, avoiding the light so Lisa wouldn't notice my red and swollen face. At first she thought I might have been in a fight. But then Grandma Sophie casually explained to Lisa that my father regularly hit his sons and his brother Nick. After that, Lisa stopped asking questions and would only shake her head in disgust.

During one Christmas, the family played Pictionary, with my father doling out the cards. With Dad on the opposing team, Lisa drew a picture of a "sacred cow." As she drew a church, a cross, and a cow, my father shouted out, "Scared cow!"

"All right," Lisa said. "Who cheated? And who doesn't know how to read?"

Kurt and I exchanged nervous glances, and tried to give Lisa the high sign to shut up and let it go. My father could blow up at any time.

Kurt's wife, Angela Lascola, became Lisa's buddy. They both realized that Kurt and I were at odds with our dad. Angela and Lisa confided in each other. "You'd have to be in this family and live in their world to believe it," Angela told Lisa. And she was right.

Lisa noticed that Christmas brought out the best in my father. Just as she saw the violence, she saw kindness. He would go to the neighborhood churches and collect addresses of needy families. He'd put together boxes of food, a turkey, and canned goods and include an envelope of cash. He'd drop off the boxes himself, though he preferred to give anonymously.

But you'd wonder, Is he doing it for the families or to soothe himself? Does the good balance out the evil? There was that side of him, one of pure kindness, and that's why we held out hope. You'd think the kindness and good deeds were a sign of a change coming about.

Then there were the notes. The big joke was whenever Lisa and I came home and there was a note posted on the door: "Frak, call me!" The note had to be from my father. Only he could misspell his and his son's name that badly.

Throughout our turbulent relationship, I kept my anger bottled up around my wife. Lisa was out one day and got a flat tire. She called me to come help her, but I was busy with my father.

"I can't come right now," I whispered in the phone.

"What the hell?" she said. "I'm stranded out here."

That night at home, I was eating a cheeseburger, and Lisa got in my face.

"Why didn't you come help me?" I ignored her, so she shoved me. "I'm talking to you!"

I stared blankly at her as I slowly squeezed the cheeseburger.

As it oozed through my fingers, Lisa said, "Okay, I'm done talking now."

I was working with my dad that day and it bothered me tremendously not only that I couldn't go out and help her, but that I couldn't tell her that I had just caught a couple of cracks to the face. Lisa got angry and started yelling and hitting me. I tried not to pay attention to her, so I walked out the door. When I returned I told her, "Please don't ever hit me again. I will never lay a hand on you, so please don't hit me."

17.

SET UP FOR A FALL

The Calabrese crew entered the 1990s making up for the money Philly Beans had stolen. At any given time, my father had between five hundred thousand and a million dollars in juice on the street, with collections ranging from 3 to 10 percent per week. Crew members like Ralph Peluso presided over a modest group of bookmaking agents. Peluso's bookies carried three hundred to five hundred active gamblers. Dino the Greek from Cicero handled additional bookie action and

juice for the Chinatown crew, and Ralph Conte and Johnny Nitti contributed their own group of customers. Counting the bookies and the juice loan collectors, my father's operations had risen to at least a couple dozen crew members earning and working the streets on his behalf or else paying street tax through their own operations.

My father blamed Uncle Nick for letting the Philly Beans Tolomeo situation get out of hand. He was angry at his other crew members, demanding that they contribute out of their weekly take to help make up the difference for his lost income.

Thanks to Philly Beans, the Calabrese crew was now on the federal law enforcement radar. Philly Beans' cooperation with the Feds gave them fresh information on how my father ran his crew. The FBI needed to stage an undercover investigation to unearth more facts. Agents decided to key in on Matt Russo, who operated an auto repair company on the border of Elmwood Park and River Grove. Russo's M&R Auto became a regular hangout for the Calabrese family.

The Feds staked out M&R by renting a room across the street, from which to take photographs. Could M&R be just another Outfit front? Elmwood Park Outfit lieutenant Joe "the Builder" Andriacchi, among others, had his car worked on at M&R, proving that even made guys needed an honest mechanic. Russo proved to be the ticket.

My father enjoyed hanging out at Matt's shop. Matt was viewed as a stand-up guy. In addition to his thriving auto repair shop, Russo was involved in the career of an Elvis impersonator. Matt was seven years older than I, and we became close friends.

Russo soon settled into his own illegal operations when he hired a tow truck driver to field the increasing number of calls for towing service. M&R's new tow truck driver introduced Russo to a grand theft auto scheme that involved making duplicate keys to his customers' cars. After fixing their cars, once they were back with their owners, the cars would be boosted for easy cash.

Matt boasted to his new driver that he was in tight with our crew and thought that he would get my father's blessing and slip him a piece of the action while John Fornarelli, a young car detailer, rented the space next door to Russo.

The tow driver paid Russo cash on the spot—two thousand to eight thousand dollars per vehicle. It was not suggested that they chop up the stolen vehicles for parts. The tow truck driver stated he had a source "somewhere down south" who would take the vehicles whole.

After moving dozens of stolen cars, Russo received a visit from the FBI and was taken to a nearby hotel room, where he learned that his tow truck driver was actually an undercover FBI agent. Both Matt and Fornarelli were caught red-handed. In addition to the auto theft ring, the undercover agent had worked out a side deal where Matt and Fornarelli would supply him with a couple of kilos of cocaine and machine guns.

It was time for Russo to play ball and cooperate. But in the scheme of things, the FBI viewed Russo as a small fish and had their eyes on a bigger prize: the Calabrese crew.

Matt freaked. Two thoughts jumped into his head. First, setting up my father could prove fatal, and second, my dad and I hadn't done anything wrong. We knew nothing about the tow truck scam. My father had warned Russo against doing anything illegal in his presence that would draw heat. The Bureau reminded Matt that he needed to save himself. Russo reluctantly agreed to wear a wire to help the FBI put us away.

Oblivious at the time to what was really going down, I wanted to get into the detailing business. I found out that crew member Ralph Conte could get me valuable car dealer accounts if I could locate a garage to set up shop.

My father approached Russo about the possibility of taking over Fornarelli's detail shop next door. Russo told my dad that Fornarelli had already agreed to vacate the premises, especially after making improvements, including installing a new garage door.

So when I approached Fornarelli about giving up his space, I was surprised to learn that Russo had already told John that the

Calabreses had insisted on taking over his spot. For his trouble, Russo would give Fornarelli ten thousand dollars to move out.

My father and I confronted Matt and asked him why he had told Fornarelli he was being muscled out by us, which wasn't true. Russo (wearing a wire) explained that the new partnership with me would bring him extra money, which he desperately needed. Much to Russo's relief, my father bought the story.

It was a golden opportunity for the Feds. As they set up across the street, we were directly in their sights. They needed to document a few more illegal predicate acts* and our crew could be looking at a possible Racketeer Influenced and Corrupt Organization Act (RICO) indictment. Much to everyone's surprise, our new detailing shop was on the level and separate from the juice loan activities. When my father expressed reservations to Russo about his tow-truck-driving friend, Matt assured him that he used the driver only once in a while.

As it turned out, my dad had previously dealt with the mysterious driver. One afternoon after Uncle Nick had given my father the tow driver's business card as one of Philly Beans' potential new customers, he took the card and dialed the number.

The man on the other end of the line was agitated. "Who is this? Who is this?"

My father hung up the phone. "Don't deal with this guy. He's an FBI agent or an informant."

"How can you tell after one call?" I asked my dad.

"A real tow truck driver wouldn't be asking, 'Who is this?' He'd be used to getting calls at all hours for tows. I'm telling you he's no good."

When Matt tried to arrange a juice loan for his tow truck driver through my father, Dad refused. "I ain't givin' nobody no fuckin' money," he told Russo, "and if *you're* doing something wrong, I don't want to know about it."

---

*A predicate act is an offense or a class of offenses that prosecutors must prove in order to achieve a conviction under the federal racketeering statutes.

My dad's warnings to Matt fell on deaf ears. Russo was already in the bag with the FBI. Under surveillance, my father and I weren't doing anything unlawful. But how long before Dad gave in to temptation?

At one point when my father had a problem with a bumper, Matt pulled him aside and told him, "I can get you a bumper real cheap. . . ."

To which my father replied, "You better not be saying what I think you're saying, Matt."

"Oh no, Frank. I'm just joking around."

When I opened up my new detail shop, my dad helped me strike a deal with the Celozzi-Ettleson Chevy dealership in Elmhurst to do some warranty work on their used cars. It proved cheaper for them to farm out their work to M&R than to have their own union shop repair, wash, and detail their used inventory.

Next, I hired neighborhood pal Johnny Marino, and brought in Lisa, who was pregnant at the time, to help out. M&R Auto and Detail was on its way! Whenever a used car from the dealership was brought in, Russo would do the necessary automotive work—oil change, new tires, tune-up, and other basic repairs—then pass it on to Marino and me to wash and detail so that it would look spotless on the lot. The dealer paid Russo and M&R for each car. Russo would then pay me my percentage for the wash and detail work.

In the beginning, whenever I would return finished detailed cars to the dealership every week, they would hand me a check to take back to Matt. One day Russo told me that the dealership was going to start mailing in their payments.

"Why mail the check?" I asked. "I'm there all the time. I can just pick it up." I didn't realize that payments based on fraudulent services and sent through the U.S. Postal Service would constitute mail fraud, strengthening the FBI's case.

While Matt was under pressure to set up our crew, it wasn't long before my father let greed get the better of him. On two separate occasions, he took the bait.

Russo approached my father and said he was behind in paying

his back taxes. Rather than back off and not get involved, my dad instructed Kurt to go to the bank and withdraw the necessary funds. While lining up a loan for Russo, he convinced Matt to hand over a small percentage of M&R. My father struck a deal whereby his family would pay only for parts to get our cars serviced until Russo repaid the money.

Next, Matt told my father that he was in danger of losing his house. He was three months behind on the mortgage payments and the bank was ready to foreclose. Matt was in tears telling him that he didn't know what his wife and three kids were going to do. My father responded by buying the house and putting it in Kurt's and my names. He directed Matt to sign a promissory note saying he would pay my father rent every month. In the meantime, Russo could buy back the house for the same price he sold it for—or less if its value went down.

I was put in charge of collecting Matt's monthly house payment. One Saturday night Matt told me that he didn't have the money and had no idea when he could pay. It was likely a ploy orchestrated by the FBI to see whether or not my father or I would physically threaten Matt. Instead, I quietly offered to advance the payment until Matt could make good. When my father found out that I fronted the payment, he arranged a sit-down with Matt and me.

"Matt," my father said in an even tone, "if you're having a problem paying me, come right out and tell me. We can work it out. I can't have my son going out of pocket. That ain't right."

Then my father turned to me and angrily shook his finger. "And you, I oughta break your legs for youse bein' so fuckin' nice."

To the chagrin of the FBI, the wrong guy, me, was threatened on the wire.

My father had been magnanimous toward Russo for a share of the business, but Dad's predatory instinct soon took over. He demanded 10 percent of what Matt and I generated in the detail shop. On the back of each invoice would be a code: a circle on the back meant ten dollars; a check mark meant twenty-five bucks; a line denoted five dollars.

My father told Matt and me that there would be three ends that would profit from the M&R deal. The first would be for him and me. The second would go to Matt. And the third would go "somewheres else." "Somewheres else" meant the Outfit.

Matt and I were essentially paying my father extortion, and in true Outfit style, my dad wanted payment in cash!

I was gutted that my latest business venture had just been co-opted by my father. I knew at that point that I needed to get out from under the new business. The FBI was anxious to move in on its target. One more development could reel in the Calabrese family on racketeering charges.

One day I received a call from a friend at the Chevy dealership. Management had noticed that some of the automotive repairs on the cars sent to M&R weren't completed as promised. The bills were padded with fake charges. When I confronted Russo about it, he denied any wrongdoing.

I felt the walls closing in. My father was extorting me, and my business partner was defrauding our biggest customer. In frustration, I put Johnny Marino in charge of the detailing operations and exited the business. I went to work for the Chevy dealer as a car salesman. I didn't mind the long hours. In the end it was better to work long hours selling cars than being my father's stooge at M&R.

But it was too late to walk. I was already set up for a fall.

The last straw came when the manager at the dealership told me that a car that was supposedly serviced by Russo had been sold to a newspaper columnist from the *Chicago Tribune*. When the reporter realized that all of the work had not been done on his car, he threatened to expose the dealer in the newspaper. I phoned Matt.

"What the fuck is going on? Why aren't you doing the work on the cars?"

"I did the work."

"Matt, I just inspected the car myself. You *didn't* do the work."

There was a pause on the other end of the line.

"Matt, meet me at the Chevy dealership at seven thirty," I said.

Meanwhile, my father stopped by the shop to see Matt. Marino was there. It was dark outside.

"Let's go," my dad told Russo. "We're going for a ride. Follow me and you ride with Johnny." My father wanted Matt to look at a car, so he enlisted Matt and Johnny to help him drive it back to the shop. Marino was behind the wheel with Matt in the front seat. When my father pulled his car over by a bridge over a river, he waved to Johnny and Matt to pull over, too. As my father walked over to Johnny's car to get the directions straight, Matt became hysterical. *"What is he doing?"*

"Just relax," Marino said. "Let's see what he wants."

Matt was convinced my dad was going to kill him and throw him in the river. But nothing happened. After the incident, Matt sat motionless in his car in front of the shop for several minutes.

Russo didn't show up at the dealership that night to meet with me. He didn't show up for work the next day, either. A couple days later, when I stopped by his house, I found the place empty. Russo and his wife and kids were gone. He had turned himself in to the FBI and joined the Witness Security Program.

With both Russo and Tolomeo in the hands of the Feds, all hell was about to break loose inside the Calabrese camp.

18.

FLORIDA

After Matt Russo went missing, my father and I concluded that he was cooperating with the FBI. Now Uncle Nick's question—Why was there a mirrored one-way glass window facing M&R Auto from the house across the street?—was answered. If Matt was a beefer, it was only a matter of time before indictments dropped. My father was feeling the heat, so he arranged a visit to his ex-brother-in-law, Uncle Ed, for a consultation.

I knew that if my father went to see my uncle Ed, Hanley might not be eager to help. A few years back, Uncle Ed

came to my father when a bookie and a few of his South Side friends beat up his son Tommy at a local nightclub, hitting him across the head with a beer bottle and putting him in the hospital. When Uncle Ed asked Dad to take care of the guys, Dad put him off. Business was booming at the time of the incident, and while my dad knew the culprits, he said "he was working on it."

Uncle Ed was still the president of HEREUI, the hotel and restaurant employees union. At one time the Justice Department considered HEREUI to be one of the most corrupt unions in America, although Uncle Ed had not been convicted of a crime. His powerful union gave him the ear of politicians and judges, including guys like then congressman and chairman of the House Ways and Means Committee Dan Rostenkowski, activist Jesse Jackson, Mayor Richard M. Daley, and President Bill Clinton.

Nervous about Russo rolling over, my father approached Ed on the premise that he was still working on finding his son's assailants. He broached the subject of his own problem: What should he do if the Feds launched a RICO case against him?

Uncle Ed's response wasn't exactly what my father wanted to hear. Since there were no murders involved, his best bet was to take off and go into hiding for seven years until the statute of limitations expired. If my dad had been more receptive about Ed's troubles with his son, he might have been more helpful.

The crew explored ideas of making my father disappear, including staging a fake assassination. Uncle Nick would shoot dozens of bullet holes into one of his cars and afterward, torch it. My father would drive south and set up base camp down in Florida, where he already owned a warehouse and a winter home. Inside the warehouse were modest living quarters with a shower, a cot, and some clothing. He already had enough cash stashed to live comfortably in Florida for seven years.

Rather than elaborately stage his death, he decided he would secretly escape. The timing couldn't have been worse for me. Lisa was due to give birth any day. Now my dad, whom I had been avoiding for weeks since I walked away from the M&R debacle, was demanding that *I* drive him down to Florida to help him get settled. We would drive up the Florida coast, where I would grab a plane back to Chicago, but probably not in time for the baby's birth. At first I protested.

"Lisa is going to have our baby any day now—"

"You mean you're not going to do this for your *father*?" my father asked incredulously. "You *have* to do this for me! What's more important than your dad?"

Adhering to my father's wishes put me between a rock and a hard place. I feared that telling Lisa or my mom where I was going and what I was doing could brand them as accessories. Lisa wasn't pleased when she heard the news. I winced as I lied to my mother when she asked about my plans for the baby's arrival.

My father and I spent an entire day packing up the van, lining the inside wall panels with six hundred thousand dollars in cash. As we were ready to begin the long drive to Florida, the reality of my dad being a fugitive sank in—I wasn't going to see my father for at least seven years. Part of me was sad, but as I thought more about it, I became *ecstatic*! Getting rid of him for seven years would solve my problems and would be well worth the grief and aggravation I would take for missing the birth of my child.

As we drove the van south across state lines, I was dressed casually in my bright blue, green, and yellow workout pants. I had donned a red sweatshirt with the arms cut off. My shoes were the pink, green, and yellow Zodiac loafers that my friends teased me about.

On the road, my father enjoyed eating at truck stops and staying at Super 8 motels. When we rolled into one truck stop over the Kentucky border to eat, the whole restaurant stopped what they were doing and gazed at the sight of two Chicago gangsters. What a sight we were: me, muscular, wearing loud leisure sweats, Technicolor shoes, and sunglasses, standing a full head taller than my mobster father. My dad, stocky and buff, was also wearing sunglasses. Then he looked up at me and hissed in a whisper, "You stoopid motherfucker!"

"Whaaaa?"

"I told you to blend in. Look at you! The whole fuckin' place is staring at that outfit!"

When we made it to Florida, my father was set. He and I unloaded the money and his collection of aliases and phony ID cards. My father was prepared for his brand-new life underground and on the run. Plus he had a winter home in nearby Port St. Lucie. He was already familiar with the area.

The next morning we both drove up the Florida coast so that I could fly out of a different city. I had mixed emotions at the airport. I was sad to say farewell to my dad. Yet I could hardly believe I was breaking away. It was bittersweet.

As we hugged and kissed at the airport gate, my father had tears in his eyes. He couldn't let me go. It was the same scenario all over again. The Good Father, the loving father, stood before his eldest son. And it felt good. On the flight home, I thought over the prospect that things were going to change for the better. My father could come back in seven years having missed me terribly. We would have another shot at a normal father-son relationship.

One week later, as I sat at the breakfast table at my mother's house, I heard someone open the back door. I jumped up to find it was my dad, back from Florida. Having no control over his crew, his family, and me was too much for him to handle.

"I'm a man and I ain't runnin' from fuckin' nobody," he muttered.

My jaw dropped to the floor in disbelief. I was crushed with disappointment. The planning, traveling, and high drama had dissipated into thin air.

My father was back to stay.

19.

I TOOK THE MONEY

By the winter of 1991, I was hiding and avoiding any contact with my father. We hadn't spoken in months when I drove to Grandma Sophie's place at 3645 North Pacific Avenue in Chicago, north of Elmwood Park. Sophie was living in one half of the duplex owned by my father, while my mother lived in the remaining half, 3643, with Kurt and Nicky.

I took the stairs down to my grandmother's basement, where in the past my father, my uncle, and I had set up shop, meticulously keeping the crew's books. I walked over to a special wall unit we had built. Instead of ordinary drywall, there was a panel of Peg-Board over plywood, set in place by drywall screws instead of nails.

I unfastened the drywall screws and removed the Peg-Board-and-plywood panel, revealing a secret storage space. I was careful not to touch the guns that were hanging inside. I reached for a light blue duffel bag that was hanging next to them. The duffel bag was filled with bundles of currency, wrapped tightly in increments of ten thousand dollars, nine thousand in hundred-dollar bills, the remaining thousand in fifties. At the top of each bundle, on each outer fifty-dollar bill, was a symbol scrawled by my father in red pen, a code he used to keep track of the money and denominations he had stashed inside his many hiding places all over town. My original plan was to save the outer fifties with the red writing so that when I returned the money, I could replace the identical marked fifty-dollar bill back on top. My father would be none the wiser.

I was taking the money to open a restaurant. My plan was to become a success on my own. I figured that if I could earn enough money to replace what I took, and once I had a couple of successful businesses under my belt, maybe my father would respect me or at least leave me alone. I didn't want to resort to Plan B, which was simply to take the money, grab my family, and run like hell.

I estimate that I took between six hundred thousand and eight hundred thousand dollars. I didn't bother to count it. I wasn't stealing from my father or the Outfit. This was money I felt entitled to after years of counting quarters, doing the books, making collections, strong-arming late clients, backing up my uncle, and, especially, taking punches and putting up with years of physical and verbal abuse from my father. I knew that my dad owed me a sizable chunk of money from the ventures we were partners in, like the rehabbing and reselling of houses. I knew I would never receive my cut, and that I was going to get stiffed the same way my father cheated Uncle Nick and Ronnie Jarrett when they co-owned the hot-dog stand.

Although we hadn't communicated in months, my father had no reason to suspect that I would steal from him. (Had he known, he would have come after me and killed me.) As the weeks and months passed after I took the money, my dad didn't come around looking for his cash. Over the next eighteen months, I spread the money around town. First I invested in a couple of restaurants. I helped start La Luce on West Lake at Ogden and became a partner in Bella Luna, a popular pizza-pasta place on North Dearborn, owned and run by my childhood friend Danny Alberga.

I also spread my father's wealth among the family. I gave fifty thousand dollars to my youngest brother, Nicky, who wanted to attend college in Boca Raton. Next, I gave my mother thirty thousand dollars. Then I put money down on a house for my family. The rest I put aside, blowing it on trips to Vegas with my friends, snorting cocaine (a habit I'd picked up), and financing a small coke-dealing operation around town. Soon I was running my own tiny crew, starting out small and running the operation with the same spirit my father ran his with, carefully and discreetly.

Although law enforcement had me under surveillance at both restaurants, I stayed one step ahead, careful not to get caught dealing or holding. There were numerous traps set up by the DEA using informants to try to smoke me out and make me incriminate myself. But I didn't take the bait. My father had groomed me to be cautious and smart, and I based my drug business practices on what my father would have done lending money. Be secretive. Be careful not to become overextended. Deal only with people you trust, and move the merchandise quickly.

One guy who I suspected was cooperating with law enforcement wanted to meet in person. I sent a message back: "If I want to meet people, I'll join a social club." Later I found out he *was* cooperating with law enforcement, which reinforced my rule of selling only to people I knew. But with my caution, I still made two mistakes: (1) throwing my money around like a *spaccone*, behavior that was contrary to what I had been taught by my dad, and (2) getting high on my own supply. As the drug sales mounted and the restaurants began doing well, my plans to replace my father's money evaporated. The drugs had given me the courage to decide *not* to return the money.

My father watched from afar the success I was enjoying.

I heard he was impressed with how well both restaurants were doing. My father had no idea how much money it took to get a restaurant started, or how much I kicked in to become a partner at Bella Luna. Soon he began coming around, asking questions, and we started talking again. I could tell he was trying to figure out how *he* could get involved. I lied to him about how much money it took to get La Luce off the ground. I put him on the payroll for a few hundred bucks a week to stave him off.

Back then I was rolling in money. Danny Alberga, the owner of Bella Luna, and I were driving around one time looking at restaurant equipment because we were remodeling the place. We were out on Madison Avenue, where there were a lot of homeless people. I had a brand-new white Jeep with the top off because it was the summer. We were coming out of one of the restaurant supply stores and I told Danny, "Check under the seat. I got some money I forgot about."

Danny reached under the seat and there was a brown paper bag with twenty thousand dollars inside, two bundles of ten thousand apiece.

"Are you fucking nuts?" Danny screamed. "There's twenty dimes in here!"

At this stage, Lisa knew better than to ask me about money.

There were a lot of things she didn't ask about. To her, less information was more. It's not that she wanted to be lied to; it was just that she didn't want to hear it. Yet had she known I was using cocaine or that I'd stolen from my dad, she would have left me.

Lisa was barely a drinker and staunchly opposed partying with drugs. One time we went to Boston. At the hotel, I went out on the balcony and smoked a joint with my friends. The husbands and wives all smoked, but not Lisa. She was so angry that we got into a big fight on the plane ride home.

Soon the pieces added up: clues like finding a rolled-up twenty-dollar bill and folded slips of paper in the drawer. When Lisa confronted me, I denied using, claiming the items belonged to one of my friends.

Danny Alberga didn't approve of my drug use either. But I was making money selling, and was damned lucky I didn't get caught. Had my father known what I was up to with his money, the old man would have killed me.

At first my drug use was a weekend-warrior thing. I'd do only a line or two on Friday nights. I was having problems with my father and got more into it. I blame myself. When I began selling, my use spiraled.

I would often come home pasty white and clammy, with my heart racing. Lisa would find my stash. One time she taped a *Twelve Steps to Sobriety* pamphlet to the spot where she had found drugs. A couple of times she flushed thousands of dollars' worth of cocaine down the toilet.

My cocaine use put a strain on my family life. Around the time our second child, Anthony, was born prematurely and was confined to the neonatal unit, I was buying small quantities, converting them into ounces, and selling to my select group of people. With my father's juice loan and gambling operation, I needed to keep *my* drug business very low profile so that the two of us never crossed paths.

Alarmed at my increased use, Lisa tried to enlist the help of family members.

She called Kurt, who met her at the Chicago Board of Trade, where she was working. In a restaurant across the street, she told Kurt that I was hurting a lot. Kurt had his *funge* face on and never got back to her. He was having his own problems with my father. Then Lisa cried to my mother, but she would not get involved. Of course, she couldn't go to my father or Uncle Nick.

Kurt did confront me about my drug habit.

Like Lisa, he didn't do drugs. We had a conversation. But he didn't know how to talk to me about it. He never told me that Lisa had spoken to him. I found out later. They had an intervention of sorts, but that didn't work out too well. When I was selling drugs, we were moving around from house to house. My life was chaos.

Cocaine made me feel I could think clearly. Then I learned there are two kinds of users. There's the addict and the abuser. Had I been an out-of-control rent-snorting addict, Lisa would have left me immediately. But I was the abuser and would continue to use until I dealt with the issues concerning my father. That's probably why Lisa cut me some slack.

After I stole the money and started the restaurants, my relationship with my father thawed again. Dad was visiting the restaurants to hang out. He would sit in the back and drink a little wine.

I saw that my father was enjoying our revived relationship. Now that I was no longer involved in his crew, we could make a go at it. The only problem was how to return the money before he noticed it missing. If I could get the money back to him, I'd be home free.

I loved seeing my father play the proud papa, fielding compliments from friends and associates about how well I was doing with the restaurants.

One winter night in 1992, after he'd had too many glasses of wine, I elected to drive my father home. Father apologized profusely. "Thanks for driving me home. You know I don't mean to be such a pain in the ass."

"No, Dad, I don't mind. I'm enjoying this."

Getting out of the car, we stood outside my dad's home. He cried, kissing me and telling me how much he loved me. Father and son enjoyed a long embrace.

"I love you too, Dad," I said. "This was a nice night."

"Yeah, but you know," my father said, breaking away from the embrace and grabbing me by the shirt, violently shaking me. "You gotta quit bein' so fuckin' nice. *You gotta quit bein' so fuckin' nice!*"

20.

THE THOUSAND-YARD STARE

Spring 1995. It was eleven o'clock in the morning on a summer weekend. I was living in Elmwood Park when my father and Kurt appeared outside my locked screen door. When the two of them arrived, I could see the swollen cheeks and redness in Kurt's eyes. I knew right away it was about the money.

Uncle Nick, Kurt, and I were the only people who knew the hiding places for my father's money. Once my father noticed it was missing, he immediately accused Kurt and slapped him around. He knew that Kurt was more fearful of him than I was. After grilling Kurt, he found out what he suspected: it was I who had taken his money. For months afterward, he would continue to blame Kurt, convinced he had played a part in the scheme, which wasn't true. He threatened Kurt that whatever money I didn't repay, he would be on the hook for it.

I gazed at Kurt standing on the porch, then at my father. I saw the cold, glassy look in my father's eyes. It was as if he was transfixed by something far in the distance. The Thousand-Yard Stare. My father was in Outfit throat-slashing mode. I knew this because my father had taught me to look into the eyes of my opponent. The eyes were the window to the soul, except what I saw in my father's eyes wasn't a soul but icy rage. He knew who had taken his money.

My two children, Kelly and Anthony, were standing in the hallway with Lisa. They had no idea what was going on, and my father wouldn't come into the house, which was a very bad sign.

He wanted me to come outside. I'm thinking, Do I run upstairs and get my gun, then go outside? Maybe I should shoot him through the door. Or should I just go outside and talk to him? With Lisa and the kids in a possible crossfire, I stepped outside unarmed.

Word was already on the street that my father and I had butted heads, but were back on speaking terms. My father was unaware that I had partied with and sold cocaine. Had he known that, he would have killed me instantly.

As soon as I stepped outside, he grabbed me by the arm and began pulling me down the street. A full head taller than my father, I did not resist or raise a hand against him.

He gave me a few openhanded cracks to the face.

"You took my fucking money."

At first I denied it.

"Yes you did. You fucking took my money."

My father hit me again with the cupped hand to the temple, disorienting me, nearly knocking me down. I had to remain on my feet; otherwise my father might stomp me.

"I know you took it," he whispered furiously, inches from my face. "I got a gun over there in the truck. Confess right now or else I'm going to go get it and shoot you in the fucking head. You don't understand the predicament you've put me in. It's not my money! It's Angelo's money. How am I going to explain it to him?"

I knew my father was lying. I had to think fast.

"Fuck it!" I screamed. It took him aback. "I spent it all. Make an appointment with Angelo, and I'll go shoot *him* in the head."

My father looked at me like I was crazy. "We can't do that."

"Why not? Fuck him! He isn't right with you. You don't like him anymore. That guy doesn't respect you. I say we kill him. Let's go do it together."

My father let go of my arm. "No. I'll talk to him."

Being busted by my dad for stealing the money was one thing, but what followed, the decree, chilled me to the bone.

"From now on, I own you. The restaurants are mine. Your house is mine. Everything is mine. You will report to me three times a day and do whatever I say until you pay me back my fucking money."

I couldn't believe it. Everybody was trying to get away from this madman. Now I was his again.

Once my father found out that he'd been robbed, he systematically set out on a mission to recover as much from me as he could. Our father-son relationship became strictly a business arrangement. I was no better off—actually, I was worse off—than one of his deadbeat customers on the street. Financial reparation came in waves as my father tightened the screws. First he took back approximately ninety thousand dollars in cash left in the till, followed by another ninety thousand in drug money that I recovered off the streets. He then credited another hundred thousand to my "account" that he owed from our home-remodeling projects. Add in the boat, the new dump truck, and two snowmobiles, it all belonged to my father now, not to mention my stake in both restaurants. For the coup de grâce, he grabbed my white Jeep, replacing it with an old beater that I would drive as a daily reminder of my transgressions.

My father took back the money I had given my brother Nicky to attend college in Florida. Retrieving the money that I had put into the two restaurants became a stickier issue, particularly with

Danny Alberga, owner of Bella Luna. Danny had already had serious reservations when he'd agreed to bring me in as an investor in the first place.

Alberga told me, "I just want to make sure this money has nothing to do with your father. I don't need the aggravation. If I need money, I'll go to the bank and borrow it like anybody else. I don't want or need your father as a partner."

At the time I bought into Bella Luna, I was partying hard, snorting and throwing money around by taking my friends on trips to Vegas, and laying down three-thousand-dollar roulette bets. The partying stopped once my father lowered the boom. Now the investment that I'd made in Bella Luna came crashing down. Just after my father discovered his money was stolen, Danny got the phone call. It was my dad.

"You gotta meet me in the morning for breakfast."

"Sure. What's going on?"

"Just meet me in the morning."

Danny recalled a breakfast he'd had with me, my dad, and Johnny Marino at the American Eagle on Grand Avenue the morning after a night of serious drinking. My father had ordered a half a cantaloupe. When the waitress brought the fruit cut in squares rather than intact, he went ballistic.

"Does this look like a fucking half a cantaloupe to you?"

He angrily wiped the table clean with his arm as plates, food, coffee, and cutlery went crashing to the floor. Danny and the group left the café hungry.

The next morning Danny met my father and me at a coffee shop in Franklin Park. I hung my head low and sat on my hands. Danny sat in the booth facing my father and me.

"We're gonna order breakfast," my father ordered, "and when we get done, we're gonna talk about stuff."

When the waitress came over, my dad and I ordered, while a nervous Danny asked for a cup of coffee.

"What do you wanna talk about?"

"My son put money into your restaurant that didn't belong to him. How much money did he put in there?"

Danny looked over at me, not wanting to throw me under the bus. "What *did* you end up giving me, Frankie? I don't remember exactly."

"Over sixty thousand."

Danny and I locked eyes. Sixty grand? Alberga was into my father for sixty grand? I had just thrown my best friend to the wolves.

"That money belonged to his grandmother," said my father, but Danny knew the score. Nothing was ever the old man's. Drive up in a fancy car, it was never his, belonged to a friend. Now it's Grandma's money.

"The long and short of it is," my father said, leaning in, "this money has to be returned." Alberga was left with few alternatives. Mess with a gangster. Throw me, his best friend, to the lions. Or pay the loan back. Three weeks later, after finalizing a bank loan, Danny, like a true friend, arranged another sit-down with my father.

"All right, Frank, I got the loan. Who should I make the check out to?"

My father shook his head. "No, no, no, no, no, no. What goes out as cash comes in as cash."

With the loan amount sitting in the bank, Danny had to cash checks over time around town to pay my father his money. This meant that Dad was going to become a fixture around Danny's restaurant. He would arrive every Friday like clockwork, during the restaurant's busiest time. My father's presence created a distraction and made it difficult to work. One Friday evening, surrounded by customers and frantic waiters and waitresses, my father did one-handed push-ups in the middle of the floor. Another night while Danny was in and out of the restaurant delivering pizzas, my father was planted at a front table gazing out the window.

"You doin' anything wrong here, Danny boy?"

Alberga was no fool. He knew what my father was getting at.

"Look, Frank, I have thirty-eight dollars in my pocket. I'm delivering pizzas. I've been here since nine thirty this morning. If hard work is a crime, arrest me now."

"It's just that there's a truck across the street in that vacant lot with tinted windows, its back end facing us. They're watching the place."

"Frank," Danny maintained, "I'm clean. Nothing's going on. You should talk to your son."

One of the pretty waitresses, Janice from Atlanta, teased my father. "Do you know Ferlin Husky, the country singer? You look just like Ferlin Husky."

As my father sat and joked with a couple of his friends having dinner, he told her, "Ferlin Husky? I can sing you some Ferlin Husky songs." And he did.

Danny knew my father's reputation as a killer, and warnings by both Kurt and me only heightened Danny's concern. He had to get my dad paid off as soon as possible and was trapped until he managed to gradually siphon the rest of the sixty thousand dollars to him. My father was showing up regularly, bringing in friends and demanding special service and pizza deliveries to his lawyer's office.

Finally Danny was down to the final five thousand balance. During a busy Friday evening my father walked in, and Danny handed him five grand in twenties rolled up in a tight wad, just as a waitress walked by. My father angrily pulled him aside.

"Don't you ever fucking hand me my money in front of people again! From now on we go into the bathroom." My father examined the bankroll and shook his head. "Can't you give it to me in hundreds?"

After the final payment, my father brought up the subject of interest on the loan. Danny had had enough. Stashing a pistol in his pants just in case, he motioned my father back into his office.

"Let's stop right there," Alberga explained. "This was never a loan. I went to the bank and borrowed the money. You got your cash. If there's anybody who owes you money, it's your son. As far as I'm concerned, I've given you back his investment. This is what's owed and that's it."

Back under my father's thumb, I was the walking dead. I wanted to run away from it all. I was numb; I didn't care about anything. I toted a gun everywhere I went. Living in constant fear of my father, I anticipated the worst. I would park blocks away from my house to give the appearance I wasn't home.

One night I was walking home, drinking a can of beer. I saw this big guy, a neighbor, working on his car with the garage door open. I finished my beer and threw the can on his lawn. "Hey," he said to me, "ain't you gonna pick up that beer can?"

I turned around and slowly pulled the gun out of my pocket, knowing the rule: If I pulled it all the way out, I had to use it. As I moved toward him, he froze and got scared. "Fuck you," I said, and I turned and walked away. Then I caught myself. "What am I doing?" I walked back over, and he was looking at me with his eyes wide open. "I'm sorry, sir, for throwing the beer can. I'm sorry for yelling at you, and I'll pick it up." I couldn't believe what was going through my head. I wasn't thinking clearly.

Although I routinely parked my car blocks from home, one evening, in a hurry, I slipped, leaving my car in the driveway. At about ten o'clock, the doorbell rang. Peering out the upstairs window, I saw my father's white Bronco. Telling Lisa to stay with the kids, I walked past a window to get to my bedroom, where I kept my 9 mm Beretta. I needed to be more safe than sorry, not knowing if my dad would try to force his way into the house. I lay low as he rang the doorbell repeatedly, then walked back to his car. In the past, I would have jumped out the back window and run. Watching from the darkness, I could see the fury in my father's steps. Hiding from my father had worked before, but as the saying goes, I could run but I couldn't hide. My father drove away.

To steer clear of my father, I immersed myself in work at the restaurant (a public place where my father couldn't attack me). Arriving early and leaving late, I hunkered down as my father turned up the heat. He would show up each day to bark out orders and keep tabs on me. He got angry when he found out that I had given my mother a job at La Luce.

I put her in the restaurant in the daytime, and she loved it. But my father made her quit so he could collect the money I was paying her. He was checking on me and would call at all hours.

One day my ma told him I was out running errands. That night he called me at home.

"What's going on, Son? How's the restaurant doing? Why don't you come and meet me so's we can talk?"

The tone of voice that I heard was that of the loving father. After being paid back some, maybe he'd gotten over my stealing his money.

As I pulled up to my father's car, my dad motioned me over. "Park your car and take a ride with me."

I got into my father's car and we drove until he parked a few blocks away from one of the work garages in Elmwood Park. As my father and I walked into the work garage gangway, a feeling of dread ran through me.

Oh my God, is he setting me up? That can't be. He's the good dad now.

As I opened the door of the garage and walked in first, my father turned the lights on and slammed the door behind him.

Suddenly I saw the Thousand-Yard Stare. Holy shit, I'm dead. My father grabbed me by the throat.

"You motherfucker, you lied to me. Where were you? After you took my money, you still don't listen to me. I seen you that fucking night, standing in the hallway of your house not answering the door. Nobody does that to me!"

He reached for a gun, a .38 snub-nosed revolver, encased in a black dress sock. (The crew kept guns in thin socks to eliminate fingerprints.) With one hand he grabbed my shirt and pulled me toward him, and with the other he stuck the gun in my face against my cheek.

"This is only getting worse. I'd rather have you dead than disobey me."

I asked myself, How am I going to get out of this? He's going to kill me. I started crying and begged him to please help me, saying that I was a bad person.

"You're right, you *are* a bad person," was my father's response. As I tried to hug my father, once again, to his pleasure, I became the wallowing subservient son.

At least he didn't shoot me. On the ride back, he punched me in the face. I was numb; I couldn't defend myself. They just kept on coming, punch after punch, to the point where I welcomed the pain. I was thinking that at any moment he would change his mind, pull over the truck, and kill me. But he didn't. Once I walked away, I knew that from that day forward I could never trust my father again.

21.

BUSTED

July 1995. As a result of the FBI's investigation into Matt Russo and M&R Auto and Detail, on the day the statute of limitations was due to expire (on the final infraction), the grand jury handed down a RICO indictment against members of the Calabrese crew. RICO is a federal law that provides for extended penalties for acts performed by an ongoing criminal enterprise. The RICO's "predicate acts" committed by the Calabrese "organization" included high-interest juice loans, extortion in the form of street taxes on businesses, and illegal gambling.

Looking back, it was weird getting arrested. The phone rang at 6:00 a.m. It was Agent Kevin Blair speaking in a calm, low voice, informing me, "This is the FBI and we have the house surrounded."

Blair's call took me by surprise. Keeping the grand jury indictments sealed allows the FBI and other law enforcement agencies time to serve warrants and make arrests before a suspect can flee the jurisdiction. The question remained, What was I being busted for?

I wondered if it was the stuff I was doing with my father or if it was about my selling cocaine. Was it the FBI *and* the DEA? If it was about the drugs, I had a big problem because my dad didn't know I was dealing and using. If it was about my father's stuff, well, at least I wasn't getting the rest of the crew in trouble by attracting the FBI.

With the house surrounded, both the FBI and I wanted the apprehension process to be as simple and painless as possible. I managed to stay calm. Blair's instructions were succinct. Come downstairs and accept the arrest warrant. I was cooperative and cautioned Blair that once I came down the stairs he was going to see me open a closet door and turn the alarm off on the front security gate. No gunfire. No resistance. As I calmly opened the front door, the agents refrained from storming the house. Lisa, dressed in her nightgown, was frightened and upset but maintained her composure. (According to FBI agents, it's the spouses who can be the most abusive during a mob arrest.)

While everyone kept their cool, Blair and the agents asked me if I needed to put on any clothes. Did I need to brush my teeth? Did I have any firearms in the house? After informing the officers about a skeet shooting shotgun and the Beretta 9 mm pistol in the bedroom, I led the agents upstairs, and asked, "Can you do me a big favor? Both of my children are sleeping in their bedrooms. Can we please be quiet? They're little kids. I don't want them startled."

Accompanied by two agents, I entered my bedroom and surrendered the two firearms. An agent stood outside the bathroom while I dressed and brushed my teeth. Once I finished I turned to the agent.

"What's the arrest for?"

"Old stuff . . . RICO violations."

I felt a wave of relief. No mention of any recent drug dealing. Once downstairs I grabbed a sweatshirt while a distraught Lisa stood at the front door.

"What do you want me to do?"

"Call my father and tell him—"

"No," interjected an agent. "We've got your father."

"All right, then call Kurt and—"

The agent shook his head. "We've got your brother, too."

"You know what, Lisa? Why don't you just wait for me to call?"

I didn't bother bringing up Uncle Nick. An early riser, he had already stepped out for his morning coffee. His wife, Noreen, let in the agents, and they searched Nick's three-flat from top to bottom, including the crawl spaces. He later turned himself in on advice of counsel.

As the agents walked me outside, they placed me in cuffs before putting me in the backseat of the car. Toward the end of the twenty-five-minute drive downtown to the federal building, I chuckled as we passed another government sedan with my dad sitting in the backseat. I gave him a nod. We hadn't spoken in months.

Before taking the crew members to the marshal's lockup, they put me in a holding cell. What followed was a parade of family and crew being led in by agents. Next to arrive was my dad. Although we were estranged, I wanted him to know that I was concerned about him. We exchanged pleasantries. I asked how he was feeling. Was he okay?

This was another time when I thought our relationship could change. Maybe this arrest will mellow my father and wake him up. He'll see his sons standing up for him, while at the same time he'll have our backs. We'll stand together and get through this. He probably feels god-awful and responsible that Kurt and I are mixed up in this.

Next Kurt was escorted into the holding cell. He was tossed, his hair and clothes disheveled.

"What happened to you?" I asked.

"Didn't they drag you out of the house?" Kurt asked.

Kurt turned to Dad and asked him the same question.

"No," we replied in unison, shrugging.

"They let me change, brush my teeth, and get ready. Why?" I said.

"You let them into the house?" Kurt asked.

"That's what you do when they hand you a warrant for your arrest."

Kurt turned to our father. "Did you let them into the house?"

"Yeah."

Kurt looked perplexed. "Didn't you tell us to not let anybody into the house?"

When the FBI came to Kurt's front door, he refused to let them in. His wife was in her nightgown, screaming from the window, "Get the hell out of here. Leave my husband alone. He's got nuthin' to do with nuthin'."

Once Kurt opened the front door, he was bum-rushed by the agents and dragged into the middle of the street, placed on his stomach, and handcuffed.

My father and I burst into laughter. "Now you're a tough guy, huh?"

The Calabrese RICO arrests turned into a reunion. After me, Dad, and Kurt came Philip "Pete" Fiore, one of the crew's primary collectors. Then Uncle Nick. Even the guy doing the fingerprinting was jovial.

"I've got good news and bad news," one agent told Kurt. "I just heard from your lawyer."

"Yeah? What'd he say?"

"He said, 'The good news is, don't worry about a thing. He's going to get you out. But the bad news is it might take ten years."

Once Kurt and I were fingerprinted and photographed, the photographer pulled out a book filled with signed mug shots. He asked Kurt, "Do you think your father will sign this?"

"I wouldn't ask him," Kurt cautioned. "He'll never do anything like that."

Back at the holding cell, I took ribbing about my pink, green, and yellow Zodiac shoes.

When my dad returned, the photographer came by the cell. "Hey, Frank, thank you!"

"No problem."

"What did you do?" Kurt asked him.

"The guy asked me to sign something for him."

I laughed at the look on my brother's face and the thought of Dad signing some copper's scrapbook filled with autographed mug shots. While he and Fiore whispered to each other, they kept an eye on the overhead security camera. I rolled up the sweatshirt I'd brought along, tucked it under my head, and took a nap. The crew and I would spend less than a day in jail.

Back in Elmwood Park, Lisa and Angela exchanged frantic phone calls. Angela had spoken to Diane, who suggested they come to her house in Oak Brook to discuss the next step. Diane seemed calm, asking if Lisa had called "our" lawyer.

"I didn't know *we* had one," was her rookie response.

After the arraignment, the mug shot photographer from the cop shop warned me that there were reporters outside the federal building. "I'm gonna make sure you guys get out the back door."

Once the marshals ushered us out the back door, we were immediately spotted. As the photographers and reporters gathered, I proposed we split up and run for it. I remember running through one of the nearby hotels. It was funny. My dad, Uncle Nick, and Kurt ran up a set of stairs, and I slowed down like I was going to talk to the press, but as soon as they caught up, I started running again until I saw my dad, Nick, and Kurt coming down a set of stairs ahead of me. I tried to get the press to follow me while everybody else could escape. At one point, we all bumped into one another like the Keystone Kops. We dashed through a few rooms and lost the pack of reporters chasing us. I saw my father that night on the news running in his Bermuda shorts.

Considering it was my first major arrest, it was surprisingly not too painful—until I overheard a conversation in the next room that gave me pause. One of the agents asked my father, "Why don't you help your kids?"

"My boys can take care of themselves," he responded coldly.

That bothered me. So much for standing together.

Before appearing in front of the magistrate at the arraignment, Agent Blair sat me down.

"Look, Frankie, you've got to make sure nobody gets hurt."

"I don't understand."

"You guys better not hurt anybody."

"We're not gonna hurt anybody," I assured Agent Blair, and added, "By the way, do you think I can get my guns back? They're not illegal."

"You've got bigger worries," Agent Blair replied.

It had taken five years for the FBI to nail the Calabrese crew, because the FBI takes its time gathering information . . . as long as the law allows. The Bureau is in no hurry to make an arrest unless an operation is immediately endangering the general public. Otherwise, FBI Organized Crime squads take as much time as they need, whether it's months or years. Federal prosecutors prefer to walk into a courtroom with nothing less than a slam-dunk case.

The 1995 Calabrese RICO case had its inherent weaknesses, especially the charges against Kurt. There was the possibility that Matt Russo might not come across as the most credible witness. In a pretrial victory, the judge ruled that the Calabreses couldn't be referred to as "the Calabrese Street Crew," insinuating the group's association with the Outfit.

After the arrests, the Calabrese RICO case didn't attract much publicity in Chicago's newspapers. Had we contested the case and fought, Kurt might have skated, especially if my dad and uncle had pleaded guilty, with one of the conditions being Kurt's severance. Instead, the crew, led by the intimidating Frank senior, decided to plead out and let Kurt fend for himself. The entire process—the bust, bail, plea-bargaining, and final sentencing—would last two years.

By the Fourth of July holiday in 1997, I had conceded that I needed to speed up the process so that I could begin serving my sentence and get on with life. Rather than postpone the inevitable with various delays, it was time to face the music, make a deal, and go inside. I needed to free myself from the clutches of cocaine and my father. Using drugs, I figured, was the surest way to have my bail revoked, so my strategy was to test positive for cocaine and ask for drug treatment. Blowing off a meeting with my presentencing investigation officer, after which I'd "pee dirty," would seal my fate. I hoped that would convince the G to send me off for eighteen months of drug treatment, which would be credited toward my sentence. This would be done on the QT, without anybody finding out. I would make my escape from my father while doing my time. But convincing the government of my drug addiction would take some doing. After I intentionally missed my presentencing meeting, the government was still skeptical. Not everyone who asked got shipped off for drug treatment.

On the night of July 3, I was in Elmwood Park at the annual street festival and feast, manning a booth and frying calamari with Danny Alberga. Lisa, the kids, and a few friends were with Danny and me. The calamari was selling briskly.

Suddenly from out of nowhere I felt a vise grip on my left wrist. Startled, I looked over to find it was my dad with his cold deadly stare. As I tried to pull away, he squeezed my wrist tighter, then leaned in and whispered, "I got two guys trained on you. Don't try to run. Come with me. I just wanna talk to you."

With Lisa and Danny looking on in disbelief, I scanned the crowd in search of two shooters. Would he gun me down in public? Rather than call his bluff and possibly endanger my friends and children, I relented. "Let go of my wrist so I can put down the fry basket. Then we can talk."

As we walked toward the parking lot, I scanned the crowd again for any gunmen, and realized there were probably none. We found a remote spot near the lot to sit down and talk.

"What the hell is going on with you, Frankie?" my father asked. "I got a call from your presentencing officer. She told me you missed your appointment and she couldn't get hold of you. She's concerned. I told her I'd find you and bring you in right away."

Knowing that I would soon be going to jail, I decided it was time to confess.

"Dad, the reason I'm playing around with the PSI officer is so I can get a court date and have my bail status revoked and start doing my time. That way after going to the MCC [Metropolitan Correctional Center], I can enter a drug program and get eighteen months off my sentence. In two weeks I'm going to court, and they're gonna lock me up."

I gazed into his puzzled face. I could see the wheels turning. With me in jail, he would lose control of his son. I had known since we began butting heads that he worried that one day I might turn on him. I knew more than enough about my father to put him away for life. But that wasn't my intention.

"I'm gonna be straight with you. I've been selling and doing cocaine for a while . . . but on my kids, it's over. That's why I need to start my sentence. I need to get away and get clean."

My father's face froze in disbelief and anger. My cocaine confession took him completely by surprise.

The morning I left to go to court to stand in front of the judge for violating my bond, I knew two things: One, I would never do cocaine again. Two, Dad was not going to contribute a dime toward my defense, and we would have to sell the house. I was on my own financially.

I had already cashed in my retirement savings from my city job to retain counsel. Money was getting tight. Any money on the streets from dealing cocaine was gone. I was out of the restaurants and delivering pizzas part-time at Armand's just to get by. If it hadn't been for Lisa's job at the Board of Trade, our household would have had no money.

That morning I showered and picked out a set of clothes—pants, shirt, and sport coat—that I assumed would be stored in a federal prison property box for the term of my sentence. Saying good-bye to the kids proved difficult.

"What's wrong?" my young daughter, Kelly, asked with her younger brother Anthony, looking up at me.

"There's nothing wrong. I'm going to work, and I love you guys very much." Lisa's grandmother left the room crying at the sight of me hugging my children.

As I walked to the train that would take me to the lawyer's office across the street from the federal building, several thoughts occurred. I would miss my wife. I would miss my children's formative years growing up. But I was ready to do my time. I anticipated it. I was upset with my father. I was numb, living life by going through the motions. It was a long walk to the lawyer's office from the train station. As I ambled through the morning rush-hour crowd, commuters bumping into me, I realized it would be my last taste of Chicago for the next few years.

When I walked into my lawyer's office, there were my parents and Lisa. I was upset that my dad was there. It was evident that he was there to put on the "dutiful father show" for the judge. Since I was going to be sentenced and incarcerated first, he was wondering how I would handle doing federal time.

He pulled me aside into an adjoining office for a last-ditch effort at a heart-to-heart. As the "Good Father," he gave me a tight hug and held back tears. "I don't know how you came to start doing that shit," he said, referring to my cocaine habit. "But you broke my heart."

"I'll make you a promise if you make me a promise," I said. "I will stop doing drugs and do my time if you promise to step back from the Outfit so that we can work on building a new relationship and a new life."

We embraced tighter, and tearfully agreed to mend our ways. After prison we would begin anew, both professionally and as father and son. As I crossed the street on my way to my sentencing hearing to surrender, I squeezed Lisa's hand, feeling good about the pact I had just made with my father.

I appeared in front of the judge twice. The first time was after my bail was forfeited as I surrendered to the court. With no bail, I was sent directly to the MCC. A short time later, I reappeared in front of the judge for sentencing as my father stood next to me.

In front of the judge for a second time, a deal was struck: fifty-seven months in federal prison. My PSI officer had recommended forty-seven months, but in my rush to begin serving, I succumbed to the G's demand of ten more months. I agreed to the fifty-seven months, not counting good behavior. I should have fought it, but I wanted to just go inside and do my time.

Accepting my fate, I was contrite. I admitted my mistakes to Judge James Holderman and reiterated that I was willing to "do my time like a man and pay my debt to society." As I spoke, the judge put his pencil down, leaned back in his chair, and looked me square in the eyes. He then asked a series of questions to make sure that the government hadn't pressured me into waiving my rights by accepting a plea. The judge expressed concern that I had used the same law firm as my father and that I was pleading out along with him.

When my dad stepped up next to speak to the judge on my behalf, Holderman put his head down and resumed writing, not once looking up. My father spoke about being godfather to twenty-five children, declared his love for his sons, and added that he was a senior citizen with serious health issues. I stood off to the side in shackles, clad in a jumpsuit. I shook my head in embarrassment at his theatrics. He concluded his speech with a tearful request, asking for a final concession.

"Do you think I can give my son one last hug?"

My eyes rolled heavenward as my body went limp in his tight embrace. Once I was led away in shackles, out in the hallway, Lisa and my mom wept while my dad's response was, "So . . . you guys wanna get something to eat?"

Mom drove Lisa back to the Elmwood Park train station and apologized for her son leaving her in the lurch, while Lisa wanted only to comfort her mother-in-law after she had seen her firstborn son reenter the MCC. Parked at the station was the pathetic old beater that Dad, an avid car collector, had lent me to drive after taking away my white Jeep.

Two weeks later, a pair of FBI agents showed up on Lisa's doorstep and asked if she had any additional information about my father or me. "No, thank you," Lisa responded as she closed the door, doubled over with stomach pains from stress.

Not long after, Johnny Marino showed up with a cryptic message that resembled a ransom note. It was a list of necessities that would be "paid for" provided that Lisa presented the correct receipts and invoices.

"Who asked you to bring this to me?" she asked Marino, who sheepishly shrugged.

"No thanks," said Lisa, handing the note back to Marino.

Later, a box arrived on Lisa's doorstep from the MCC. It contained my shirt, pants, and sports coat. The sight of my life reduced to a cardboard box of clothes set off a flood of emotions. Dread over the struggle that she suddenly faced as a single parent with two small children. Her love for me, and the hate she felt toward me for leaving our family in the lurch. Then the guilt over the relief she felt at no longer having to watch her husband self-destruct before her very eyes.

22.

COLLEGE WITH GUNS

If someone had told me as a kid that I would eventually work with the FBI, let alone forge a close professional relationship with someone like Agent Michael W. Maseth, I would have thought that person was nuts. On the other hand, had that same all-knowing someone told Mike that *he* would become an FBI agent, he might have been equally surprised.

According to Mike, chasing Outfit gangsters wasn't his original career path. He first showed an interest in law enforcement at age twenty-six, in 1996. As a young criminal-defense and personal-injury attorney in Columbus, Ohio, he received a phone call from his mother, who worked as a secretary for a high school vice principal. Two FBI agents had dropped by the school to speak with the students on Career Day.

"I hope you don't mind," Mike's mom said, "but I gave the FBI your contact information. They're looking for attorneys. It sounded like something you might be interested in, so they're sending you an application."

While John Fecarotta was dodging Uncle Nick's gunfire that September evening in 1986, Mike was attending high school in western Pennsylvania, where he was a popular student leader. As the drum major and a "terrible" euphonium player with North Allegheny High's 350-piece school band, Maseth marched halftime at the Gator Bowl and Cotton Bowl football games, and various other collegiate sporting events. After graduating from high school, Mike earned a bachelor of arts degree in history and a minor in philosophy at Allegheny College. But it was the law that had been calling Mike since his elementary-school days, when, as a smallish youngster, he was a probing debater with a questioning mind. After earning his bachelor's degree, he was accepted into the Capital University Law School in Columbus, Ohio, in 1992.

I would later learn from Mike that he received his law degree in 1995 and began working for two small firms. He stayed focused on criminal defense but expertly handled DUI cases. He had his first encounter with the FBI while defending two clients arrested by the Bureau for bank fraud. To Mike, the FBI agents seemed like levelheaded people who enjoyed what they did for a living—unlike him, wanting to pull his hair out representing drunk drivers.

Mike filled out a three-page FBI questionnaire and later completed the more detailed personality test, after which he heard nothing from the Bureau. He hadn't thought about the FBI application for about nine months and assumed there was no interest. What was the likelihood that he would be accepted? He figured not very high.

But in the summer of 1997, the FBI contacted Mike for a full-scale interview, to be conducted by three agents. After he passed the polygraph test, they asked if he was interested in becoming an agent. In March of 1998, the twenty-seven-year-old was set to report for agent training at the FBI Academy in the shoreline town of Quantico, Virginia.

Around the time I was starting my prison term, Mike put his stuff into storage, and off he went, going back to dorm life with a roommate, eating in a cafeteria, sharing a bathroom with four other guys, and going to gym class. It was like college with guns, except that Maseth had never fired a weapon in his life—which was fine because he didn't arrive at Quantico with any bad firearm habits.

Mike completed his training by taking an intensive seventeen-week program. He crammed to get through written exams, took extensive firearms training, and learned how to drive at high speeds. He soon found Quantico to be more about camaraderie than competition.

In week six, Mike was asked to rank all fifty-six FBI field offices from top to bottom in order of where he would most like to work. As is the custom at Quantico, when a budding agent steps up to receive his marching orders, he reveals his top choice to the class before opening the envelope. Mike's first choice was Kansas City, the locale closest to friends and family. He flinched when he read his destination aloud. Our town, Chicago, wasn't even a top ten choice; it ranked twelfth on his original list.

Mike spent his first six months of service in Chicago on a revolving training squad doing two-week stints working with a variety of different teams, including Bank Fraud, Terrorism, High-Tech Crime, Street Gangs, Bank Robbery, Public Corruption, and Organized Crime.

When the time came for a permanent assignment, Mike was originally optioned to Wire Fraud, but his training supervisor had other ideas. His superior, once a handling agent in Chicago for famed mob informant Ken "Joe the Jap" Eto, recommended that Mike be sent to the Organized Crime squad. Perhaps the supervisor felt his law background might supply a fresh investigative perspective.

It was always our belief that the Organized Crime squad used older, more experienced agents. What prompted his boss to send Mike to one of the two Bureau OC squads that operated out of Chicago? What could the world of organized crime possibly offer a fresh-faced rookie agent like Mike?

The old Organized Crime office in Chicago was on the eighth floor of the FBI's 219 Dearborn Avenue headquarters downtown, housed in the federal building. Mike found that his new FBI digs resembled the set of 1970s police sitcom *Barney Miller* more than that of Efrem Zimbalist, Jr.'s 1960s white-collar drama, *The FBI.* Only his supervisor, Tom Bourgeois—and later John Mallul after Tom retired—had his own office. Bourgeois was a top agent. He grew up in a law enforcement family, and his father was an FBI agent killed in the line of duty. Tom was two years old at the time.

According to Mike, the squad room during the 1990s was more like a bullpen than the cubicles of today. When he arrived there were nine agents in OC1. Four aged computers were stashed in the corner for community use. Not all of them worked. There were no regular Monday-morning staff meetings; people worked on top of one another, and it was up to each individual to stay current on what was going on elsewhere.

This free-for-all environment meant that Mike didn't have to corner a specific person if he had a question or a comment. He now had a *roomful* of mentors. A rule of thumb was that questions or observations were taken to other squad members first before going to the boss. Outside of dealing with secret informants (who were referred to only by their code names), investigating was about throwing things out in the open and getting different takes from the peanut gallery. If somebody heard a particular name from four desks up, it was up to that agent to speak up: "I'm dealing with that guy, too. Let's talk about it."

While we worked the same streets alongside the other Outfit crews, there was healthy competition between the two Chicago FBI squads for who would deliver the next big takedown. Mike was assigned to OC1. Mike's "competitor," OC2, had scored a major coup in 1992, which involved flipping a bookmaking and gambling kingpin, William Jahoda. This resulted in LCN (La Cosa Nostra) figures being convicted on gambling and racketeering charges, including Outfit consigliere Rocky Infelise.

Mike's path and mine were about to cross, at least on the streets. Mike's first official Organized Crime squad assignment involved shadowing Johnny Apes's lieutenant, Jimmy DiForti. DiForti worked in my father's crew and had been indicted and was set to stand trial for the murder of a juice loan deadbeat named Billy "the Pallet Man" Benham. In addition to shadowing DiForti, Mike was ordered to conduct surveillance on our crew lieutenant Ronnie Jarrett.

While Mike was tailing Ronnie in the Bridgeport area, another squad agent supplied directions from another vehicle on a two-way radio. Mike soon learned that giving chase in the real world (as opposed to drills at Quantico) was not easy. Jarrett, as usual, drove erratically, sometimes speeding up to fifty miles an hour the wrong way up one-way streets.

"Quick! He's making a left here," the voice emitted from the radio, "and a left there. No, no. Now he's going right!"

My father taught me to always know my backstreets. While I grew up knowing the avenues and alleys of every neighborhood in and around Chicago, Mike had no idea which street was which. Navigating into a dead-end alleyway and driving in circles, he fell three miles behind the chase and pulled over to the curb. He couldn't find his ass with a road map that day and sat in his crummy old square box Bureau car, exasperated. What the hell had he gotten himself into with this job? He was out of his element. He didn't know anybody in Chicago and needed to get up to speed quickly and figure out who *were* these guys in the Chicago Outfit.

Mike was having difficulty getting into the groove of the squad. After the botched surveillance, Mike approached Chicago Police Department detective Bob Moon, who served on the squad as a task force member. Moon and Detective Al Egan were veteran cops whom the Feds trusted when they needed local intelligence: the inside scoop on particular mob hangouts or information on who had been arrested and on what charges.

"Listen, Bob, help me out. I'm lost!" Mike said. "I don't know what the hell I'm doing. I don't know who these guys are. You gotta explain it to me."

Moon was a down-to-the-bone blue-collar Irish Catholic cop. We knew the name, and that he was a Chicago copper placed on the FBI's Organized Crime task force crew. He once infiltrated our crew through one of our members, Louis Bombacino, posing as a juice loan customer. Both my father and my uncle Nick had dealt with Moon. He was round, short, and stout, with a bald pate and glasses. According to Mike, he was one of the funniest guys in the office, with the driest wit. While sitting at his desk, he called up the archdiocese as Pope John Paul II lay dying. He asked to speak with the bishop so he could submit his name for consideration to replace the ailing pope. But to us, Bob Moon was no joke.

Not only did Moon answer Mike's many questions and supply him with important details, but Bob made him feel more at ease in the squad room. Moon gave Mike a detailed history of the Outfit and a who's who of the players involved with Ronnie and DiForti. As it turned out, Ronnie was becoming a key figure in a new investigation of the Calabrese Chinatown crew. Although Jarrett was not a made guy—he was only half Italian—he had done sufficient jail time and whacked enough people to make him a well-established name within the Outfit.

Mike knew Chicago had a long, colorful history of corruption between organized crime and the police that dated back to the days of Capone. Chicago was tainted with plenty of dirty cops like Richard Cain, Michael Corbitt, and Bill Hanhardt—high-level guys who were in the pocket of the Outfit bosses.

It was hard to know whom to trust inside the police force while working with the OC1 squad. Law enforcement never really knew which cops, judges, politicians, or moles my father had in his pocket. As a result, it was wise to keep interdepartmental cooperation among the Bureau, the Chicago PD, the U.S. Marshals, and the Cook County Sheriff's Department strictly to those you knew and trusted firsthand. Now that Mike was in the mix, it would only get crazier when we eventually bumped heads.

23.
THE MCC

Plea agreements regarding the RICO charges were reached by me, my father, Uncle Nick, and Kurt on March 21, 1997. Crew members Louis Bombacino and Philly Beans Tolomeo—the latter having fled to witness protection—also pleaded out. Co-defendant "Pete" Fiore would try his luck in court, and serve ten years.

By July, I felt I could do my time as long as I was away from my dad. I had violated my bond by using drugs, so I was the first inside. My plan: attend drug rehabilitation in Yankton, South Dakota, with the judge's consent, applying the time toward my sentence.

I reported to the Metropolitan Correctional Center in Chicago in late July 1997, the first stop inside the federal penal system. After MCC, the Federal Bureau of Prisons would assign me to a prison within five hundred miles of my home to accommodate my family. My mission was simple: serve my time and return home to mend fences with my wife and family, and leave behind my life with the crew.

Conversely, going to the MCC was something that my father wanted to avoid. He ordered his lawyers to have him report directly to the Federal Correctional Institution at Milan, Michigan, to begin his 114-month sentence. To ensure a quick and smooth transition, he was eager for the rest of his family—Kurt, Nick, and me—to plead out alongside him and not go to trial. Kurt pleaded guilty to a tax charge and was sentenced to two years. My father's rap to Kurt was that if he didn't do this, my dad could get sixty years, while Kurt would get a relative slap on the wrist or be sent to a boot camp. What kind of son would risk his father having to serve sixty years? Being too old for boot camp, Kurt was sent to FCI Oxford in Wisconsin. Not long after, Kurt was put on a bus back to the MCC, where he served eighteen months.

In finalizing my plea bargain, the main snag was the fine attached to my fifty-seven-month sentence. My father's fine amounted to around $750,000, which he arranged to pay in part by forfeiting Grandma Sophie's property rather than touch his own cash. After settling his own fine, he promised through his attorney to pay my fine, but only if I agreed to plead guilty along with the rest of the family. My fine came in at $150,000. Nick's was closer to $25,000, and Kurt's came near $5,000.

The upside of my dad's offer was that I could keep the equity in my home, which meant that Lisa and the kids would still own a home while I "went away." Foremost in my mind was the pledge that Dad had tearfully made to me at the attorney's office that once we were released, he would step back from the Outfit, repair our relationship, and legitimize his business dealings. The big if was that I would have to trust him to come through with the

$150,000 for my fine in exchange for pleading guilty and not going to trial.

Except for doing a night for brawling, I had never served any time. After going through intake, on my way up to the MCC's thirteenth floor with four ominous-looking black inmates, I had no idea what to expect. Violence? Racial tension? Inedible food? I walked toward a steel door with a long vertical window. Inside I could see the tiers, a Ping-Pong table, and no guards. Just guys walking around in their shorts.

I walked to the door and stopped. I saw a bunch of guys pointing at me. I figured, Okay, this must be it. I'm the new guy. I'm going to have to prove myself. Once I entered, I realized they were pointing at the door to tell me it was open.

The MCC's room accommodations were basic: two bunks, toilet, small desk with pencils and paper, and a cellmate. The environment was more open than I had pictured. Lockdown was ten at night until five in the morning.

The guard who signed me in didn't like Italians or my family, so he put me with a guy that nobody else would cell with. I was sitting on my upper bunk when this animal hulk walked in. He was a humongous, hairy white Indiana hillbilly, close to fifty years old. He looked at me and growled. They called him Bear.

One look at Bear during my first night inside, and I slept clutching a pencil for protection. After a few days, Bear opened up to me. We talked and got along. After his wife died and a hooker screwed him out of a lot of money, he threatened to kill her. Then he threatened the judge and nearly strangled and killed his last cellmate. The guards were terrified of him. I bought him food and threw popcorn into his mouth like an animal in the zoo. The guards got a kick out of how fast I tamed him. Trouble was, he didn't bathe.

After I dragged Bear into the shower and took a scrub brush to him, if anyone got near me, he became protective . . . like a mother bear. When I moved from the thirteenth to the seventeenth floor, Bear was heartbroken. But the move was good for me.

I joined friends from Brooklyn's Bensonhurst and the West Side of Chicago, and a kid from Elmwood Park.

Prison is about fiefdoms, turf, and control. You stick with your kind, whether by race, nationality, area code, county, region, or lifestyle. I was assigned to the kitchen, while my pals Pat and Joey worked the laundry. As the minority, the Italians confined themselves to the same small area in the day room.

I spent nearly five months—July through November 1997—at the MCC. I missed my family and friends, but after a couple of weeks inside, my mother visited me. She was surprised at how relaxed I was. Yet I discouraged visitors. At my insistence, Lisa rarely came, alone or with the kids. Whenever I got a visit, even if it was for a few minutes, it put me back. I'd go upstairs, and it was like starting over.

The kids had a tough time being away from their dad. They were six and seven at the time. They had questions for which Lisa had no answers. While she had little faith left in our relationship, she needed to hang in there for the kids.

Before going inside, Uncle Nick ran into Lisa at a social event. A man of few words, a somber Nick offered reassurance that I would find the way to live drug free amid the turmoil. He shook his head sadly, and admitted, "The boys should never have been involved, and shouldn't be in jail."

Life inside was better for me than working the streets with my father, but I kept in touch with him to see if he was serious about going straight. He was intensely interested in and fearful of the MCC. What was it like? Was I okay doing my time there? Was it difficult?

While my uncle was sent to FCI Pekin, Illinois, a few hundred miles away and a higher-security institution, my dad was admitted to FCI Milan in October of 1997. I was still waiting to "get designated." Designations were big news at the MCC. The assignments were regularly posted on a community bulletin board. It was like trying out for football, seeing if you made the team. Every day the list went up, I would run over to see if my name was on the list. One day I saw it: "Frank Calabrese, 06738424, Milan, Michigan."

Frank Calabrese? FCI Milan? That can't be right.

I approached one of the counselors. "Excuse me, but I think they made a mistake on this list. That's my father going to Milan, not me."

The counselor reviewed the list and looked up. "Nope. That's definitely you."

Milan, the *same prison*? That can't be!

At first I thought the FBI was trying to punish me. After talking to veteran inmates, I learned that with multiple defendants on a case, spreading people around different federal lockups was difficult. The government often made concessions for out-of-state families by bunching family members into one institution for visiting convenience.

My heart sank at the thought of having to do time in the same facility as my father. My plan to start a new life was derailed. The idea was to put *more* distance between me and him. Now here I was, done in by a random glitch in the Federal Bureau of Prisons system.

Being transported to Milan would give me time to think. I had no choice but to make the best of the situation. My time at Milan could be well spent working things out with him and seeing if he would live up to his two promises. So far he hadn't come through with the money for my fine. Now, would he live up to his commitment to retire from the Outfit, or would he continue his manipulative and controlling ways?

I was about to find out.

24.

A CHANCE TO STEP UP

I was in prison.

The trip from the MCC in downtown Chicago to FCI Milan had one stopover. I arrived by bus at USP (United States Penitentiary) Terre Haute, Indiana, and then flew on "Con Air" into Michigan. It was November 1997 and transportation was shut down for the Thanksgiving holiday. Because the Terre Haute facility was under lockdown, I spent my entire stay in the SHU, the Secure Housing Unit. This was my first stay in the hole.

For sixteen days before I boarded the plane for Milan, I stayed locked down in one of USP Terre Haute's older wings. It was filled with Cubans from Fidel Castro's Cuban Crime Wave purge of the late seventies and early eighties. These were criminals who had been dumped onto American shores like Al Pacino's Tony Montana character in *Scarface.* Lockdown was twenty-three hours a day with one hour of "rec" outside in the frigid cold. Consistent with the high security, rec was spent in an outdoor cage. It took only one session for me to beg the guards to let me back in with the Cubans and the cockroaches. Meals were slid through a slot three times a day. Inmates were issued one set of clothes that could be swapped out every couple of days. Showers were offered every three days. I scored a couple of dog-eared paperback books off a cart that squeaked by my cell. I spent time doing push-ups on the bed to avoid crushing roaches on the floor.

Terre Haute was the appropriate stop for me to consider my dilemma. Was my father going to change or, more important, was he going to *step up*? Would he step up and stand behind his sons, by paying my fine and looking after Kurt, who had opted to sacrifice his freedom for his dad. It was also time for *me* to step up and become proactive, if not for myself, then for my family. Federal prison would be the great equalizer. The prison yard would be the place where I would judge my father not by his promises, but by his actions.

When I walked into FCI Milan, I noticed that a large part of the prison was old. There was an outdoor yard with a new gymnasium and three large housing units. There were cells and tiers but no bars. Milan's cells had electronic doors. Going through intake, I was fortunate to get an outside cell unit rather than one facing inside that was part of a noisy dormitory. In a matter of days, I had gone from sitting in the cold darkness of a two-man cell in the hole in Terre Haute to moving into a modest two-man room that looked more like a college dorm than a prison cell—and with no cockroaches.

I had met a guy at the MCC who advised me, "When you get

to Milan, make sure you get a job quick!" Once I made it through Milan reception, the guard in my unit tested a bunch of fresh "fish" inmates on their first days. He assigned us to cleaning detail in the cell block unit. Most of the guys ignored him and didn't show up, but I, along with a couple of guys, cleaned the window frames with toothbrushes. I did what he said and after that he didn't mess with me. The guys who didn't show up, he fucked with them all the time.

The first night, as the new Frankie, I unloaded my "property" in my cell. I noticed the obvious differences between the MCC, USP Terre Haute, and FCI Milan. Milan offered freedom to roam the yard until the 9:00 p.m. count. There were few internally locked doors. There was very little signing in and out. Movement wasn't predicated on having to be escorted by a guard. While there was a "hole," there was no fear of being shot from a gun tower if an inmate stepped onto the grass or wandered into places that were designated "out of bounds" because of regulations and sight lines. I got lucky when my cellie (cellmate), Lenny LaLiberte, showed me how to eat healthier and lift weights, which became an important routine in my recovery.

Once I hit the Milan yard, it was time to seek out my dad, who lived in an adjoining unit. (The old Frankie would have avoided his dad for as long as possible.) My father was excited, telling everybody that I was coming and that we were the best of pals. It was a good sign and a good start.

I got lucky again when I scored a job in the commissary that a biker from Cleveland named Johnny Ray helped me get. So now I had a regular job and spent time playing softball and hanging out with the bikers.

Inside my new environment, I concentrated on reinventing my relationship with Dad. Seeing my progress pumping iron, he joined me on the weight pile. We reminisced together about growing up in the old neighborhood and how he had won a weight-lifting contest years ago in jail. He joined me at substance-abuse meetings, and we attended Catholic Mass together.

Over the first couple of months, we mainly stuck to talking

about the daily routine of prison life. Whenever the subject of leaving the street crew behind came up, he assured me that his Outfit days were over. Whenever I broached the subject of his promise to pay his sons' fines, he denied making such an arrangement through his lawyer.

His denial was the first red flag that I spotted in testing our relationship. A second red flag came when he approached me with news that "a friend" had located Matt Russo, who would be approached with a sum of money. In exchange, Matt would recant his story and testify that my dad was innocent. Then I was to lie on the witness stand.

"I think we can beat this, Frankie."

"You're gonna force me to get on the stand and lie for you? You do realize that once I'm up there, the government can ask me any questions they please."

"I can always subpoena you."

Because Matt Russo had been tracked down by one of his soldiers, I became convinced that my father was still active on the streets. Then one day he let it slip that the Catholic priest had allowed him access to the phone. The priest's line wasn't monitored. An alarm went off in my head. Was he manipulating the priest with a newfound "interest" in Catholicism so that he could keep in touch with people on the street?

For a while, we both lived on the first floor of G-Unit, sixty feet apart. Then we were getting in each other's way. I noticed he was increasingly short-tempered, especially after I nixed the idea that we share a cell. I soon discovered that he was reading my mail. Collecting it from an unsuspecting guard, he intercepted a letter from Kurt, who had halted contact with him after feeling hoodwinked by his guilty plea. Kurt asked in the letter how I was holding up being in the same prison with our father.

"What's worse?" Kurt wrote sardonically. "Losing your freedom or being in jail with Dad?"

Taken aback by the tone of Kurt's letter, he returned it to the guard, who passed the opened letter on to me, explaining that my father had seen it first. When I confronted my father, a heated argument ensued. After our row, we became estranged and didn't speak for days. As I walked past him on the yard, we bumped shoulders and kept on walking. I noticed the cold murderous Thousand-Yard Stare in his eyes.

But inside the prison walls, I no longer feared him.

By early 1998, my father was going through cellmates in rapid succession. Everything had to go by his rules: No eating in your bunk. Take your shoes off before entering the cell. Wash your hands after you pee. If you opened the window, he'd close it. At times his cellmates would come to me to complain. Some were afraid that he would get angry at them. I defended my dad, careful not to reveal the strain between the two of us. I needed to maintain a facade that we were friends while I evaluated his actions and true intentions.

25.

TWO CHOICES, NEITHER ONE GOOD

Inside the limited confines of the prison universe, I could take my father only in very small doses. I didn't care for his jailhouse buddies. He mostly hung around made guys. They would sit in front of the boccie courts, complaining about how awful prison life was. None of them worked jobs or took classes, because most had money coming in from the streets deposited into their prison accounts. If any of them had a job, it was a menial

assignment, like emptying a trash can twice a day. My dad's chore was filling a napkin holder at a certain table in the chow hall.

By January 1998, I was enjoying a plum job at the prison commissary. Whatever kept the prison running, especially food and clothing, was shipped through the commissary. I took my job at the commissary quite seriously. Not long after I began working there, more commissary guys shipped out. I moved up quickly in seniority.

There were many benefits working in the commissary, including access to new clothes and a new jacket for the winter. I made sure I shared new stuff with my father. Rather than scamming or shortcutting, I learned that perks came from hard work.

My restaurant experience proved invaluable for working there. I assisted the correctional officers in ordering supplies, and because I had been in the food-preparation business in Chicago, I called various companies to send samples. Next I helped reorganize the warehouse.

Commissaries were the only enterprise that brought profit into the federal prison system other than Unicor, the furniture factory. With the help of the inmate staff and me, the Milan guards won the prize for running the most profitable commissary in the federal system, earning them a five-hundred-dollar check each and a beer and pizza party.

The entire Milan facility held 1,200 men, and through my hard work, I earned a seat on the prison commissary board, representing my 250-man unit. It gave me influence as to where a portion of the profits from the commissary would go. On behalf of the men in my unit, I lobbied for new televisions, exercise mats, and certain brands of toothpaste and toiletries.

Things were going well at the commissary until I heard the news: my father had been hired to work in the commissary. The prison guard in charge of hiring was an Italian guy who thought he had done me a favor by showing respect and giving him the job.

It was the last thing I wanted. I pulled my dad aside.

"Why do you wanna work at the commissary, Pa? You've got

your job putting the napkins in the container. The commissary is hard work."

The staff welcomed him because he was my father. As part of the job, each employee was assigned an aisle to stock every day, and because I had gained seniority, I was assigned the easiest aisle. Since my father was the new guy, he received the most difficult aisle, with the heaviest cans and boxes to stack. To help him, I switched aisles, and because I worked days *and* evenings, each night I would stock both aisles before he arrived at work the next morning.

In came my father, acting like King Farouk, sitting around with his feet up on the order desk, taking occasional naps.

I pulled him aside. "You gotta start looking busy."

"But there's nothing to do," he said. "This is such an easy job."

He got a big kick out of working at the commissary because he got to pick through the fruits and vegetables first. The staff maintained a small kitchen in the back where we'd cook Italian dishes. On a few occasions, the guards brought in food from the outside so that my father and I could cook them a genuine Italian meal.

Those were "Good Dad" days. He loved to cook. We made pasta and sausage and peppers and red gravy from scratch. I made my Italian fish salad, which the guards loved. Cooking with him, I thought once again, maybe there's hope for better days.

As the guards looked the other way, I reminded him to be tight-lipped with the other inmates regarding the special perks we enjoyed at the commissary. "Please don't say anything. These are privileges that we work hard for."

When he began bragging to the other inmates about his easy job, that pissed off the COs. I got into it with him about it.

"While you're out there telling everybody the commissary is an easy job, I stock *both* of our aisles every night! I took the hardest aisle and gave you the easiest."

"What did you do that for?"

"Because you're my father!"

Working together in the commissary marked the first time he was required to *take* orders instead of *giving* them, especially from his own son. In the eyes of FCI Milan, we were now equals. Whenever a delivery truck came in, the inmate staff would hop up on the dock to run forklifts and move boxes. We were busting our asses while my dad stood around with the guards, pointing and supervising. One day I walked up to him:

"Listen, you wear the same khakis as me. Why don't *you* get up on the dock and help us?"

I got the Thousand-Yard Stare.

My father had a learning disability—and is probably dyslexic. It was difficult for him to read the order sheets. Out of pride, though, he didn't want anyone to know. At first, inmates went out of their way to help him, but soon the rest of the commissary staff grew tired of his antics. It came to a head when a female CO took him to task and my dad got back in her face. I looked over at the commotion. The guard was ready to write him up. I approached her.

"Look, do me a favor. I know you want to send him to the hole and fire him, but let me talk to him and see if I can't get him out of here."

The CO agreed to give him one chance.

Later that night, I took him aside on the yard. "Dad, you've got to go."

"What do you mean?"

"You got in her face. She was going to write you up and send you to the hole. But I fixed it so you could walk in there, quit, and get your other job back, and it doesn't go on your record."

My father became indignant. "I don't need *you* fixin' nothin' for *me.* Got it?"

Our relationship slid from bad to worse. Each time I gained a little distance, he closed the gap.

His multiple personalities reared their various heads behind prison walls. He could be very likable. The guys loved the Good Dad and the Street-Smart Mobster. But the cold stare of a hit man chilled them. We were polar opposites while inmates assumed we were of similar temperament.

Inside prison, the smallest things were magnified. During a

"Movie Day" for the commissary workers, a video was brought in from the outside and shown in the backroom. Since it was only a TV hooked up to a VHS player, the guards were willing to look the other way. I invited Dad to watch *Face/Off* starring John Travolta.

"Come in and watch a movie at the commissary. *But don't say nothin' to nobody!*"

Movie Day was another perk that could turn into a political hassle among the general population. But after he hit the yard inviting his friends, one of the guards approached me. "Frankie, what the fuck?"

I met Dad on the boccie court. "What the hell are you doing?"

"What?"

"Who are you inviting to Movie Day? I told you to say nothing. Please, this isn't like you. You used to know how to keep things to yourself. What's going on?"

After receiving his nearly ten-year sentence, my father continued to waver on his promise to pay my $150,000 fine. Whenever the subject came up, he would wave it off or change the subject. With the arguments and friction we were having, I remained convinced that my father was not going to come through.

Life was hard on the outside for Lisa and the kids. Other than my father giving Lisa six thousand dollars—in exchange for a signed promissory note and a lien on the house—my family received no support from the Calabrese family or crew. With only her job at the commodities exchange, Lisa fell months behind on the mortgage and lost the house. When the house was sold, he collected his six thousand. After the government took its share toward my fine, Lisa was left with nothing. People assumed my dad was taking care of Lisa and the kids while I was locked up. Losing the house proved to be the last straw. Lisa filed for divorce, and she and the kids moved in with her grandmother.

With news of the divorce, I hit rock bottom. I'd lost everything—my family, my house, my savings, and now my marriage. Yet despite the money stashed away in Chicago and the property, it was clear: my father was not going to pitch in to help.

Once he was transferred to H-Unit while I was still in G-Unit, I enjoyed the distance. One evening I was lying in my bunk with the lights out when I suddenly opened my eyes. I was startled by a daunting figure standing in the doorway of my cell.

"Psst. Frankie."

"Dad! What are doing here? You're not supposed to be in this unit."

"The guy let me in. He knows me."

It was the final straw. I was divorced, broke, and locked up, and now my biggest nightmare was inside my unit, breaching what little privacy I had. How much worse could it get? I needed to confirm my suspicions and find out if he was active on the streets.

I used my connections on the outside to find out what was going on. The news wasn't good. It was terrible. Not that I was surprised, but my father was very much in business. The assurances were lies. I found out he had Ronnie Jarrett running the crew and that both Ralph Peluso and Michael Talarico were reporting to Ronnie. But what shocked me was that he had Nick Ferriola booking for him.

I needed to make a decision. With my hopes dashed, I sat for weeks in my cell, sickened that he was lying to me. I couldn't confront him over what I had discovered. That would only endanger the lives of those who had supplied me with the information. I knew I couldn't trust him to do what was right or what was best for the family.

I thought about going to my counselor to get transferred so that I could wash my hands of him. I could lie about wanting to be closer to my kids or say that I didn't feel safe at Milan anymore.

I scrapped both options. I knew that once Dad, Uncle Nick, and I were released, the streets wouldn't be big enough to hide on. Once released, my father would remain out of control, the crew would be revitalized, and there wouldn't be a damned thing I could do to stop him. Somebody had to stop him; otherwise nothing would change. After some consideration, my situation boiled down to two impossible alternatives.

Do I play this out and take it to the streets so that when we both get out, one of us ends up dead while the other rots in prison for life? Or do I contact the FBI and offer to help keep my sick, manipulative, sociopathic father in jail for life?

I hated both options. Contacting the FBI meant not knowing exactly what was in store working with law enforcement. The FBI was convinced that it had shut the Calabrese crew down. But I knew better. I'd have to convince the Bureau otherwise. Could the FBI be trusted? Were the agents competent? Would they even believe me?

I had two choices, neither one good: Kill my father before he killed me or reach out to the FBI.

26.

THE MOMENT I SENT IT...

Knowing that I couldn't live with myself if I killed my father, I decided to reach out to the FBI. But how? In prison, where privacy was nonexistent, I needed to be extremely careful about how and with whom I communicated. Choosing the right method was a matter of life and death.

A phone call to the FBI was out of the question. Outgoing calls were taped and monitored. If I was going to take the plunge, not one person or entity could be trusted, no inmate or cellmate, no guard or counselor, not the warden himself. Being exposed as a beefer was equal to a death sentence.

Dad had already received one anonymous piece of hate mail threatening him. He suspected it was from Uncle Joe, which gave me an idea. I would send the FBI a letter. This would be the safest way to move forward.

My plan was simple: compose a one-page letter, typed, unsigned, and sanitized so that, although my name was on it, no one could positively confirm that I sent the letter. I took every precaution while typing the letter, stashing crumpled drafts in my shirt.

Sending a letter was my only option. Prison authorities rarely, if ever, read an inmate's outgoing mail. I was aware of the Outfit reach inside law enforcement. The letter had to be a complete secret. Whom should I send it to?

I scoured my PSI forms and court documents for any particular FBI agents assigned to my case. One name stood out: Agent Tom Bourgeois. He had worked on the RICO case involving Matt Russo. Bourgeois was not only a supervising agent on the Organized Crime squad, but he was gung ho and seemingly untouchable. Although it was a shot in the dark, I felt that reaching out to Bourgeois was a fail-safe way to deal with my father. If my mail was intercepted, I could blame my embittered uncle Joe or the FBI, who often used disinformation campaigns to divide and conquer organized crime.

I walked into the empty prison library early that morning to type my letter. It wasn't in my nature to cooperate with law enforcement. It was viewed as weak. The FBI was seen as an adversary whose resources were potentially limitless. Before now, the thought of assisting them was out of the realm of possibility. But I realized that my relationship with my dad was at a dead end.

July 27, 1998. After a couple of horrible weeks watching him maintain his facade, I dropped the letter into the Milan prison mailbox knowing I was taking a life-altering step.

The moment I sent it, I knew I had crossed the line. Cooperating meant I would probably have to give up Uncle Nick for his crimes, and that was agonizing.

The final draft of my letter read in full:

> ATTN: Thomas Bourghois [*sic*]
>
> I am sending you this letter in total confidentiality. It is very important that you show or talk to nobody about this letter except who you have to. The less people that know I am contacting you the more I can and will help and be able to help you. What I am getting at is I want to help you and the GOVT. I need for you and only you to come out to MILAN FCI and we can talk face to face.
>
> NOBODY not even my lawyers know that I am sending you this letter, it is better that way for my safety. Hopefully we can come to an agreement when and if you choose to COME HERE. Please if you decide to come make sure very few staff at MILAN know your reason for coming because if they do they might tell my father and that would be a danger to me. The best days to come would be TUES. or WEDS. Please no recordings of any kind just bring pen and lots of paper. This is no game. I feel I have to help you keep this sick man locked up forever.
>
> FRANK CALABRESE JR.
> 06738–424 inmate #
> UNIT G-Right
> FCI MILAN MICHIGAN

Months passed. I received no response. I kept my guard up just in case the letter had been intercepted. One day a CO called me aside and whispered to me, "SIS called and they want you to come over right away." The Special Investigative Service office housed the prison police force.

I feigned surprise. The request had to be about the letter. The SIS chief ushered me into a small windowless room with a table and a few chairs. A few minutes later FBI Agent Tom Bourgeois walked in and sat down.

Bourgeois had his doubts about me and decided to put me to the test. There were legal issues and a lot of questions. Did my attorney know about my sending the letter? What were my intentions in writing the letter, and what did I want in return? Was I unhappy doing my time? Had my father and I had a falling-out?

Was I willing to wear a wire?

I said no to the wire because I felt my father was way too smart and careful. He wouldn't talk about any of his activities with the Outfit and the crew, or if he did and if he "caught the play," he would kill me like he would kill anybody else who betrayed him.

But after a couple of weeks of reflection, I changed my mind. I felt I had to wear a wire after all.

After a second FBI interview with Agent Bourgeois and another agent, Scott Brooks, I agreed to wear the wire. Then Assistant U.S. Attorney Mitch Mars asked to speak with me. In November 1998, Bourgeois returned to FCI Milan with Mars for a third FBI meeting. After a short meeting, both were satisfied that I would go the distance.

When Agent Bourgeois returned to FCI Milan for a fourth time in January 1999 with fellow agents Kevin Blair and Mike Hartnett, I "gave" the FBI the 1986 John Fecarotta hit. I detailed the planning my father, my uncle, and I had done before the hit and conceded that Uncle Nick was involved. I admitted to Hartnett that I had retrieved the gun from the sewer.

The first meetings with "Tyler," my new code name, were fruitful. The facts about Fecarotta's death passed muster with Mitch Mars and the prosecutors at the U.S. Attorney's Office. As Tyler, I could provide the Feds with any possible communications or street crew activity going on between Dad and the outside world.

In January 1999, Agent Michael Maseth was assigned to my case, which centered on my pledge to testify against my father. I took one look at the boyish Maseth and shook my head. This guy looked much too young to be an FBI agent. Had I made the right decision? Was the Bureau taking this operation seriously enough? In February, I alerted Maseth that crooked cop Michael Ricci and another policeman named Anthony Doyle were going to visit my father in FCI Milan to discuss what was going on with some evidence. As a result Mike and the squad obtained a wiretap order from a judge and went fishing for information.

With new light cast on the death of Fecarotta and with me implicating my father and uncle, the FBI went to work. It was time for the Bureau to reopen the case and retrieve a golden piece of evidence stored in the Chicago PD evidence locker for thirteen years: the bloody gloves worn and dropped by Uncle Nick. The handing over of a piece of the bloody gloves to the Feds for DNA testing became of particular interest to a couple of Outfit moles (and personal friends of my dad). Retired cop Mike Ricci had moved over to the Cook County Sheriff's office from the Chicago Police Department to become head of the Home Monitoring unit. Anthony "Twan" Doyle, a veteran CPD officer, worked in the evidence room and had computer access to information about the Feds' interest in the gloves.

Once the FBI was alerted through me and other sources that the mob was aware of the bloody gloves, a plan was hatched. Young Agent Maseth would act as a decoy to exploit any mob leaks that might have developed among Ricci, Doyle, and my father regarding the Fecarotta murder.

It was common knowledge among the feds that Deputy Ricci "was kinky" and cozy with the mob, and especially with my father. The two had been partners in a hot-dog stand, and Ricci didn't care who knew about it. So Agent Mike reached out to Ricci, who manned the administrative post with the Sheriff's Department.

Mike visited Ricci at the Sheriff's office in April 1999 posing as a naive rookie and brought along female agent Tracy Balinao, who looked just as youthful. Mike pulled out a picture of Jimmy DiForti and handed it to Ricci. At the time, DiForti was out on bond and was supposed to be on home monitoring, but due to an administrative snarl, he wasn't.

"This guy is a mobster," Maseth told Ricci, "and he's out on $2.5 million bond. Why isn't he on home monitoring?"

Maseth and Balinao were sent to play dumb. They didn't care about DiForti. Their mission was to "tickle the wire" to see whether or not Ricci would tip off my father about any pending investigations, especially the reopened Fecarotta case and the gloves. Mike noticed on Ricci's office wall a picture about the notorious Scheussler-Peterson murders, a case resurrected from 1955, when three young boys were found dead and molested in a ditch. Through the toil of detectives like Ricci, the case was reopened, and the killer was arrested and convicted in 1995.

"You know what's interesting?" Mike said, pointing to the framed photo. "With today's technology, we can actually go back thirty years to solve cases using DNA. In fact, we're working on a couple of cases that go back years."

Ricci nodded with interest.

Two days later, Maseth phoned Ricci again, prodding him further. "Listen, Mike, can you do me a favor? Forget I was at your office talking about Jimmy DiForti. After I got back and told my bosses about our meeting, I got my ass chewed out. Forget I was there."

The ambush was set. Would Ricci and Doyle take the bait and reach out to my father?

27.

SCARPE GRANDE

As the case, now code-named Operation Family Secrets, gained traction in January and February of 1999, I gave Agents Mike Hartnett and Kevin Blair the urgent news that my father would be visited by Mike Ricci and Twan Doyle in a week. Maseth flew up to Milan and combed through tapes of my father's incoming calls. Armed with the Milan daily phone logs, Maseth listened to countless monitored prison phone calls on an old reel-to-reel tape recorder.

Scanning through the tapes, he located a conversation between Mike Ricci and my dad confirming their visit for February 19, only a few days away.

Agents Mike Maseth and Mike Hartnett, whom I had nicknamed "the Two Mikes," knew that Ricci was in deep with my father. As for Anthony Doyle, had Twan gained access to the bloody glove before CPD officer Laurie Lewis sent it off to the FBI OC1 squad, chances are he would have destroyed it. Out on the street, Frank "Toots" Caruso, Johnny Apes, and Ronnie Jarrett were put on red alert to help find the mole.

Little Jimmy Marcello was holed up in FCI Pekin along with Uncle Nick and his cellmate, Harry Aleman. Marcello was serving a twelve-year stretch for juice loans and ordering the firebombing of an Oak Park movie theater in a union dispute. Originally serving as a driver and emissary for bosses Joey Aiuppa and Sam "Wings" Carlisi, Marcello had reached the upper echelon of the Outfit. Calling the shots while incarcerated in Pekin, Marcello regularly communicated in code with his half brother Mickey Marcello. Word was out that the bloody gloves and the reopened Fecarotta case posed a tremendous problem, and the Outfit needed to know who was supplying the Feds with highly incriminating information.

The Two Mikes needed to get the wire up in the Milan visiting lounge pronto if they were going to tape the upcoming visit to my father. Here was their chance to catch two crooked cops leaking valuable information to a key Outfit figure. There wasn't a minute to waste. Instead of the necessary three *weeks* of prep work it would ordinarily take, Hartnett and Maseth had three *days* to appear before a federal court judge in Detroit, seek probable cause (PC), and line up the proper Title III Wiretap Intercept affidavits to roll tape and video the upcoming meeting.

With Maseth's growing knowledge of DiForti and the Fecarotta case and his criminal law background, he was named administrative agent for Operation Family Secrets. It was now his responsibility to take care of the technical details securing the wiretap at Milan. While Hartnett wrote and swore out the necessary affidavits in Detroit, Maseth made sure the paperwork between the courts and the Bureau was "administratively pure."

On Friday, February 19, 1999, the day of the Ricci and Doyle visit, permission for the wire had still not been granted. That morning, as Doyle and Ricci made their way up to Milan by automobile (a five-hour, 250-mile drive from Chicago), a federal court judge still hadn't given Hartnett and Maseth's wiretap the green light. The clock was ticking, with Hartnett stuck in the judge's Detroit chambers finalizing the Title III order. The delay left Maseth wringing his hands on the Milan prison grounds, where the warden held off any further action until they had permission. A holding cell next to the visitors' lounge was already set up for surveillance. With permission, Maseth would only have to slip into the adjoining room to monitor the video and sound of my father's noontime visit.

It was fast approaching noon. Mike Maseth and Kevin Blair sat in the warden's office waiting for the signed papers to arrive via the warden's personal fax machine. The operation would have to be aborted soon. Then Hartnett phoned Maseth at 11:45. The federal judge in Detroit had just signed off. The paperwork had been faxed. By 11:50 a.m., Agent Blair was waving the official paperwork—but he couldn't find the warden. He sat at the warden's desk and phoned Supervisor Bourgeois at the Chicago Bureau office.

My father was cautious during his meeting with Doyle and Ricci. The trio grabbed three white plastic chairs and huddled in the back corner of the lounge next to a hanging fire extinguisher. My dad spoke in such cryptic code that he sometimes got lost in his obscure jargon.

Here's the important stuff they discussed:

The bloody gloves weighed heavily on everybody's mind. Twan confirmed that somebody named Lewis let it leave "the warehouse" on January 13.

Referring to Jimmy DiForti as "Rota," my dad wondered whether or not Rota was cooperating. He had viewed DiForti suspiciously ever since Jimmy LaPietra carelessly broke an Outfit code by telling DiForti about our role in the Fecarotta hit.

What did he tell *Scarpe Grande* [code for the FBI]?" he asked Twan and Ricci.

It bothered him that DiForti had underboss Johnny Apes's ear. Could this be DiForti's opportunity to bury my father and uncle and skate on his own murder beef?

Caught on video, my dad referred to the bloody gloves as "the stuff being taken from the sister's purse," something that could hurt "the entire family," meaning the Outfit.

"Was anything mentioned to Pancho [Ronnie Jarrett] about the stuff being taken from the purse?" my father quizzed Doyle and Ricci. Pancho needed to be informed about the gloves situation so he could cover himself and Uncle Nick, considering the hits they'd both been involved in.

According to my father, Pancho needed to see "the doctor" (Chinatown Outfit associate Frank "Toots" Caruso) about "those things stolen from the purse" and that the "other doctor in the hospital" (Jimmy Marcello) needed to be alerted by Mickey Marcello. ("What they should do is tell the doctor they want to see her.") Jimmy could then approach my uncle and assure him that everything was under control and to stay cool. Sensing the worst, my father remarked that "something stinks over there."

"It's a shame," he said. " . . . what they should do is maybe bring her [Nick] to see a psychiatrist [Jimmy Marcello] or something. . . . Not only that, but a psychiatrist would be able to determine if she needed shock treatment or, a, a, ah, prodder up her ass. . . . Yeah, maybe a good physical."

Ironically, as my father commiserated in his ridiculous thick code with Doyle and Ricci about the dire consequences of the bloody gloves, he had no clue that the mysterious mole was right under his nose out on the Milan prison yard. Me.

Communication between my father and Doyle and Ricci continued for five more visits, until July 16, 2000, and all their conversations were caught on wiretap.

With the departure of Kevin Blair from the OC1 squad, the Two Mikes would lead the case as it gained momentum. While Hartnett remained the senior member of the two, Maseth was gaining more and more experience—and my personal trust—by the day.

As I contributed more information to the case, the Two Mikes would soon need to enlist extra agents to track down the numerous leads on the unsolved murders and illegal activities that my corroborating information provided. Speculation grew that Operation Family Secrets could be an even bigger organized crime case than the Bill Jahoda–Rocky Infelise OC2 case of 1992.

28.

THE WIRE

The FBI met with me and discussed the danger of wearing a wire on a prison yard against my father. They advised me to think hard about how best to make the approach and get him talking. The closer it came to crunch time, the more I doubted whether I could get anything out of my dad out on the Milan yard.

By then we were down together (locked up) for a year. My dad knew I was doing my time well. If he had seen me having a hard time, he would have caught on right away. So we proceeded. First off, I had to get back on speaking terms with him. Next, I had to convince him that I wanted him and me to patch up our differences. But would he talk? Was he too smart? He didn't talk about the past, and if he did, it was often in an impenetrable code.

There was one sticking point the warden and the Bureau of Prisons had with the FBI about my wearing the wire. Because the prison was constructed out of concrete, I could not be monitored, which made it impossible for the FBI to listen in. If I ran into trouble, I was on my own and vulnerable, which made the BOP legally liable. Nobody except the FBI, the Milan warden, and the head of the SIS knew that I was wired. What if I was discovered? What if I was suddenly targeted for murder by my father or an inmate (or a corrupt correctional officer) who might want a shot at a wired inmate? Six months had already passed since my first letter was sent to Tom Bourgeois. Everybody was anxious to start taping. When the warden gave his approval, it was time to get to work.

Originally I had agreed that I would record one tape for the FBI out on the yard. If I could get my dad to admit to having taken part in the July 2, 1980, murders of Billy and Charlotte Dauber, that would be enough to open the door of self-incrimination. I knew he was involved in the hit, but wasn't aware of the extent.

Billy Dauber was drafted into the Chicago Outfit in the 1970s by James "Jimmy the Bomber" Catuara, who ran illegal gambling and vice on Chicago's South Side. Dauber had a fearsome reputation as an established killer and earner for the Outfit. As Catuara's protégé, he was a suspect in more than twenty homicides and was active in illegal automobile chop shops, gambling, and prostitution.

In November 1976, Dauber, Catuara's former protégé, defected and joined Albert "Caesar" Tocco as his top enforcer. Almost two years later, on July 28, 1978, Jimmy the Bomber was found shot to death in his red Cadillac.

In 1979 Dauber was busted for intent to distribute cocaine along with a list of firearm violations. With the FBI, the DEA, and the ATF all over him, Dauber had to make a move. He and his outspoken wife, Charlotte, began cooperating with the ATF.

On July 2, 1980, Dauber and his wife left the Will County Court House trailed by three men in a work car. Those men included Butch Petrocelli and Jerry Scarpelli, members of the Joe Ferriola street crew and the Wild Bunch. The work car was a Ford Econoline van, a vehicle with a sliding side door that provided easy access for a shooter to kill his victims. To assist them and set up the victims properly, a second work car was driven by my father, who was forty-three at the time. Everything for the hit had to be covered. The Daubers had been followed for the previous two months by James "Dukey" Basile, a crew member who, because he didn't do "heavy work" (like killing people), was assigned to detail their movements and habits.

Dauber, a giant of a man at six foot six and 290 pounds, had to have his junk-food fix. After stopping at a Winchell's Donut shop with their lawyer, Ed Genson (who later defended rapper R. Kelly), and leaving a short time later, the Daubers drove off, followed by the two work cars. Moments later on an isolated stretch of road in Will County, my father swerved in front of the Daubers' Lincoln Continental, slowing it down. The van, meanwhile, quickly pulled alongside the Daubers' car, and as the Econoline's side door slid open, Petrocelli showered the car with .30-caliber shells from his carbine. As the Daubers crashed into a large apple tree, Petrocelli ordered Scarpelli to make certain the job was done. Exiting the van with his ski mask on, Scarpelli approached the motionless car, where he pumped two shots into Dauber's head. He left Charlotte alone because she was already dead. The van was driven down the road to a remote spot, where it was saturated with Ronsonol lighter fluid (the solvent of choice for Outfit arsonists and murderers) and torched to destroy any physical evidence. Later that evening the murder weapons were dismantled, hacksawed into pieces, and thrown into the Cal Sag Canal off of the Route 83 Bridge. Dauber's ATF handler, Dennis Laughrey, later recounted how he had told Billy it would be a good idea if they had protection. He offered to escort them home. Dauber had refused.

The prison yard at Milan was surrounded by a double fence with rolled barbed wire strewn across the top. Below were large jagged rocks and boulders—leg breakers—at the foot of the fencing. Inside the Milan yard was a softball field, basketball courts, and an outdoor weight pile, which were used mainly during the summer months. There were also boccie ball courts, picnic tables, and a half-mile asphalt track. Inmates could look over at neighboring farms and fields and into the prison parking lot.

Walking the outdoor half-mile asphalt track on the yard gave inmates a chance to escape the endless chatter that echoed inside the cell units. It was a secure area where my father and I could talk under the pretense of ironing out our troubled relationship. More important, my dad felt safe outdoors. While operating in Chicago, he insisted on talking "business" outside. When the other inmates saw him and me walking the yard together, they knew to keep their distance.

I got the first wired conversation rolling by bringing up what bothered me about my father's organized crime affiliations. I asked him point-blank, if the Outfit didn't kill innocent people, then how come Uncle Nick told me my dad had killed Dauber's wife? Of course, my uncle had told me no such story. It was actually my dad who had told me about the Daubers. I mentioned Uncle Nick's name just to get my father riled.

Dad's eyes opened wide. He went into a tirade, angry that Uncle Nick would run his mouth to me. I shifted the conversation to his relationship with his Outfit partners, taking an antagonistic view.

"I'm not scared of them," I said defiantly. "They're backstabbers, and if they try to come around to any businesses me, my friends, or the family have, they'll know they fucked with the wrong person."

My dad stared back at me in amazement. "Does that include me, too?"

"It depends on whose side you want to be on," I answered.

My comments about the Outfit opened the door to a wider discussion. Respecting my newfound toughness and bitterness toward the Outfit, he seemed determined to win me back to his side by talking things out with me.

When I returned to the SIS office to remove the wire, I remarked to Hartnett how difficult it was to get my dad to talk. But I felt we'd scored some hard-hitting information. We had talked more about the Outfit. I had also brought up Angelo LaPietra. We had spoken about his having to take orders and report to the various underbosses and bosses—something he resented, although he had no ambition to become a boss.

A few days later, I received the bad news. A technical glitch in the prototype digital recorder had rendered our first conversation unintelligible. The malfunction sowed doubt and disappointment. Had I done the right thing risking my life in the first place? Were these guys competent? How was I going to get my father to talk about the same stuff over again?

The FBI agents were distressed that their equipment had malfunctioned. In the future the agents made sure I had two devices rolling, using one as backup. For one session, the backup was an old-fashioned analog recorder that required me to be "wired up like a Christmas tree" and plastered with white tape on my chest. The recording device was fastened between my legs old-school-style and burned my testicles as I stood out on the yard.

The hardest part of the mission was getting back to my cell before correctional officers conducted the final count. Immediately after taping, I would leave the SIS office and scurry through a long hallway to reenter the main prison yard. If anybody spotted me coming from the SIS office out onto the yard, a rumor would spread that I was an informant.

I ventured onto the yard on Valentine's Day, 1999, for my second try. A portion of that day's conversations took place in the prison library, which explains why my father spoke in thick code that day. "Joy," "Slim," and "Gus" were code names for Nick. "The Tall Guy" and "the Small Guy" were both Ronnie Jarrett.

Jimmy DiForti was "Poker," "Rota" (Italian for "road"), "Tires" (because DiForti once had a tire shop in Cicero), or sometimes just plain Jimmy.

It had snowed earlier that day and the air was brisk as we strolled around the asphalt track. To get the conversation moving, I suggested to him that based on a *Chicago Tribune* news article a friend had sent me in the mail, DiForti might be cooperating with the FBI. Otherwise, I asked, how else could DiForti be out on bail on a murder rap, violate his bond, and be back out on the street? This was a way to get him going. Then I brought up the Billy and Charlotte Dauber murders again.

"What happened with the Daubers?" I asked.

"Don't say that name," my dad shot back.

"What? Dauber?" I repeated on purpose. "What about the Daubers?"

"Dauber was very dangerous, six feet six inches, a big fucking hillbilly, biker type," he said. In my second taped conversation, the first successfully recorded, my father confirmed that, yes, it was he who drove the Mustang "casey" (as in casing) car at the Dauber hit, while Ronnie Jarrett rode shotgun. I couldn't believe he was talking about it so freely, so I pressed on, bringing up Charlotte Dauber as an unwitting victim caught in the trap with her husband, code-named "the Farmer" by my dad.

"They didn't do it on purpose," he said. "They couldn't say, 'Hey, move over.' "

To keep the dialogue moving, I used a trick my dad had taught me on the street: pit one person against the other. At the mention of Uncle Nick again, he maintained that the acrimony between him and his sons stemmed from my uncle "poisoning" our minds against him.

Uncle Nick wasn't completely innocent, according to my father. He then singled out my uncle for shooting and killing Arthur Morawski, an unfortunate bystander, while the pair was trying to kill the drug dealer Richard Ortiz. It was Nick who gunned down "an innocent Polish guy that worked every day from nine to five."

Ortiz wasn't paying his street tax, and he skimmed money from Dad's capo, Johnny Apes. Morawski, "the innocent Polish guy" with Ortiz, was not an intended target. Then my dad admitted he was the driver in the Half and Half Murder, while my uncle and Jimmy DiForti were the shooters.

On April 10, he recalled the Ortiz and Morawski hits, which took place in July 1983. He remembered having to prod Uncle Nick and DiForti out of the car to make the kill outside the His 'N' Mine Lounge in Cicero.

Calabrese Sr.: [Ortiz] was a dope dealer and he was, uh, he was, he was lendin' money out of his own. And he belonged to Johnny [Apes] at one time.

Frank Jr.: He was Mexican.

Calabrese Sr.: Mexican . . . We used . . . to call him half and half, because he was half Mexican and half somethin' else.

Frank Jr.: Oh, okay.

Calabrese Sr.: And, uh, where he got it, his friends were sittin' right across the street.

Frank Jr.: Oh really?

Calabrese Sr.: His friends were sittin' on a bench across the street. They couldn't even describe the car. Because you see how confusing things are when people . . .

Frank Jr.: Oh yeah.

Calabrese Sr.: And he, the guy [Ortiz], they were pullin' over to park to go across the street. . . . As they pulled, I pulled [up] with 'em.

Frank Jr.: Diagonal?

Calabrese Sr.: Yeah. Diagonal like this. But I left room. . . . Right off Laramie there you could park like this on, on Twenty-second. . . . I made sure when they got out, I made sure that I didn't have to back out, that you turn right out. . . .

Frank Jr.: Okay, I understand what you're saying.

Calabrese Sr.: This was done in a matter of seconds. I'm shielding them from the street so nobody could see what they're doin'. . . . They [Nick and DiForti] both got out on the same side then.

My father went into detail about the shotguns and the shells used to blast Ortiz and Morawski to pieces.

Calabrese Sr.: Yeah, they emptied out. They, I made sure.
Frank Jr.: They were . . .
Calabrese Sr.: Empty. No, they were automatics.
Frank Jr.: Oh, they were shotguns?
Calabrese Sr.: Yeah. But they were . . .
Frank Jr.: Oh. Automatics . . .
Calabrese Sr.: Automatics . . . Yeah 'cause after they inject, we threw 'em away.
Frank Jr.: Oh, okay.
Calabrese Sr.: Yeah. In fact, that's the first thing that's done. . . . And they worked, because we went and tried 'em. Anytime you use somethin', you make sure you try it. We took on, on, we took 'em both on, uh two different nights. On, uh, County Line Road up in DuPage County . . . The forest preserve up there. On the other side of uh, of, uh, Hinsdale . . . We went over there and we tried the shotguns. They both worked. . . . They worked perfect. They didn't jam up or anything. So that's what they used. They had, uh I think four apiece, or five apiece. They had one [shell] in there and four in the chamber.
Frank Jr.: Mmm-hmm.
Calabrese Sr.: They were double-aughts, Frank.
Frank Jr.: That means what? Extra . . .
Calabrese Sr.: Bigger ones . . . Big big bearings. So them, them will fuckin' tear half your body apart.
Frank Jr.: So they must have tore them up pretty good then.
Calabrese Sr.: Oh yeah. Tore 'em up bad. Them'll tear your body up. They're called double-aughts. And you want me to tell you somethin'? The Polish guy that was with 'em was a nice guy. Okay? But he happened to be at the wrong

place. You know the—eh—uh, they were, it was said no matter who's with 'em, [the Outfit] want it done. Now if you back away and you have that opportunity and you don't, then you'd look like a fuckin' asshole.

I captured every word on tape. My father reminded me that when you agree to kill for the Outfit, you'll likely be killed if you back out. Outfit code states that if a guy working for you agrees to kill, then freezes, you have the right to kill him, too.

"We worked on that guy [Ortiz] for nine months," he told me. "We had him one time [before] by his house. Jimmy [DiForti] was lead. He was supposed to shoot him, but he froze. Your uncle was backup and afterward I told him, 'Why the fuck didn't you shoot *Jimmy* and leave him there? You shoulda shot the other guy first, then shoot Jimmy, too.' "

He explained his role in the Half and Half Murder. He talked about the Spilotro killings and named most of the "fellas" who took part, remarking that if Uncle Nick flipped to the Feds, these were the guys most apt to be hurt by his cooperation.

My dad then asked me about a new tattoo I had on the upper right side of my back. It was a tattoo of a United States map trapped by prison bars, with a pair of handcuffed hands through the bars. At the time I was taped up with the old-school recorder and was wearing a sweatshirt and a pair of sweatpants with no T-shirt underneath. He asked to see my new tattoo and, to my horror, reached for my sweatshirt. I grabbed the front bottom of my shirt and, hiding my fear, motioned to him that a guard was standing nearby. (Prison tattoos are technically against regulations.)

Calabrese Sr.: Let me see that tattoo you got on your back. Why you been covering it up?

Frank Jr.: I haven't been covering it.

Calabrese Sr.: Yeah, you did. The other day you put your shirt on, blamin' the, uh, girls in the yard. And I start laughin' 'cause I spotted the tattoo then.

Frank Jr.: But you've seen it.

Calabrese Sr.: No I didn't.

Frank Jr.: You seen it all.

Calabrese Sr.: When?

Frank Jr.: Yes, you did.

Calabrese Sr.: When did I see it?

Frank Jr.: When did you see it? You seen it when I showed you when we were sittin' out there, I showed 'em all to ya.

Calabrese Sr.: Did ya?

Frank Jr.: Yeah. And remember I says, that guy Danny said, um, he goes, he goes, I want a copy of that? Remember I showed you the copy sitting on the thing, too?

Calabrese Sr.: A copy of that tattoo?

Frank Jr.: Yeah.

Calabrese Sr.: Why are you putting all those tattoos on you?

Did my father ask to see the tattoo because he suspected I might be wired? At that moment, a couple hundred yards away from the SIS office, I had to make a quick decision. If I was found out, should I make a run for it? Should I fight him? Would the other inmates give chase and attack me? Luckily, he was just curious about the tattoo. I kept myself covered that day as a chill went through my body, and a close call was averted.

After I reported back to the SIS conference room for one briefing, Maseth could see the guilt and fear etched on my face. After a particularly long and stressful recording session, an agent held out a small bag.

"Want a cookie?"

My face showed a combination of disbelief, exhaustion, and sadness. I thought to myself, I just spent five hours out on the yard setting up my father. Do I look like I want a fucking cookie?

Not all of the conversations were confrontational. Dad liked to brag on the wire about winning every intermob sit-down, including those with Butch Petrocelli over turf or disputes and which bookmaker and juice loan collector belonged to whom. In one conversation on February 21, he showed a fondness for his old friend

Tony Borsellino and a disdain for Petrocelli, who engineered Tony's death with Joe Nagall [Ferriola]'s blessing.

Calabrese Sr.: Tony Borce, Tony Borce, when he died he was fifty years old.

Frank Jr.: He was fifty when he died? He was that much older than you?

Calabrese Sr.: He kept himself in good shape, Frank.

Frank Jr.: I was arguing with Charlie one day he says, he was arguing about the date when he died.

Calabrese Sr.: Tony Borsellino.

Frank Jr.: Yeah it didn't make sense.

Calabrese Sr.: . . . Uncle Nicky was married, we were by his father-in-law when he lived in Norridge. Remember when he lived in Norridge? We were by his house, we were sitting on the back porch. We had eaten that day, on a Sunday. I'll never forget it. And we were talking. Him and I were on the back porch talking about knowing what was going to happen to Tony that night. And right around the time that we were figuring it, all of a sudden, it was real sunny and clouds were starting to come. And I'll never forget that and I made a comment. I says, you think it's God trying to say something?

Frank Jr.: And it bothered you?

Calabrese Sr.: Oh, it bothered me. I loved that guy. . . . You want me to tell you. I tried everything to save him. I tried everything. I, I sat and I talked to Ange [LaPietra], I says, Ange that guy's a man. That fucking, fucking, that fucking what's his name, ah Butchie.

Frank Jr.: Petrocelli.

Calabrese Sr.: Yeah Butchie. He [Borsellino] was too much of a man for Butchie. And he had Joe Nagall's ear. Butchie had Joe Nagall's ear, well then half of these fuckin' guys, they're stealing. Butchie was a no-good motherfucker.

Frank Jr.: Didn't you say he tried to set you up, too?

Calabrese Sr.: Well, he tried to always have sit-downs. And we'd win 'em, every sit-down we had we won with them. They used to be called the Wild Bunch. It was Harry [Aleman], Jimmy I. [Inendino], Tony, and Butchie. They were four partners, but they were fuckin' with almost everybody. They weren't winning anything with us, they weren't winning with Johnnie Bananas. The only guys they were winning with were nobody guys. We had a card game on Laramie on the South Side that Butchie started stickin' his nose in, in another direction, almost fuckin' up our game. . . . Butchie's a big mouth. I'll never forget one day I walked up to him on Twenty on Thirty-first. Remember where that fish joint was where you buy all the stuff to go fishin' and stuff like the Canal there? It was like a little shack that sold fishing bait and stuff.

Frank Jr.: I think I know what you're talkin' about.

Calabrese Sr.: Yeah, you know where the hot-dog stand is on that, that Toots' stand is now?

Frank Jr.: Yeah.

Calabrese Sr.: Right across the street from there, on the north side of the street, before the railroad tracks there, I was walkin' down Thirty-first Street because I had to meet the little guy [Ronnie Jarrett]. And I seen him with his hood up on his truck. He had a black pickup with a camper back on it. As I'm walkin' up, he made a comment. He say, man what'd ya, why did you walk up so sneaky? I says, sneaky? I'm just walkin' up. I says what do you got? A guilty conscience about something? I never liked him. Fuckin' hated him. We sat there and talked for a while and he's telling me that he was looking for some pot for Turk [Torello]. No, because Turk was sick, he had cancer.

29.

MY FATHER'S EXECUTIONER

The Milan prison yard recordings took place between February 14 and June 1, 1999. There were eight extraordinary sessions, one every ten days or so. My father had implicated himself in the murders of Billy and Charlotte Dauber, Michael Albergo, Richard Ortiz and Arthur Morawski, John Fecarotta, and Michael Cagnoni.

Each meeting was planned by the two of us. At times I would pick the location; at other times it was his choice. While I knew how to push his buttons, I also

knew when to back off. If I pushed too hard, he would catch on. One night when my dad wasn't feeling well, we rescheduled our conversation for the next morning, which meant I had to sneak back to the SIS conference room early to tell the Two Mikes that there would be nothing that night. They would have to come back.

During one session, my father reminded me what the Outfit stood for, and described in a whisper his and Uncle Nick's made-guy ceremony. The tape revealed that he harbored doubts about swearing allegiance to his Outfit bosses.

Calabrese Sr.: Did you read the real book, the first *Godfather*? Whoever wrote that book . . .

Frank Jr.: It's pretty close.

Calabrese Sr.: They wrote it very closely. So whoever wrote that book, either their father or their grandfather or somebody was in the organization.

Frank Jr.: So you mean like when . . . you and Uncle Nicky went? They actually pricked the hand and the candles and all that stuff, too?

Calabrese Sr.: No, no.

Frank Jr.: I don't mean to laugh, Dad. It's—

Calabrese Sr.: Their fingers got cut and everybody puts the fingers together and all the blood running down. Then they take pictures. Put them in your hand. Burn them.

Frank Jr.: Pictures of . . .

Calabrese Sr.: Holy pictures. You stand there like this. There are the holy pictures. And they look at you and to see if you'd budge and while the pictures are burning. And they wait 'till they're getting down to the skin. Then they take them out of there.

Frank Jr.: What happens if you budge?

Calabrese Sr.: Then it shows your fear. You have fear. Stand there like that with your hands cupped like that. Then they say okay.

Frank Jr.: Um-hmm.

Calabrese Sr.: One guy at a time. You don't see two up there. When one guy's on it, the other guy's sitting somewhere else. In the same place but in a different room. There's a panel like that about nine guys. . . . And the guy that's the second guy in charge is the guy that talks to you. Everybody else are the capos.

Frank Jr.: They just sit there.

Calabrese Sr: They're watching you. . . . The guy that brought you in there is a capo. He is sitting at the table, too.

Frank Jr.: Him, the one that's gonna make all the promises and stand by your side and everything.

Calabrese Sr.: I got to tell you a story. . . . I told him [my capo] I didn't want it. . . . He says how come? I says because I feel that I would be strapped down and that if I wanted to do anything else I couldn't.

Frank Jr.: Yeah.

Calabrese Sr.: He says to me, No you wouldn't. I says, That's not what I hear. I says once you belong. He said you always belong. I says I would rather do what I'm doing without having to have that. I says I don't need that. I carry enough respect for myself.

Frank Jr.: Do you regret it now?

Calabrese Sr.: Yeah . . . [but] you know what I regret more so than anything? Burning the holy pictures in my hand. It bothers me . . . and the other thing that I would think would bother me is somebody give me an order to do what you says you had to do before you can get one of those, you know?

According to my dad, "the real [Outfit] model was not to hurt innocent people. In the beginning we went after guys who tried to hurt our people [Italians] or were stool pigeons. People got hurt when they didn't listen to us. They got one warning, a second, but never a third. By then it was too late."

Out on the yard, he postulated at length about the bloody

gloves and how the delay of any conclusive DNA tests was encouraging news. He explained how Mike Ricci and Twan Doyle were providing confidential information about the bloody gloves and the status of the case.

On the March 27, 1999, tape, he was hopeful that there wouldn't be any repercussions from the gloves:

Calabrese Sr.: So, evidently there hasn't been anything.

Frank Jr.: Well, that's good.

Calabrese Sr.: Now the thing that I'm happy about is it does not take that long to get a sample and go through the DNA?

Frank Jr.: No.

Calabrese, Sr.: Okay. So that means that they might be coming up with a blank.

Frank Jr.: Which would be good.

Calabrese Sr.: Which would be, I'm, I'm, it's convincing me more and more. Again . . .

Frank Jr.: You saying?

Calabrese Sr.: I put it in God's hands, Frankie.

Frank Jr.: You say the way the gloves are his, ya know, that sounds . . .

Calabrese Sr.: Yeah. Those are his gloves. He had 'em on still.

Frank Jr.: Then that's good. And if he had, ah, and if Gus [Nick] had his gloves on the whole time, that's good. 'Cause maybe . . .

Calabrese Sr.: They both wore gloves.

Frank Jr.: Maybe the blood dripped in the glove and didn't get anywhere on the car.

Calabrese Sr.: I think it got mostly in his sleeve, Frankie. There was not a bloody spot, because when I, when I got there, there wasn't a lotta blood there.

Frank Jr.: Oh, so see, okay . . .

Calabrese Sr.: The watch, [Nick] had the watch on, that had a little blood on it.

Frank Jr.: Okay. So . . .

Calabrese Sr.: Yeah, it had to be this way. 'Cause I kept the watch. I took it in my pocket.

My father was hostile toward my uncle because Nick bad-mouthed him prior to their reporting to prison, and arranged to use a different criminal law firm. When my dad befriended an inmate and made man named J.R., who had transferred from FCI Pekin to Milan, J.R. told my dad that Uncle Nick openly blamed him for the jailing of his sons. That Nick aired dirty laundry to someone outside the family angered my father. He was concerned that if my uncle bad-mouthed my father to Jimmy Marcello, the Calabrese brothers would be seen as a "problem." At that point they would be expendable, resulting in Marcello having them both whacked, much like the Spilotro brothers.

Uncle Nick and I had spoken prior to my being locked up. He admitted he was tired of "the life," and had been for a long time. Being a gangster had lost its luster, and he wasn't getting rich working on his brother's crew.

On the March 27 tape, I discussed my uncle again. We mentioned Nick's stupidity for signing Fecarotta's gambling winnings form. To gain my father's trust, I pretended to side with him against my uncle.

Frank Jr.: And I mean that's the other thing. I just think of all the stupid things he done. Look what he did with Johnny [Fecarotta]. He signed the fucking gambling thing.

Calabrese Sr.: Yeah.

Frank Jr.: How stupid could you be?

Calabrese Sr.: Out of town. I'm the one that told him, what'd you do? He said, I signed it. I says, did you know what you did? You committed yourself to being there. Oh, I never thought of that. I said, he made you sign it, why didn't . . .

Frank Jr.: [*Laughs*]

Calabrese Sr.: . . . You tell him to sign it?

Frank Jr.: He knew him, right? He had his number.

Calabrese Sr.: Oh, everybody has his number. Frank . . . don't you think they got his number now? If he's doin' like stuff . . .

Frank Jr.: Yeah.

Calabrese Sr.: They're lookin' at him [in Pekin]. What are you? Fuckin' crazy? Watch this guy when he gets on the street. Watch him. . . . Keep an eye on him.

Frank Jr.: I know, I know.

Calabrese Sr.: Tell you something? I hope the best thing he fuckin' does . . .

Frank Jr.: Is move.

Calabrese Sr.: . . . is move. Go back to Las Vegas where he wants to go.

Frank Jr.: Least then if he signs somethin' now, he's, uh [*laughs*], he could say he lives there.

Calabrese Sr.: Yeah.

Frank Jr.: I know. I been thinkin' a lot of stupid things he did. That's what concerned me about the gloves. Because . . .

Calabrese Sr.: Frankie, do you know what the most, the, the stupid thing he did . . .

Frank Jr.: Yeah.

Calabrese Sr.: . . . that I can't get out of my system? I forgive him for it, but I can't—is take my family and try to turn 'em on me. I would never do that to anybody. There's no way that I would go to a guy's kids and put hate in his kids to 'em.

Once in a while, my dad would eyeball me if I was a little too specific about certain events. Whenever a question raised a red flag during our conversation, I would stare back at him, look him in the eye, and act dismissive.

"Then fuck it! Let's not talk if you're gonna act that way." That would reel him back into the conversation. I couldn't push anything; nor could I ask about anything out of line. I was on my guard because my father was good at reading people. Sometimes he'd challenge me or look at me funny.

"Why bring that up?" he would ask.

The thought of him catching on constantly ran through my mind.

Before each encounter, Agents Maseth and Hartnett presented a wish list of subjects, some stemming from previous conversations. If my dad happened to drift into certain hot topics, Maseth might ask me for more detail on a specific murder or a particular act next time. At times their wish list was extensive.

I had no control over the recorder. They turned it on when I left the SIS office and turned it off when I returned. That was because in prior federal cases, guys turned the recorder on and off whenever *they* chose. The original tapes were valuable in court only if they were unedited.

After six months of nerve-racking intensity, my prison yard chats were starting to suck the life out of me. By June 1999 it was apparent to the Two Mikes that the mission was becoming too dangerous for me to continue. It was time to get me out of Milan. Six months of wearing the wire had drained me. I was beaten down. I needed rest. After my release from prison, if I was agreeable, I could return to visit my dad under more controlled and less dangerous circumstances.

The FBI's next plan was to transfer me to a federal facility in Florida under the guise of enrolling me in a drug-rehab program. By November 1999, I would be eligible to be released to a halfway house in Chicago to begin to rebuild my life.

I wasn't looking forward to the final taping session on the evening of June 1, 1999. The process had become so overwhelming that I was second-guessing my ability to hide my emotions.

My father and I spoke about letting go of the hard feelings between us. We talked about my working alongside Ronnie Jarrett once I got out. We talked about keeping in touch and which codes to use to communicate secretly. I went along with the conversation, feeling disappointed and guilty. Sadly, this conversation proved that Dad had no intention of keeping his promise to step away from the Outfit. He had big plans, and if I was going to be a part of them, I was expected to "earn" my place on the crew again.

Calabrese Sr.: But what I'm, what I'm gonna, what I may wanna do is, is what I wanted to tell ya is, is, ah, I make sure you partners with Ronnie someday.

Frank Jr.: Ah . . .

Calabrese Sr.: But you have to earn that, Frankie. But I tell you now right up front.

Frank Jr.: All right.

Calabrese Sr.: And, ah, he's a good guy and, ah . . .

Frank Jr.: We ain't gonna have to answer to nobody else.

Calabrese Sr.: Nobody else. No fucking body else. No, nobody else. No, we're not answering to nobody else. Did any, did anybody else fucking supply us? Only one guy . . .

Frank Jr.: I don't know where all your friends are right now. I mean . . .

Calabrese Sr.: And you can bet soon as Joy [Nick] gets out, she's gonna go try to dirty Ronnie's ears up. If she hasn't dirtied his ears up yet.

The session ended on a lighter note as my dad joked about Mom's reaction when he first joined the Outfit back in the early 1960s.

"I'm not gonna slap myself on the back," he said to me on the yard, "but when I got around these people in the sixties, okay? That's when your mother . . . remember she made the statement when I got around them in the sixties I lived like Dick Tracy."

The night before I was transferred from Milan to a drug-rehab program at the federal prison in Coleman, Florida, we shared an emotional moment with tears running down my dad's face. Me, I was ready to cry, but for a different reason. I was deceiving my father. I finished the betrayal of my father by leaving him with the impression that I was won over, and would return to the fold once I was released.

Frank Jr.: Can't dwell on the old stuff.

Calabrese Sr.: No.

Frank Jr.: Ya gotta talk about the new stuff.

Calabrese Sr.: The thing is, ya got to do, is you gotta get out there and keep yourself out of trouble. That's the most important thing. . . . And, ah, then, I will, ah, I will tell you something little by little. There's no sense now because you're gonna be gone for another maybe ten or twelve months yet. And, ah . . .

Frank Jr.: Plus you still think I'm not gonna come back.

Calabrese Sr.: Come back where, Son?

Frank Jr.: Well, you keep telling me, are you gonna come and visit me, are you gonna visit me?

Calabrese Sr.: No. I know you are, Frank. I'm . . .

Frank Jr.: I feel sometimes ya think I'm not gonna come and visit ya?

Calabrese Sr.: Yeah, I gotta tell ya something. I have no doubts you're coming back, Son. Ah, I think, ah, what happened in here, is you and I got to understand each other a little bit.

(*Long pause*)

Frank Jr.: It'll go by fast. It's gonna go by fast.

Calabrese Sr.: I ain't worried about that.

At the end of the final taping session, we hugged and said our good-byes. Then I crossed the yard back to the agents at the SIS office for the last time. Everything between me and him, good or bad, happy or sad, ran through my mind. I wanted to be my dad's savior. In fact, I ended up being my father's executioner.

After lights-out, I lay in my bunk and wept quietly, wishing things were different. The strain of dealing with my father had taken a huge toll on me—and it was the last time I would hug, kiss, and touch him.

30.

THREE SECRET LIVES

I transferred out of FCI Milan in June 1999 and flew to Oklahoma City, where I spent two weeks in lockdown. My cellie was a convict from Kansas City serving time on a federal machine-gun rap. He was sedated on meds. From Oklahoma City, I hopped on Con Air to Tampa, where I took a bus to the Federal Correctional Complex in Coleman, Florida. FCC Coleman consisted of four separate institutions, a low-, a medium-, and two high-security facilities, with one of the high-security facilities an all-female camp. For my last six months, I was assigned to the lowest-security facility, located next to a cow pasture. Most of the male inmate population were South American nationals plucked from the notorious cocaine wars.

I lived in a dorm and hung around two other inmates: a murderer from Alabama and a Daytona sailor busted for smuggling Haitian refugees aboard his fishing boat. Compared to the MCC and Milan, the atmosphere at Coleman was more like a camp. With its warm climate and large number of Latin inmates, the primary recreation was baseball.

I wouldn't be at Coleman long enough to complete the drug-treatment curriculum that would shave eighteen months off of my original fifty-seven-month sentence. I was granted the eighteen-month credit anyway—the only concession I gained by cooperating with the FBI. With another six months off for good behavior I served almost thirty-six months.

During the six months I spent inside FCC Coleman, my cooperation with the Bureau was kept top secret. To keep in touch with the Bureau, I placed Mike Hartnett on my "call list" under an assumed name. Only a few key people at the FBI knew I was cooperating. In early November 1999, wearing prison-issued jeans, shirt, and tennis shoes, and carrying a cardboard box with my belongings, I walked out of FCC Coleman with two hundred dollars' gate money stuffed in my pocket—sixty dollars of which went for a cab ride to the Orlando airport. I had no driver's license, so when I got to the airport, I walked up to the airline gate and handed over a special prison ID that detailed my release status.

I felt stupid. I had to tie the belt loops together with a shoestring to keep my pants from falling down. After I checked in, I walked into the airport mall to buy a duffel bag for my stuff . . . and a belt for my jeans, which were two sizes too big. I wasn't used to walking from one storefront to another without permission. I stood at the edge of the carpet of the luggage store until the girl behind the counter saw me and said, "You know, you can come in." Standing in line at one of the fast-food restaurants for a coffee and sandwich, I noticed the hurried pace of the outside world while the customer behind me marveled at my patience.

Landing in Chicago, I was met by Kurt, who presented me with a bag of Johnny's Beef sandwiches from the stand in Elmwood Park. Later we met up with Danny Alberga from Bella Luna, who arrived with pizzas. After Kurt and Danny slipped me a few hundred dollars, I checked into the halfway house on Ashland Avenue, not far from downtown. I wasn't permitted to leave the premises the first two weeks while attending reentry classes. Once I found a job, I would be required to pay rent. After a couple more weeks, I got my first four-hour Sunday-morning church pass so I could meet Lisa and the kids.

I found reuniting with my family emotionally difficult. I was nervous. Lisa and I were divorced and I knew she was dating other guys. I didn't know how she felt, but I wanted to see the kids. I hadn't seen them during the six months I had spent in Florida, nor had I seen them the last few months in Milan when I was doing the recordings.

Lisa was nervous during the ride down to see me. She had such terrible anxiety about my coming home that she had to go on meds. She wondered whether she was done with that chapter of her life. But we still had two little kids, and I think she felt I deserved a second chance. Besides, the kids were asking, "When's Daddy coming home?"

My first meeting with Lisa was cordial, a polite hug and a kiss on the cheek. Holding a large stuffed toy frog, I stood humbly before my wife and children, straight, off drugs, broke, and unemployed. Who knew where our relationship was going? Nobody, not even Lisa, knew about the Milan taping sessions or my cooperation with the FBI. I couldn't tell her. It wasn't that I couldn't trust her; I just didn't want to put that burden on her.

I remember one Sunday during a pass when the four of us went out to breakfast. Nonchalantly I pulled a Baggie of white powder out of my pocket, and suddenly shivers went up Lisa's spine. I realized what the protein powder resembled and immediately apologized.

I was working for Danny at Bella Luna, slowly getting back

into things. At first it was weird working at the restaurant. I was slow and not used to the fast pace. Soon I was granted weekend passes. I'd stay with my mother. I had my old room back. It was a strange feeling because my belongings were reduced to a couple of boxes in her garage. The halfway house would call in the middle of the night to make sure I was there.

During the 1999 Christmas holiday, events started to get heavy. First, Uncle Ed was killed in a bizarre automobile accident. He had been drummed out of HEREUI in 1998 with a promise of immunity against corruption charges. Out for a pizza, he was hit by a drunk who was driving a snow plow. My mom was devastated by the death of her brother. Then on December 23, I received a phone call at Bella Luna from Kurt.

"Did you hear what just happened? Turn on the TV."

I switched on the television. Ronnie Jarrett had just been shot in front of his house in Bridgeport. There on the TV at Bella Luna was an old mug shot of Ronnie. Underneath it the caption read, "Attempted gangland slaying of Chinatown mobster today." The news didn't say if he was alive or dead. I called Mike Hartnett.

"We know about it. If you hear anything, let us know. We'll talk later. Is everything okay?"

The hit on Jarrett broke a four-year drought of Outfit murders. Suddenly this changed the dynamic on the streets. For Maseth, the killing of Ronnie Jarrett was one of the first setbacks for Operation Family Secrets. I spoke to Mike about the incident.

Coincidentally, on December 23, Maseth had decided to do a quick check on Jarrett. Because of heavy traffic, he took an alternate route to Jarrett's Lowe Street residence. Approaching the house, Mike encountered something completely unexpected—a bleeding Jarrett lying in the street with half a dozen bullets in the face, chest, and arm. His son Ronnie junior recounted hearing firecrackers while sleeping late. Jarrett's wife ran outside screaming, too frightened to approach her fallen husband lying by his car. After rushing off the front porch Ronnie junior knelt at his father's side. Mike had missed Jarrett's killers by a matter of minutes, if not seconds.

Careful not to be made, Mike pulled alongside the crime scene and called in the shooting. He looped around to see if anybody suspicious was nearby. As Mike got out of his car to see Jarrett whispering to his son, a yellow Ryder rental truck pulled into an alley blocks away. Two men jumped out, splashed gasoline inside and out, and set the truck ablaze. Once the fireball shot up in the air, the men jumped into a black Lincoln and sped away.

Mike's thoughts flashed to me and the case. Who ordered the hit, and was it related to my uncle or me? The FBI knew the Outfit was watching Uncle Nick inside prison, while the Outfit knew the FBI was watching Jarrett. If Ronnie was fair game, the Outfit had to know that I could hurt them. I was concerned: if the Outfit had whacked Ronnie, could they kill any other member of the Calabrese crew?

A few minutes after I saw Ronnie on television, the phone rang again. It was my dad. Hearing his voice wasn't a complete surprise. We had been in frequent contact since my release, him calling the restaurant and having his associates check on me.

"What's going on?" he asked.

"Didn't you hear what happened?"

Knowing the prison phone line was being recorded, I broke the news vaguely. "You know my brother Nicky's friends, Ronnie and Tony? Their father just got gunned down in front of his house this morning. They aren't saying if he pulled through or not."

I could tell by the silence on the other end that the news had taken him by surprise. Based on his reaction, I was convinced that he'd had no hand in Ronnie's shooting. He did know that Jarrett had been whistled in by Toots Caruso and Jimmy DiForti for a sit-down with Johnny Apes.

At the time of the shooting, Jarrett was running both my father's operations and his own rogue drug dealing. While Jarrett had a fearsome reputation as a go-to killer for the Outfit, he was only half Italian and therefore not a made guy, which irritated my father. Someone as smart and seasoned as Ronnie knew better than to ignore an order to "come in," especially from the bosses. By my estimation, Dad would have been the only person Ronnie would have listened to, overriding the order to come in. Perhaps my father overestimated his standing with Johnny Apes by giving Jarrett such bad advice as to duck the meeting.

Jarrett clung to life for another month at Cook County Hospital before succumbing to his gunshot wounds. He died on January 25, 2000, effectively derailing any FBI plan to have me return undercover to infiltrate my father's Chinatown crew. Jarrett's death also changed my dad's plans to have me resume street operations while "earning my stripes" with Ronnie.

I had been home only a month or so before Ronnie got killed. If the FBI's plans were to get me back inside the crew, we didn't talk about it. I think they wanted to take it slowly. While I understood how insidious the Outfit was to families like mine, had Ronnie not been killed, I doubt I would have worked with them to put him away. Ronnie wasn't my primary concern, nor was crushing the Outfit.

Organized crime affects people and whole families, and guys like my father were parasites. I chose my battles on a more personal level. I was no cop, just one guy who had seen and heard enough.

To this day, Jarrett's case remains unsolved. Speculation flew. Some surmised that his death wasn't the work of the Outfit, but was outside and drug-related. Some said that the Outfit hired a pair of bikers to murder Jarrett. During a taped visit, Dad revealed to me that once Jimmy Marcello was transferred to Milan, he admitted to him that it wasn't only Ronnie's refusal to sit down that got him killed. The hit was sanctioned by the Outfit, perhaps by Johnny Apes, and had more to do with the drug dealing. The bosses feared that if Jarrett was arrested on drug charges, he would face a long prison sentence and become a liability if he flipped. I responded to my father's revelation with concern and questions.

"How come nobody reached out to you before killing Ronnie, your first lieutenant? Aren't you worried for yours and Uncle Nick's safety? Is Jimmy okay with me collecting money for you on the street? Is he going to send somebody after me?"

While he assured me that everything was "still a go," I

remained skeptical about my safety. Was my dad losing status with the bosses? Mike warned me to remain on guard.

Ronnie Jarrett's death only accelerated my father's plan to win me over and put me back on the street. While visiting Grandma Sophie's duplex, my stepmother, Diane, handed me a folded note tightly wrapped in cellophane tape.

"What's this?" I asked.

"I don't know."

I would receive five coded messages from Dad smuggled out of FCI Milan. The first one read:

> Smile, have Sadsack till [tell] NFy to meet Smile by the Church near Smile. At night. He will have to see Smile on Thous 10 Truck Louds [loads] per week. Curly same thing. Have Joe OL the guy who sells goods to rests [restaurants]. Get him or you. SONO will have Joe see smile. Smile can till [tell] Joe what day he would like to see Curly! The Farther [father] by the [way] will be happy if Smile will do this for him. All so have Smile go and see Cop-Ten ware he wonts to pick up food for the Priest every month. Father will like this. Ask Sadsack how much food he got from him, When he was going there. You keep 10 box's of spam ham for your self every month [one thousand dollars]. Do this right away, if you can't, see them anyway to see what they have to say. Then I will have some one come to see you and you can make him meet them whit [with] you. I would like to see you do it. Think [thank] you I love you very much, give kids kiss for me. P.S. hope to see you soon.

While my dad was an extremely poor speller and writer, the depth of his criminal cunning can be seen through the intentional gibberish.

The translation: Frank senior wants Frankie to be his eyes and ears on the street. Find out what's going on and report back. Smile is Frankie. Sono (or Sano) is his reference to himself. Sad-sack is Kurt. Cop (or Cap) is Captain D, Donald DiFazio, who ran

Connie's Pizza, a small local pizza chain my father had the arm on, collecting $500 a month in street tax. Curly is Ralph Peluso, who was paying Dad $1,000 per week. NFy is short for Neffie or Nephew, his code for Michael Talarico, Angelo LaPietra's nephew. Talarico put another $1,000-a-week street tax into Dad's pocket.

By my calculation, my father was pulling in $110,000 annually on these three accounts. Who knew what else he had going?

My father had everything worked out. His plan was to assign me these three customers: Captain D of Connie's Pizza, Mike Talarico, and Ralph Peluso. According to the note, I was to keep $1,000 a month for myself, a pittance considering that he was grossing at least $10,000 a month while sitting in prison. Another $700 a month was to go to "Skins," the code name for my mother.

The contents of the note didn't shock me as much as they revolted me. I was free again, and my father was willing to risk my freedom and Kurt's by pulling us back into the same activities that had got us locked up—for a mere $1,000 a month.

After Ronnie was shot, who was next in line? Uncle Nick inside prison? Kurt? If word got out about my cooperation with the FBI, my life wouldn't be worth a plugged nickel on the street. Was anybody *really* safe from my father or the Outfit? To get a better grip on my situation, I tried thinking like my dad.

After Ronnie was shot, I figured Dad needed to regroup quickly. If he could get me back working the streets, he'd have eyes and ears he could trust on the street plus a nice little stash waiting for him once he got out.

I now had a new dilemma: how to juggle three secret lives.

Before prison, I had led a dual life with my family and my father. Now I was living a triple existence. First, I was starting over at age forty, living the straight life in an effort to win my family back. Second, I had my father believing that he had won me back and I now worked for him again. Third, I had to continue working with the FBI until my mission was complete.

31.

THE CHANGING STREETS

When I left the halfway house in February 2000, I had two goals. First, finish the fight against my father, even if it meant working undercover for the government. Second, rebuild my life by winning back Lisa and the kids.

I knew there was a good chance that we would not get back together. I wanted to repair my relationship with Lisa, but I needed things to be cordial so that I could spend time with the kids. I knew she was dating, and although I went out when I first came home, it was infrequent.

Although I was working with the FBI, there were parole conditions I had to abide by. Release from prison requires a convict to be on constant call for parole check-ins and random drug tests. I was no exception. One of the terms of my release was to meet with a drug counselor twice a month for a year. My parole required me to call in daily for possible urine tests. If my "color" came up, I had until the end of the day to report to a designated place for a pee test.

My parole officer was one of the very few people cleared to know that I was working with the FBI. My PO met regularly with the Two Mikes and the judge for a status update to make sure I wasn't being taken advantage of by the government.

I had the burden of what to do about the cryptic notes from my dad, who was anxiously waiting for my Milan visitation rights to be cleared.

> Tell Mish [Frankie] to see Sanno [Frank senior] ias [*sic*] soon as posible [*sic*] about Skins [Dolores].

Or:

> Put everything in an envelope, put for lawyer on it give it to skins and have skins give it to who gave you this paper. You keep 1-B every month for yourself.

And:

> Hi Smiley! I know you're much happier where you're at. Sano would like you to find out about her girlfriend with the long curly hair. Tell her she knows where she belongs and you are there talking to her for Sano and listen to whatever she has to say and tell her afterward that you'll be getting back to her. . . .

And finally:

> The recipes you get from Cap—put them in a big book, put book in big envelope and live [*sic*] it next door for my wife to pick up—put for Tony [bullshit name] on outside of envelope. . . . There should be a

> 11-months [money from Captain D] of cooking in there, total of 65 recipes . . . when you go see Sanno he will tell you about it all. . . .

I had to try and find a way to communicate with my father that didn't involve Diane. After she gave me the notes, I told her that I had questions that needed answering. Whom could I talk to? She told me to call Mike Ricci. I wore a wire on him when we met. Those meetings with Ricci proved extremely productive. They established that Dad was still active, and that Ricci and Twan Doyle were helping him.

I looked over the list of the men I was expected to collect from. I liked Donald DiFazio, known around the neighborhood as Captain D. He was a good guy. Then there was Ralph Peluso, whom I'd had run-ins with in the past. I disliked Peluso, though not enough to wish my father on him. And there was Michael Talarico, whom I regarded as family. Talarico was admired by almost everyone who bet with him. He ran "a great book" and had a reputation for fairness. He didn't threaten anybody, and took more than his share of flak. When Michael mentioned leaving the street business behind, he was beaten up by my dad and Ronnie Jarrett in front of a neighborhood bar down the street from his house.

As I received the notes from Dad I would turn them over to Mike Maseth. A meeting was set up with the Two Mikes on the top floor of a shopping center parking lot on Harlem Avenue and Irving Park Road to discuss following up on the three street tax contacts from which I was to collect.

We met at different locations on the West Side of town. It's difficult to be anonymous on the street, so we would meet in cars in shopping centers. Because I'd worked the streets so long, it was likely that I would run into people that knew me or my father. The Two Mikes didn't look like regular FBI agents; they looked and dressed like a lot of my friends. Maseth blended in by looking preppy. Had I met with, say, Mitch Mars, Bob Moon, or John

Scully on the street, that would have been a different story. Those were high-profile guys.

After the clandestine shopping center meetings, I agreed to meet with extortion victims Donald DiFazio and Ralph Peluso, plus Mike Ricci. If I wore a wire, I would remain focused on collecting information on my father. I had no interest in targeting other street crews; I wanted to assist victims of my dad, so I refused to wear a wire on Michael Talarico. He was a decent man, and what Talarico did on his own was his business.

I could have busted gangsters running their scams, but it wasn't my job; I wasn't a G-man or a cop. I focused on people who were close associates and victims of my father. The FBI went along with my decision.

After I left the halfway house, I moved in with my mother. My dad called the house regularly.

"Did you see the recipes or talk to the chef?"

My mother caught wind of the calls and picked up the phone, only to be cut short by him. She knew that her ex was up to something. She handed the phone to me with a curt warning: "You best not be doing anything wrong with your father."

"I can guarantee you, Ma; I'm not getting into trouble again."

Technically I was telling my mother the truth. Yes, I was working with him, but no, I wasn't going to get into trouble. I couldn't risk letting my mother or Lisa in on what I'd been up to over the past months. Who knew how they'd react? Secrecy was important to ensure my safety. After letting him off easy with the divorce, Mom grew weary of Dad's promises of support that never materialized. Watching two of her sons do prison time was heartbreaking enough.

Being back out on the streets wasn't without temptation. When word got out that I was back collecting, offers came from a new generation of characters. There was a line waiting to replace gangsters like Angelo LaPietra, Johnny Apes, and Jimmy DiForti, who died between 1999 and 2001.

I had guys ask me to get into offshore gambling, sports betting, and poker machines. While creating the impression that I was still a gangster, I told them I wasn't interested, and politely thanked them.

Under the FBI's watchful eye, I met with Captain D to collect the extortion payments. The new agreement was to meet and collect every two months instead of monthly. One of those meetings occurred on the street in Chinatown. DiFazio was too nervous to get out of the vehicle and barely cracked his car window open. At the time, I didn't know why DiFazio was nervous about his payment arrangement. Originally, Connie's Pizza money had gone to Angelo LaPietra. After Angelo pleaded guilty and went to prison for skimming Vegas casinos, my father switched the terms and pocketed the proceeds for himself. But with Dad in prison and Jarrett and Angelo dead, Captain D was without "protection" and was being hounded by Anthony "the Hatchet" Chiaramonti. Connie's was opening another restaurant in the southwestern suburbs. The Hatchet was squeezing the pizzeria chain for additional street tax. DiFazio asked me to let my father know, so he could call off the Hatchet. I promised that I would explain the situation as soon as I saw him.

(In 2001 "Hatch" Chiaramonti parked his new BMW in front of Brown's Chicken and went in to use the pay phone. When he walked back to his car, a van pulled into his path, and a passenger exited and chased the Hatchet back toward the restaurant. As he entered the restaurant vestibule, Chiaramonti was shot five times: he took one bullet in the chest, one in the arm, and three fatal slugs to the head.)

I ran into Captain D at Bella Luna. He handed me an extra payment that was due. I put the cash in my pocket. At the time I was struggling financially, making only three hundred dollars a week while having to pay rent to the halfway house and provide more money for Lisa and the kids.

I went home, put the money on the dresser, and just stared at it. Part of me wanted to keep it, knowing the FBI would never find out. The other part of me loved my new life. While it was difficult, it was a tremendous feeling, not having to look constantly over my shoulder. I stashed the money in a drawer.

A couple of months later, I confessed to the Two Mikes.

I knew I had to tell them and that they'd have to file a report, though I hadn't spent a penny. If I kept the money, what would set me apart from my father? Turning the cash in wasn't about preserving the integrity of the case but about preserving my character. I *needed* to turn in that money.

Once I handed over the money, Hartnett blew his stack. After the money was logged in and the paperwork was filed, I stayed clean, if almost broke, for the rest of the investigation.

With Ronnie Jarrett dead, the streets were changing in Chinatown. Not having Ronnie around eliminated a huge threat. Ronnie had been a primary concern for me because of his "killer" status. His death meant one less person to worry about. I visited Jarrett's widow, Rosemary, a friend, while wearing a wire. The purpose of my visit was to try and find out who might have killed Jarrett. At first the family was cautious, as was everyone that I approached. Even from prison, my father's menacing aura loomed over the streets of Chicago. Not long after Ronnie's death, the Jarrett family were approached by associates of my father about cash and jewelry that Ronnie had been holding. They were reminded that they had a "responsibility" to give back the money and the jewelry.

I was appalled to see Ronnie's family shaken down by my father's associates, especially after the death of his loyal lieutenant. A short time after Jarrett was gunned down, Rosemary contacted me, asking if we could meet at her mother-in-law's house on South Lowe in Chinatown. It was the same house where we had done our bookwork. Rosemary had sold the house and didn't want to talk on the phone, but she had some things she wanted me to take away. I set up a time to meet her with my pickup truck.

With Ronnie's murderers at large, red flags popped up. Was the meeting a setup, a ruse to get me alone? Was Rosemary being squeezed like me to do favors for the Outfit or my dad? It wouldn't be uncharacteristic for the Outfit to use a woman to set up a kill.

I contacted the Two Mikes, who wired me with a listening device and surrounded the area. I met Rosemary in the same garage that my father, my uncle, and Ronnie used to kill Paul Haggerty and John Mendell. Twan Doyle had already taken the cars out of the garage, but there were a couple of old guns and some boxes of paperwork left behind.

I threw the stuff in the back of my truck and drove downtown, followed by the FBI. The paperwork was later tied to the crew's bookmaking associates, who included Philly Tolomeo.

While working with the FBI in 1999, wearing a wire, and collecting for my father, I thought it might be safer if I left my job at Bella Luna. While I wanted to stay in Chicago and complete my work with the Two Mikes, I decided to take up a new career as a truck driver.

I needed a backup career. I was a good driver, so I thought I'd give it a try. I ran into Jimmy Marcello's nephew, Sammy Galioto, over at Kurt's house. When he heard I wanted to drive an eighteen-wheeler, he got on the phone with—of all people—Dickie DeAngelo, the same guy who killed my father's first business partner, Larry Stubitsch, back in the early sixties. He now owned a trucking company. Dickie's advice was to get my learner's permit and come see him.

I pored over the books and manuals and passed each of my driving tests, quickly earning the necessary licenses. DeAngelo had trepidations about hiring me until he was assured that I had no interest in avenging the death of Stubitsch. DeAngelo put me on the street the very next day hauling twenty-seven-and fifty-three-foot trailers for a project at the old McCormick Place.

In between trucking assignments, I worked with the Two Mikes compiling the Milan prison yard tapes for court. I'd work four twelve-hour days for Dickie, and then I'd sit down with the Two Mikes for twelve hours on a Friday working on the tapes. If I had any more time off, I'd do more work on the tapes.

Because of their legal significance, a precise transcription was necessary. Since I couldn't be seen anywhere near the FBI

OC1 squad room in the Dirksen Federal Building, many hours were spent cooped up in suburban FBI branch offices twenty-five miles out of Chicago. Getting the conversations word for word on paper, I explained what my father was referring to in his mysterious narration. For weeks, I alternated between tape transcribing and truck driving. Soon, the FBI and the Assistant U.S. Attorneys accumulated a wealth of information about the 26th Street Chinatown crew and how it operated.

One day I got a call on the highway. It was Mike, and he was driving the Crown Victoria right behind me.

"Frankie! I *thought* that was you. You're doing a hell of a job driving that rig." Mike assured me that I wasn't under surveillance.

"That's okay," I said. "You can follow me whenever you want. That's the joy of not doing anything wrong."

32.

A ROYAL PAIN IN THE...BACK

While I was working with the Feds transcribing tapes, Maseth and Hartnett had their sights set on Uncle Nick, who was serving his time for racketeering in FCI Pekin, Illinois. Armed with evidence from my prison yard tapes and the visiting room videos Maseth filmed with my father, Doyle, and Ricci, the Two Mikes were ready to use the bloody gloves to smoke out my uncle.

In mid-1999, Hartnett and Bourgeois had already journeyed to Pekin to serve a search warrant on Uncle Nick, to conduct a DNA swab, and to X-ray and photograph his left arm. They were trying to match his DNA with the bloody gloves, and the X-ray could reveal any bullet fragments that might be embedded in my uncle's left forearm.

Hartnett and Bourgeois waited in the examination room as the door opened. In walked a very jumpy Nicholas Calabrese. He submitted to the X-ray of his left arm. After the medical examiner took the exposures and went off to develop the film, Hartnett collected Uncle Nick's DNA by swabbing the inside of his mouth.

Hartnett had never administered a DNA test before, and while one or two swabs would have sufficed, he was anxious not to screw up and placed *eight* finished swabs inside the evidence container.

A few minutes later, the X-ray technician returned and slapped up the finished exposures onto an X-ray reader on the wall. The film revealed bullet fragments in Uncle Nicky's forearm.

"We need to talk," Hartnett said solemnly. "We've got you on the Fecarotta murder. You can choose to help yourself."

Nick bowed his head in anguish. Without admitting guilt, he asked the FBI to supply him with a list of lawyers he could trust and to arrange a visit with his wife and children under the pretext of "medical considerations."

Two weeks later, Nick received an unannounced follow-up visit from Hartnett and Police Detective Bob Moon. They informed my uncle that while they were awaiting DNA tests on the bloody gloves, they were confident the results would link him to the 1986 murder of Big Stoop. The FBI's mission was to convince my uncle to cooperate and testify against his brother, to verify the information they had gathered with me from the Milan yard and the visiting room.

Hartnett and Moon met with a chilly reception. "Forget it," Nick told Hartnett. "I'm not interested. I got nothing to say to you."

Despite the discovery of the bullet fragments and a positive DNA test, he was still a loyal Outfit soldier who couldn't possibly rat out his mob family, no matter how much contempt he had for his older brother.

The trip proved to be a setback. Hitting Uncle Nick with a brash ultimatum may not have been the most effective strategy. Moon's presence had rubbed him the wrong way, as they had known each other from a previous arrest. Outfit mobsters had a history of not rolling over at the first sign of legal problems, and my uncle was no exception.

Nick was living under a dark cloud. He had been estranged from my father for four years, since 1995. The two hadn't spoken. My uncle had cut his ties by hiring a different law firm than the rest of us. He began to feel isolated and underappreciated. My dad was toying with putting the word out to Jimmy Marcello in Pekin through Mike Ricci, Mickey Marcello, and Ronnie Jarrett to keep an eye on my uncle. Mickey and Ronnie were alerted that Nick had a potential problem with a murder beef. Uncle Nick's allegiance came with a price. Back in 1997 Jimmy had already arranged for the Outfit to pay Nick's family four thousand dollars cash every month to keep him quiet.

Law enforcement authorities suspected that Nick's life was in danger at Pekin, being close to Marcello and Harry Aleman. At one time, Harry and my uncle were cellmates, but once Nick was linked to the Fecarotta hit, the Feds issued a separation order and transferred Aleman out of Pekin.

When the FBI showed up a third time, it was to obtain a handwriting sample to connect my uncle to the Cagnoni bombing. Marcello was in a nearby room visiting with Mickey when he spotted the agents meeting with Nick. Nick did the writing sample without uttering a word to the agents. Then he abruptly left the room.

Another potential breach of security occurred when the Feds suspected there was a plan to murder my uncle inside FCI Pekin.

The warden called Hartnett and told him about a letter that had been hand-dropped in the prison's SIS office. It said that Nick was under investigation for a Chicago murder and that the Outfit was concerned he was going to flip, which would hurt Jimmy and Mickey Marcello. The note was completely specific and on point—a pretty serious threat.

A young inmate from Cicero jailed on drug charges and eager to gain status with the Outfit boasted to a cellmate that he knew about a gun that was smuggled inside to kill my uncle. After the young inmate's cellie slipped a note to a guard, correctional officers moved Nick into protective custody, while Jimmy Marcello was ushered into lockdown. Questioning his safety, my uncle realized he should seriously consider cooperating.

Another potential problem arose when Mike Maseth received a call from a captain at FCI Milan: an "interesting piece of paperwork" had crossed his desk. "Why is Nick Calabrese being transferred to Milan?"

Mike was stunned. Nick was en route to Milan and would be in the same prison with my father. After a few desperate phone calls, he was taken off the transport flight and detoured to the federal prison in Ashland, Kentucky.

As Nick settled in at FCI Ashland in northeastern Kentucky, on January 15, 2002, the FBI arranged another visit through his counsel. After a great deal of back-and-forth communication, my uncle surmised that he was out of options and that his situation with my father and Marcello was only going to get worse. He made the fateful decision to turn against his brother, although how cooperative he would be—and exactly how much he knew—was yet to be determined by the Feds.

"Until he actually starts talking," Maseth told his fellow agents on the squad, "we don't know if he has anything or not."

It was dangerous for the FBI to debrief potential inmate witnesses inside their own prison walls, so a predawn rendezvous was arranged at a nearby Bureau office. Waist-chained and cuffed on the pretext of being sent out for medical treatment, my uncle was escorted from FCI Ashland under cover of darkness.

Maseth, Hartnett, Bourgeois, and Assistant U.S. Attorney Mitch Mars drove their anonymous rental car into Ashland, a small Kentucky town nestled on the banks of the Ohio River.

There was eeriness in the air. In the predawn darkness, the first sight that caught Maseth's attention was Ashland's towering oil refineries. It was a scene straight out of the movie *Robocop* as tall orange flames shot out of ominous industrial smokestacks that peppered the mudflats of the turnpike.

The rental carrying the lawmen zoomed down the pitch-black highway. They were driving so fast that a Kentucky cop came out of a roadside doughnut shack, chased them, and pulled them over. As the policeman approached the driver's side, Hartnett reached over from the front passenger seat and slapped his FBI ID up against the window. Because the Two Mikes were in plainclothes and they'd been traveling seventy-five in a twenty-five-miles-per-hour zone—and carrying guns—there was a real chance of a blue-on-blue shoot-out.

Standing by the driver's-side window, the cop yelled, "Do you know what the speed limit is?"

Hartnett and the police officer exchanged cold stares. Then the cop blinked. Looking down at Hartnett's creds, he answered his own question.

"Well I guess you do. Listen, you guys be careful out there."

As the officer waddled back to his cruiser, the agents spun gravel and sped back onto the highway toward the tiny courthouse office a few miles away.

Once Nick arrived, he was shuffled in, accompanied by the heavy jangle of chains and shackles. He was escorted into one of the smaller rooms. In a separate office, Nick's lawyer, John Theis, met with Assistant U.S. Attorney Mars and Agent Bourgeois and hammered out last-minute details of their agreement. The Two Mikes joined Nick in the cramped room. There was an awkward silence. Suddenly, my uncle sprang out of his chair and bellowed, "That's it! I can't do this. I just can't do it!"

Hartnett abruptly stood up and yelled, "Sit down!"

From that point on, Uncle Nick wouldn't respond well to Hartnett and his by-the-book style. But with Maseth, it was a different story. After a few minutes of quiet, Mike calmly asked him, "Is there anything you need, Nick? Can I get you something?"

"It's just my back. It's killing me. I've always had problems with my back."

Mike explained to Nick that as a young boy, he had undergone fusion surgery on *his* back. The two exchanged tales of chronic pain and lumbar stiffness. It was clear that if Uncle Nick was going to make a deal with the Feds, he would be most comfortable working with Maseth. Nick later told Mike that Hartnett's outburst reminded him of his brother, Frank, who would scream at, slap, and humiliate him in public.

Mars, Bourgeois, and Nick's attorney emerged from their conference. It was agreed that if Uncle Nick told the FBI the truth and it resulted in substantive convictions, the Feds would go to the judge and explain that he had been helpful and would subsequently put in a good word for him regarding his sentencing.

Starting that January 15, to Mike's amazement, my uncle provided the FBI with names, precise dates, and lurid details about a variety of unsolved gangland slayings, beginning with the Fecarotta murder. There was the killing of Emil Vaci in Arizona. The Ortiz-Morawski Half and Half Murder in Cicero. The Tony and Michael Spilotro executions in DuPage County. Nick supplied information that pumped new life into another long-dormant case: the 1974 cold-blooded hit on businessman Daniel Seifert. The Seifert murder involved Tony Spilotro, John Fecarotta, Jimmy LaPietra, Chinatown Outfit assassin Frankie "the German" Schweihs, and another slippery, colorful Grand Avenue mob boss, Joey "the Clown" Lombardo.

The FBI was caught off guard. The Bureau had been completely unaware that this unassuming, bumbling lackey had been privy to dozens and personally involved in fourteen hits. It was clear to the Two Mikes and prosecutor Mitch Mars that their latest star witness would serve up a bounty of substantiating information that implicated high-ranking Outfit kingpins—like Lombardo and Calabrese senior—plus a host of top earners and soldiers, and a couple of dirty cops.

After their first twelve-hour debriefing session, Maseth and Hartnett were exhausted. They were astonished that Nick's memory was so precise. His inside knowledge of the Outfit and Calabrese crew murders was vast. And my uncle was a made guy. The so-called mob experts had categorized Nick as merely a gofer and a driver for my father. The Two Mikes' fledgling Operation Family Secrets investigation had taken a major turn, first with me opening the door, and now with my uncle Nick kicking down the walls.

Operation Family Secrets was about to rise to a much higher level and into the realm of a major organized crime inquiry. For the unprecedented information that my uncle gave up, the Two Mikes had to chase down and substantiate every detail. It was time to put together a crack investigative team that would, for the first time since Elliot Ness, put the entire Chicago Outfit on notice.

33.

PANDORA'S BOX

After Maseth and Hartnett flipped Uncle Nick in the tiny courthouse office in Ashland, Kentucky, the Two Mikes were overwhelmed with what lay ahead. Both agents were blindsided by my uncle's dramatic admissions. Before going to prison in 1995, Nick had only one prior: a weapons charge that was dropped.

They didn't know that the Calabrese crew was also Angelo LaPietra's murder squad, and they didn't know

that my father's crew had a higher purpose inside the Outfit. They understood we were a prominent street crew and we had a good juice loan business and would resort to violence. But the FBI didn't know our crew were *the* go-to guys when Angelo LaPietra wanted someone murdered. When Angelo was tasked by the bosses to hit someone, these were his guys.

Keeping off the FBI's radar was an indication of how careful, low-key, intelligent, and at the same time treacherous my father was at conducting business. Until Pandora's box was opened, nobody figured my soft-spoken uncle was a serial hit man like my father. Nick's information reinforced and corroborated my father's prison yard admissions on the Ortiz-Morawski, Dauber, and Albergo hits. Nick also linked him to the Michael Cagnoni bombing by recounting an incident when he had injured his hand by testing explosive devices.

With devastating testimony from my uncle and me, Operation Family Secrets opened the door for the FBI to prove that the Outfit functioned as a criminal enterprise whose reach extended well into interstate commerce. If the Bureau and the DOJ could indict Outfit bosses, made guys, and soldiers for a series of murders, gambling, juice loans, street tax, obstruction of justice, and crimes linked to interstate commerce, the results would be devastating for organized crime.

To be found guilty of racketeering under the RICO Act, as established in the U.S. Code, Title 18, Chapter 96, a person must have committed two of thirty-five listed crimes within a ten-year period. Twenty-seven of the cases related to the Outfit were federal, with the other eight being state crimes. In the past hundred years of the Outfit's existence, this would be the first time it could be indicted for violating RICO statutes. And the first time a made member was held accountable.

Could the Two Mikes be the guys to bring the Outfit down?

The FBI allows agents to run investigations on a one- or two-agent basis, and if substance is shown, a larger unit will be enlisted. Maseth and Hartnett needed to meet with Supervisor

Bourgeois to get him to sign off on an expanded squad to cash in on my and Uncle Nick's revelations.

Unlike high-profile FBI agents like Bill Roemer and Joe Pistone, who wrote popular true-crime books, Maseth and Hartnett were just two young agents building an investigation. Bourgeois knew they had a strong case and were gathering an inordinate head of steam.

Soon Mike was promoted to co-lead case agent. Maseth and Hartnett had to sell their colleagues on joining their budding investigation and build a team. Although the Two Mikes had a hot case to offer, many of the agents were assigned to their own investigations or were busy readying cases that were about to go to trial. Once Agent Bourgeois gave them the go-ahead to expand operations, Maseth and Hartnett needed to select their team and entice the right associates to join them.

By early 2002, they had their crew set up. According to Mike Maseth, it was like assembling a fantasy baseball team. After they listed the murders, the Two Mikes completed another list of squad members who might want to work with them. They needed to attract certain agents with certain skills to fill specific needs. Operation Family Secrets pursued crimes that were sprawled over three decades. Maseth and Hartnett needed personnel willing to put in long hours without clock-watching or whining about overtime.

Mob prosecutors Mitch Mars and John Scully (later joined by T. Markus Funk) came from the U.S. Attorney's Office. They would serve as the prosecution team. Bill Paulin, Laura Shimkus, and Mike Welch would make up the IRS portion of the squad. (No investigation was complete without those dreaded IRS agents.) Veteran FBI agent Ted McNamara brought his encyclopedic knowledge of the Outfit landscape and an uncanny knack for pulling up valuable needle-in-the-haystack wiretap transcripts and case files. Agent John Mallul jumped over from Chicago's OC2 squad. He had been instrumental in cracking the William Jahoda–Rocky Infelise case in the early 1990s. Mallul scored a civil RICO complaint against a labor council that controlled twenty locals and twenty thousand union members for LIUNA, the Laborer's International Union of North America. LIUNA's board of directors included mobsters Bruno and Frank Caruso and relatives of Joe "the Clown" Lombardo, Johnny Apes, and Vincent Solano. Mallul succeeded Bourgeois as OC1's squad supervisor after Bourgeois's retirement.

Agent Anita Stamat was also recruited and became the squad's criminal anthropologist. She was in charge of translating coded Outfit messages and correspondence. Agent Tracy Balinao was a skilled field investigator and Bureau liaison for victims and eyewitnesses. Other "first-round picks" included Trisha Holt, Dana DePooter, and Andrew Hickey. Luigi Mondini and Chris Mackey made major contributions when they joined the squad in 2004. Lastly, Bob Moon and Al Egan, two veteran detectives from the Chicago Police Department, were added to the task force.

With eighteen unsolved murders to reconstruct and numerous surveillances to organize, the Operation Family Secrets squad quickly increased from seven to sixteen people. But it was Maseth and Hartnett who maintained primary contact with my uncle and me as their two star witnesses.

For security reasons, they decided to debrief Uncle Nick at FCI Ashland in Kentucky because there was less foot traffic there than at Milan or Pekin. Although Nick had been in Kentucky for months, he was no longer surrounded by a support group of wiseguy inmates like Jimmy Marcello and Harry Aleman. In Ashland, Nick was isolated from his Outfit brethren.

The information flowed constantly, but the FBI could talk to him only for a prescribed period of time. Each debriefing session with Nick lasted ten or twelve hours. There were very few breaks and no time for ritzy lunches. The agents lived on candy bars, vending machine grub, and fast food. In the beginning, the debriefings took place in Ashland, but later they were moved to an undisclosed location.

Mike didn't know what to expect. For forty or so years, my uncle had been programmed not to talk to police. Sitting in a room with three FBI agents, a federal prosecutor, and a defense lawyer, my uncle had a lot of nervous energy. Uncle Nick was jittery and worried because, like me, he was about to do something that he had never imagined.

The FBI became extremely judicious about whom they chose to do business with. When Salvatore "Sammy the Bull" Gravano was arrested in 1998 on drug charges—seven years after becoming a government witness—the Department of Justice began driving a harder bargain for mobsters willing to cooperate or enter WITSEC (the Witness Security Program). One of my main concerns was whether or not the Bureau (or another government agency further up the food chain) would ever cut a deal with my father, putting *him* back on the street. Such an arrangement would endanger the lives of both Nick and me.

But it was extremely unlikely that my father would flip; putting him back on the street was a near impossibility. Short of revealing who killed JFK and Jimmy Hoffa, the most he could hope for was a slightly more comfortable cell inside a federal penitentiary. My uncle showed remorse for his crimes during his debriefings. His return to society as a productive and nonviolent citizen was plausible.

During the debriefing process neither my uncle nor I knew that the other was cooperating, much less talking with the same federal agents. It was vital in the investigation that we hadn't compared notes or shared information, and that neither of us knew of the other's whereabouts or involvement in the case.

For Mike Maseth, having a made member from the Outfit available to build a RICO case and close high-profile unsolved murders was a once-in-a-lifetime opportunity. Now he had to decide how best to dispense the vast amount of information on his all-important official 302 report on my uncle.

In the 302, the FBI writes down what happens in an interview. Since Nick was giving Mike forty years' worth of information, Mike decided that if they were going to debrief Nick through several interviews over a long period of time, they wanted the 302 to make sense and have a broad context. They wanted somebody to read the document five years later and understand how everything tied in. Instead of doing a bunch of individual 302s every time Nick and Mike met, they compiled one gigantic 302, a chronology of what Uncle Nick told them throughout his briefs.

Maseth's jumbo 302, which spanned 120 pages, would become the bedrock upon which Operation Family Secrets was built. It would become the road map that Mitch Mars and the U.S. Attorney's Office would use in assembling their case in federal court.

34.

LIFE ON THE SQUAD

The Two Mikes got into a heated discussion in the parking lot at the new White Sox ballpark, where the squad was conducting a search for the body of Michael "Hambone" Albergo. It was a big production that resembled an archaeological dig, and based on Uncle Nick's information, the key area was roped off for excavation. The female agent in charge of investigating the Albergo murder and overseeing the digging operation approached Maseth with a question. She said the Evidence Response

Team (ERT) needed to know how deep to dig. Only Nick knew the answer, and because Mike was Nick's handler, Mike was put on the spot. Hartnett had warned Mike not to contact Nick with too many specific questions. It would, in his opinion, be counterproductive to their ongoing debriefing relationship with him.

Yet the agent at the site insisted, and she had a full crew waiting for an answer. Feeling squeezed with so much personnel and equipment on the scene, Mike got on the phone and made calls before getting through to Nick. As the ERT began their work, Hartnett overheard Mike telling someone that he had just spoken to Nick. A visibly upset Hartnett pulled Maseth aside.

"Didn't I tell you *not* to call Nick?" Hartnett asked his partner. "You know, if you screw this thing up, it's *my* ass."

"Calm down. It's my ass, too," said Maseth. "Besides, I'm taking a beating out here, and all I want to do is help solve the case."

Later that night a set of bones was found at the dig site. By midnight, they were dusted and laid out. It looked like the remains of vertebrae and a spine. The next morning, a Sunday, Agent John Mallul pulled up to the command center with the office's special agent in charge (SAC).

"John," Maseth said wearily to Mallul, "I've got good news and bad news. We did find some bones, but the vertebrae seem too small to be human, and the skull we found looks to be that of a German shepherd. I'll let you tell the SAC."

Albergo's body was never found.

But not all of Uncle Nick's leads went cold. In recalling the details behind the Cagnoni bombing, he remembered that the license plate of the decoy car used in the blast came from a 1950 Ford that was later traced through police reports to have been stolen. Nick's claim that he and my father had staked out Cagnoni's business on South Damen Avenue at Blue Island Avenue two weeks before the murderous explosion was backed up by an old FBI 302 surveillance report that placed my father, John Fecarotta, and Frank Santucci in a parked car behind a building, half a block from Cagnoni's place of business. (After scoring such useful data,

Mike promised himself he would not complain about having to fill out and file multiple 302 forms.)

Later, Uncle Nick precisely recalled the use of a K-40 antenna stashed inside a parked car on the expressway, which detonated the brick-sized chunk of malleable C-4 explosives placed under Cagnoni's Mercedes. Squad investigators matched the make and model of similar parts of an explosive device that was used in the attempted bombing murder of another Outfit victim, Nick Sarillo.

After the painstaking process of piecing together events involving the eighteen previously unsolved homicides (although it was revealed by the government during sentencing that Uncle Nick detailed nearly two dozen slayings on Mike's jumbo 302), the investigation entered another phase between 2002 and April 2005—that of consolidating data and evidence for arrest and trial. Locating precise wiretap conversations proved to be the most time-consuming. When Agent Luigi Mondini investigated the Emil Vaci murder and the Outfit's attempt to whack the Spilotro brothers in Vegas, he needed certain wiretaps made there in the 1980s. The police in Nevada hunted through their archives, and when they dispatched the material to Chicago, Luigi wound up with a large stack of congealed reel-to-reel tapes. After baking the tapes in an oven to restore their usability (similar to what recording studios do to rescue decades-old vintage music masters), Luigi monitored hours of irrelevant material to find one pertinent four-minute conversation. It could take weeks to score one brief piece of tape. The tech room, where agents worked and reviewed wire transmissions, was so small that they could barely maneuver around the equipment.

When Mike mentioned in passing to Agent Ted McNamara a series of obscure phone conversations that may have taken place between Jimmy Marcello, Rocky Infelise, and Joe Ferriola regarding Little Jimmy's gambling activities, McNamara dropped by Mike's desk a few days later with a set of transcriptions of wiretaps that took place in 1986. Maseth was stunned. Here were the two noteworthy recordings off the wire between Marcello, Infelise, and Ferriola.

McNamara and Agent Anita Stamat had tremendous recall and discovered and understood the criminal activities of Jimmy Marcello, including the video poker machine business he had with his brother Mickey. While the Two Mikes had my uncle and me to navigate them through the coded lexicon of the Calabrese crew, Stamat, as the case agent for the Marcello inquiries, had to go it alone in cracking complex Outfit communication codes.

Chris Mackey, the agent in charge of gathering data on the late Angelo LaPietra, accumulated over ten thousand pages on the Hook alone—which needed to be meticulously reviewed before it was handed over to the Assistant U.S. Attorneys.

When I first saw how many agents had joined the investigation, I was concerned that it might compromise my identity. But this was not the case, and the inquiry remained top secret.

In November 2002, when Uncle Nick was scheduled to be released on racketeering charges, he suddenly disappeared from the federal prison system and was moved to a secret location for an indefinite period. While friends and family (especially the Outfit) waited for my uncle to rejoin his wife and kids in the suburbs, speculation turned to certainty. He had flipped and was about to become the first made Outfit guy to cooperate in court. Now when anyone typed "Nicholas Calabrese" at www.bop.gov to find out his whereabouts, he or she got nothing. Uncle Nicky had vanished into the ether—in the system one day, gone the next.

A year later, Jimmy Marcello was released from FCI Milan after serving eight years and seven months of his original twelve-and-a-half-year sentence. Marcello took a job with a nursing home operation called DVD Management. By then rumors of a major FBI investigation had escalated.

By 2004, change was in the air. Mike Hartnett was promoted and moved to New York City. At first he continued working in the Organized Crime unit in New York, but he was later reassigned to the Manhattan Terrorism unit. In the wake of Hartnett's departure, Luigi Mondini became my new handler, while Mike stayed on with Uncle Nick. Just as Maseth had earned his stripes with Hartnett, Luigi was doing the same and was upped to co-lead agent status. Now the burden of investigative leadership fell more on Maseth.

Family Secrets loomed over Mike's career. While other agents were racking up arrests and solving dozens of crimes, he was confined to working one case. How that would bode for his career with the Bureau, particularly if Family Secrets didn't pan out, no one knew. The Bureau brass in Chicago and Washington kept a close eye on the progress of each Organized Crime case. Family Secrets became a make-or-break situation for Mike. It was the only major case he'd been assigned since leaving the academy six years prior. Questions arose on the heels of Hartnett's departure. What if the operation were to fizzle before going to trial? What if the jury didn't buy into what my uncle and I testified to on the stand? What if the Outfit hired a dream team of attorneys and torpedoed the government's case? Had the case become too sprawling and complicated for a jury to comprehend? These factors weighed heavily on Mike as the squad soldiered forward.

Another unfortunate loss came after the death of CPD officer Bob Moon in 2004 after a bout with cancer. Moon was the king of practical jokers on the task force and a morale booster. For instance, he and a former agent named Diane would go at it back and forth. On Diane's fortieth birthday, Moon broke into her car and poured confetti into the air vents. When she started up the car with the air conditioner already on, her car's interior was blasted with confetti.

Soon after, Diane retaliated. When Moon showed up at his car in the parking garage after work, an attractive female stranger walked up to him and said, "I'll take a lesson."

"What?" Moon asked.

"I'll take a lesson."

"Sorry, I have no idea what you're talking about."

The woman pointed at Moon's license plate. Courtesy of Diane, Moon's custom license plate frame now read, "Sex Instructor, First Lesson Free."

Every agent on an FBI OC squad had to rotate for complaint duty. Every squad member took his or her turn answering phone calls, which sometimes involved talking to people with mental problems.

"I'm being followed. The aliens have come down to get me."

Bob Moon savored such calls. He told the other agents, "Send them to me."

"Hello. This is the communication department. How may I help you? Now sir, slow down please. . . . Before you go any further, I need to know if you have the implant chip or the headband . . . and the serial number? . . . 666? . . . Okay, now grab a pen and paper because I'm going to direct you where to go to get it fixed."

Moon gave the caller the phone number to the CPD detectives' unit.

Mike, now the lead agent for Family Secrets, remained a constant target for intra-squad pranks.

One time before going out of town to debrief Uncle Nick, he left his overnight bag in the squad area. As soon as Mike and John Mallul arrived to debrief Nick in Ashland, Mike checked into his hotel room and opened up his suitcase. He noticed he didn't have any underwear.

The next day a package for Mike arrived at the hotel. Mallul stood in line for twenty minutes to sign for it. The squad had stolen Mike's underwear and overnighted it back to him in a FedEx box with some documents. These were the same trusted colleagues who locked Mike inside the Porta-Potty one night during the Albergo dig.

Mallul jumped into the car and threw the box at Maseth.

"Next time tell those guys to keep me out of the crossfire of their crazy-ass schemes."

35.

THE TERRIBLE TOWEL

In the months leading up to the indictments, the FBI's goal was to weave the murder charges in with the other RICO predicate acts (loan-sharking, gambling, and extortion) to show the Outfit operating as a singular criminal enterprise. Until the date of the Family Secrets indictments, there had been more than 3,200 mob murders in a hundred years in the Chicago area, resulting in only twelve convictions. No made member of the Outfit had ever been convicted of a mob homicide. No made member ever testified.

On April 25, 2005, the proverbial shoe dropped when the grand jury unsealed a United States Department of Justice indictment in which fourteen defendants were charged with organized crime activities. Eighteen previously unsolved murders (plus the attempted murder of Nick Sarillo) served as the indictment's centerpiece.

For the first time the Justice Department targeted the Outfit as a criminal enterprise as opposed to prosecuting acts committed by individuals. As Patrick J. Fitzgerald, United States Attorney for the Northern District of Illinois, said, the indictment "is remarkable for both the breadth of the murders charged and for naming the entire Chicago Outfit as a criminal enterprise under the anti-racketeering law. It is a textbook example of the effective use of the RICO statute to prosecute an assortment of crimes spanning decades." Of the fourteen defendants indicted, eleven were "charged with conspiracy, including [committing] murders and attempted murders, to further the Outfit's illegal activities such as loan-sharking and bookmaking, and to protect the enterprise from law enforcement." This, simply put, represented the most extensive mob-murder prosecution in American history.

The April indictments pointed an accusatory finger at what was left of the Outfit's leadership. The roster of eleven primary defendants was as follows:

1. James Marcello, who had been released from FCI Milan in 2003, was listed as a member of the Melrose Park crew, and presently acting boss of the Chicago Outfit. Marcello would stand trial for his involvement in the 1986 murder of the Spilotro brothers.

2. Joseph Lombardo would have to answer for his role in the September 1974 murder of Danny Seifert.

3. Frank Calabrese, Sr., was listed as a member of the South Side 26th Street/Chinatown crew. In many ways my father became the star defendant of the group, the most reviled, and the defendant against whom the FBI had assembled the strongest case. The first murder of eleven he was indicted for was the killing of Michael Albergo, dating back to August 1970.

4. Nicholas W. Calabrese was listed as affiliated with the South Side 26th Street/Chinatown crew. Although Nick was cooperating with the FBI, he was indicted and would stand for his crimes, including the murder of John Fecarotta and thirteen others.

5. Frank Schweihs, known as Frank the German, was a feared enforcer and street tax collector and a murderer and extortionist. He was one of the most dangerous members of the Outfit and rivaled my father in notoriety, cruelty, and treachery. Michael Spilotro told his family that if they saw Frankie Schweihs lurking outside the family property, they should call the police immediately.

6. Frank "Gumba" Saladino, a member of my father's South Side 26th Street/Chinatown crew, committed murder and other criminal activities on behalf of the Chicago Outfit. Saladino had done a lot of overtime with a knife and fork, weighing in at four hundred pounds. When served with his indictment, he was found dead in a motel room in the northern suburb of Hampshire where he'd been living for two months.

7. Paul Schiro was arrested in Arizona. "The Indian," a jewel thief, burglar, and killer, served as the Outfit's conduit to the southwestern United States. He was listed as an associate of Frank the German and Tony Spilotro while the Ant was serving the Outfit in Vegas. Also responsible for the Vaci homicide.

8. Michael Marcello, or Mickey, allegedly operated an illegal video poker gambling business with half brother Jimmy Marcello under the name M&M Amusement.

9. Nicholas Ferriola was the son of Joe Ferriola and a member of the South Side 26th Street/Chinatown crew. He was accused of "delivering messages to associates of the enterprise and collecting money generated by extortion demands" for my father while he was inside FCI Milan.

10. Anthony Doyle was one of two corrupt law enforcement officers who the Outfit had in their pocket. "Twan" was a former CPD officer who kept my dad informed by passing messages and supplying important confidential information about my uncle and Jimmy DiForti to determine if they were cooperating with law enforcement.

11. Michael Ricci, a retired CPD officer, was subsequently employed by the Cook County Sheriff's Department. He collaborated with Twan Doyle and my father, passing messages about the bloody gloves that linked Nick to the murder of John Fecarotta. He was indicted on one count of making false statements to the FBI.

Of the eleven defendants, seven were singled out for committing murder or agreeing to commit murder on the Outfit's behalf. They were my father, my uncle, Jimmy Marcello, Joe Lombardo, Frank the German, Gumba Saladino, and Paul Schiro.

Through their involvement in M&M Amusement, three additional Marcello associates—Thomas Johnson, Dennis Johnson, and Joseph Venezia—were charged, raising the number of those indicted from eleven to fourteen. Each was charged with one count of conducting an illegal gambling business. The Johnsons appeared in FBI surveillance photos carrying video poker machines.

Besides the murders and attempted murders spanning decades, the racketeering crimes named in the indictments included juice loans (charging 1 to 10 percent interest per week), illegal gambling, violence, intimidation and threats, obstructing justice, using fictitious fronts to hide criminal proceeds, using coded language and names for fellow conspirators and victims of their crimes, monitoring law enforcement radio frequencies to detect law enforcement presence, using walkie-talkies while conducting criminal activities, acquiring explosives and explosive devices, maintaining hidden control of labor organizations and assets, maintaining hidden interests in businesses to receive untraceable income, and maintaining written records and ledgers for loan-sharking and bookmaking activities.

The official press release showed that the Bureau meant business and that the investigation that started a few years earlier when the Two Mikes reopened the Fecarotta murder case had blossomed into a high-priority attack on the Outfit.

"This unprecedented indictment puts a 'hit' on the Mob," said Patrick Fitzgerald. "After so many years, it lifts the veil of secrecy and exposes the violent underworld of organized crime." With strong words, the FBI and the U.S. Attorney's Office, through these indictments, were sending a stern message to organized crime.

"While there have been many successful investigations during the past quarter-century resulting in the arrest and indictment of high-ranking members of the Chicago Outfit," said Robert Grant, Special Agent in Charge of the Chicago office of the FBI, "never before have so many in lofty positions in the Chicago mob been charged in the same case."

Many were convinced that my father's harsh and abusive treatment of Kurt, my uncle, and me had dragged the low-key and publicity-shy Outfit into a high-profile prosecutorial shoot-out. The words of Vito Corleone in *The Godfather* echoed throughout the streets of Chicago: "A man who doesn't take care of his family is not a man."

Once the indictments dropped, two of the primary defendants—Joey the Clown and Frank the German—went on the lam. It would be eight months before Schweihs was arrested in Berea, Kentucky, forty miles outside of Lexington. The seventy-five-year-old Schweihs was nabbed as he left the town house he was sharing with his "younger and attractive" girlfriend in her sixties.

Lombardo remained a fugitive for nine months until he was apprehended in January of 2006 after leaving the office of Dr. Patrick "Dr. Pat" Spilotro. Lombardo had a couple of after-hour appointments with Dr. Pat to fix an abscessed tooth and perform a bridge adjustment. During his months on the run, Lombardo played cat-and-mouse with the judge (and the press) by feeding letters and communiqués through his lawyer, Rick Halprin, denying any involvement in acts of racketeering, murder, or violence "in anyway [sic] shape or form."

Agents Tracy Balinao and Luigi Mondini began the search for Lombardo on a Sunday, the day before the April 25, 2005, indictments were unsealed.

They went to arrest him at his place of business. Then they went to his home and to the Italian clubs. They searched up and down the streets and could not find him. He sent letters through his attorney to the judge, saying that if the FBI and the court gave him certain considerations he would come in.

Nine months later Balinao and Mondini set up surveillance and, with their car, T-boned Lombardo's car in an alley. He was a passenger. The agents had to yell at the driver—who was quite elderly—to put the car in park. Joe the Clown was polite when he was apprehended, dressed like a homeless person sporting a beard, looking like Saddam Hussein. At first he wasn't going to tell the Feds who he was, but he had a driver's license on him with his name on it. He didn't want to get the guy who was driving into trouble, so the FBI took him to their office and fingerprinted him. The agents found him to be very personable, and Luigi tried to get him to talk by speaking a little bit of Italian.

With the MCC full for the night, Joey was taken to the Chicago Police Department lockup to be held. Once there, he was more conversational, recommending restaurants in the area. The next day, he was set to be moved over to the MCC. Joey had made friends with the folks in the lockup, and warmly greeted federal agents. Gone was his homeless look. "See?" he said. "I shaved for you. I got all nice."

As charming and amusing as Joey could be, the FBI was aware of his vicious side. He's personable and nice, and people love him, but if he's crossed, that's it. The wiretap of Lombardo meeting with Morris Shenker shows the other side of Joey, when Shenker, a St. Louis mob attorney and Las Vegas casino investor, was warned by Lombardo during a 1979 money dispute:

Lombardo: How old are you, Morris?
Shenker: Seventy-two.
Lombardo: If they come back and tell me to give you a message and if you want to defy it, I assure you that you will never reach seventy-three.

Other than some idle speculation, no one knew I was wearing a wire until I made the grievous error of telling my brother Kurt, who passed it on to his lawyer. This misstep put the investigation in serious danger. Standard procedure is that the only person who should know that you're cooperating is *you*. You can't even tell your wife.

When my Bureau contacts found out that I had leaked it to my brother, their first reaction was "expletive deleted." The agents didn't yell at me, but they did ask, "Do you want to get killed?" That's essentially what it came down to. Kurt got out before me, while I was still inside with my dad. Thank goodness the information didn't spread and nothing happened.

The Feds did hear on one of the wires before indictment, around 2003, that Jimmy Marcello had made a comment about my wearing a wire. Marcello said, "Don't talk to the kid," and he ran his fingers up and down his chest as if he had a wire on. I don't know if Marcello was guessing or was certain.

Originally, Uncle Nick suspected that the FBI's sudden flood of information came from Jimmy DiForti and not from me, since the FBI couldn't play, and never played, any of my Milan prison yard tapes to my uncle. He was in the dark as to my role in the case, but after Nick figured out it was me, he apparently wasn't angry, and said, "I should have known. I knew what he grew up with. I grew up with the same guy so I understand what he had to do."

The gulf of time elapsing between Uncle Nick's flipping in January of 2002 and the spring of 2005, when the indictments and arrests landed, was occupied by the intense prep work that goes on between the gathering of evidence and the trial. Once everything pertinent to the case was collected and cataloged, it was time for an important road trip—the delivery of 1.2 million documents, which were assembled, boxed, and loaded into two tractor trailers.

Mike, Luigi, and Chris Mackey were to escort two separate truckloads of documents between Chicago and Washington, D.C. The evidence would be digitally scanned on state-of-the-art equipment and archived in D.C., a painstaking process, since some of the documents dated as far back as 1958. The older documents were extremely brittle and could easily disintegrate.

The agents methodically numbered the boxes and carried the boxes on dollies and loaded the truck. Leaving Chicago early on Saturday morning, they followed the truck to Pittsburgh, where there was a stopping point because under the rules mandated by the Federal Motor Carrier Safety Administration, the driver was allowed to drive only eleven out of fourteen work hours.

Agents Mondini and Mackey led the expedition in a Crown Vic in front, followed by Mike and another agent named Smitty bringing up the rear. The truck steadily advanced to D.C.

When they drove to D.C. the first time, they were expecting to see people waiting on the other end, ready to take the stuff off the truck. But Chris, Smitty, Luigi, and Mike unloaded the entire first shipment themselves.

On the second trip to D.C., the group passed through Pittsburgh again on January 22, 2006, a date to remember for Pittsburgh NFL football fans. It was the day the Steelers won the AFC Championship by defeating the Denver Broncos 34–17 in Denver and secured a spot in the Super Bowl.

The Pittsburgh FBI office was on the south side, and with so many rivers and bridges to cross, the truck and trailer caravan had to navigate through the city's bar district. The Steelers had won the championship less than an hour before.

The caravan was stopped by police at the site of the mass celebration. The roads were blocked. The streets were packed with crazed Pittsburgh Steelers revelers. Passage seemed impossible. Yet the three FBI vehicles snaked their way through the crowd. The locals didn't part like the Red Sea. Instead, they swarmed the truck and climbed aboard, dangling from the side of the cab. The agents and the driver had no choice but to forge ahead at a snail's pace.

They "badged" their way through to get to the office in time. It was pure mayhem. Fans were jumping onto the side of the truck, hooting and hollering, waving the Terrible Towel. The driver did pretty well. The more he beeped his horn, the more the crowd loved it. Fortunately, the hordes didn't turn the truck over.

Two weeks later Mike's team, the Steelers, behind quarterback Ben Roethlisberger, went on to win the Super Bowl by defeating the Seattle Seahawks 21–10 at Ford Field in Detroit. Next up, Operation Family Secrets advanced to the finals and on to the trial stage as well, where a team of Assistant U.S. Attorneys would lace up and take the field to prosecute the Operation Family Secrets defendants in a federal courtroom.

36.

WHAT HAPPENED TO MY FATHER?

Daniel R. Seifert was the man who could connect the dots between the Central States Teamsters Union Pension and Welfare Fund and the Chicago mob. The murder of Seifert outside his Bensenville, Illinois, plastics factory in September 1974 ran markedly against the grain of the usual Outfit killing. The news media jumped on the story because it was a gangland murder of an ordinary businessman who wasn't a mobster. Second, the killing was shocking because it happened in broad daylight, in front of Seifert's wife, Emma, and his four-year-old son Joe.

Throughout 1971 and 1972, Danny Seifert, a high school dropout turned successful entrepreneur, was president of International Fiberglass, Inc., a fiberglass-molding company that was backed by a suspicious group of "investors" that included Irwin "Red" Weiner and Milwaukee Phil Alderisio. Seifert first met Weiner when he did carpentry work for him, and soon he entered into a three-way partnership with Weiner and Alderisio. Later Danny and Joe Lombardo formed a close friendship. The Seiferts were so smitten with the Clown's act that they named their youngest son Joe.

Weiner subsequently sold a portion of his share of the business to Tony Spilotro, Frank Schweihs, Allen Dorfman, and Lombardo. As a no-show employee, Lombardo would come in to hit the heavy bag in the office, crack jokes, and chat on the phone.

Headquartered in Elk Grove Village, International Fiberglass became an Outfit-infiltrated company financed with a loan from the Central States Teamsters Pension Fund. In February 1973 Seifert discovered that illegal mob money was being laundered through International Fiberglass's books, and he left the company. When Lombardo, Spilotro, Weiner, and Dorfman were investigated by a grand jury for criminal fraud, Seifert was to be the prosecution's star witness. These "gentlemen" had plenty to be concerned about because the $1.4 million loan obtained by Weiner through his good friend Allen Dorfman came from the Central States Teamsters Pension Fund and would lead back to the Outfit. Seifert then gave federal investigators proof that Alderisio and Lombardo (the latter, through two canceled checks) were silent partners at International Fiberglass. Seifert would document fiscal wrongdoing using checks deposited to the company books that were kicked back to Lombardo under the guise of reimbursing him for back wages. By 1974, as indictments loomed, the Outfit deduced that the knowledge of the canceled checks could have come only from Seifert and that he would testify against them in court. It became obvious that something had to be done.

On September 27, 1974, three cars showed up early at Plastic-Matic Products, the Bensenville plastics factory that Seifert now operated. Joe Lombardo and Jimmy LaPietra arrived in a brown Ford LTD. John Fecarotta and Tony Spilotro drove up in a white-and-blue Dodge Charger. Frank Schweihs drove a third, unidentified car that was never found. The ambush was set. Danny Seifert showed up for work with his wife, Emma, and toddler son Joe. As Emma and her son walked into the office ahead of Danny, three gunmen dressed in hooded sweatshirts and ski masks burst through the back door. They grabbed Emma and little Joe and locked them inside the bathroom. The assailants told Emma that they were there to rob the place.

Emma screamed, but obviously not loudly enough, because Daniel didn't hear her. When Danny walked into the office, he was thrown to the ground in the entryway, hit with the butt of a gun, and severely beaten. Before the assailants could handcuff Seifert and shoot him, Danny bolted out the glass door, streaking it with blood, and was chased by the three masked men in the parking lot of the plastics factory. Screaming for help and running for his life, Seifert burst into the adjoining office building and yelled for somebody, anybody to call the police. When one worker picked up the phone, a masked gunman aimed a shotgun at him and told him to put the phone down.

Danny raced through the premises with the gunmen in hot pursuit. By the time he made it out the door and back into the parking lot, he had been shot in the leg. He fell to the ground. The next shot was a point-blank shotgun blast through the back of his head. As the shooters bolted from the scene, someone called the cops. There was a police call out for a pink LTD, but when officers drove by a Key Pontiac dealership, they saw a brown Ford LTD and some guys getting into the Dodge Charger. An unsuccessful chase ensued. The brown Ford LTD was later found with ski masks and a pair of handcuffs left behind. The abandoned car had been altered as a mob work car complete with a supercharged engine and revolving license plates. During the crime-scene investigation, one woman identified Fecarotta in a photo lineup as a man who had been casing the Seifert factory. Another female witness identified Spilotro as being one of the occupants of the blue getaway car. Emma told the cops she was convinced one of the masked men was Lombardo because of his height and stocky build and because she recognized that "Joey was a boxer and very light on his feet." She was sure he was the one who had pushed her and Joe into the bathroom. A salesperson at an electronics store, CB Center of America, picked Lombardo, Fecarotta, LaPietra, and Schweihs out of a photo lineup as being in the store buying police scanners that were later linked to the getaway cars. Joe had signed the receipt for the scanners as "J. Savard"; Savard was the maiden name of Frank Schweihs's wife.

When the brown LTD was retrieved, its ownership was linked to a bogus business called Acme Security, whose address was identical to that of a plumbing company called Minotti Plumbing. Minotti was owned by an acquaintance of Lombardo's.

In spite of the evidence collected during the Seifert murder investigation, and the fact that a witness was later told by Lombardo at a driving range, "That son of a bitch won't testify against anybody now, will he?" no charges were originally brought against the shooters. Also, the case against Joe the Clown, Tony Spilotro, and Allen Dorfman in the matter of International Fiberglass, Inc., and their alleged unlawful use of Teamster pension funds was dropped due to the lack of evidence needed to bring the case to a grand jury. Without Seifert's testimony, the government's fraud case fizzled.

When the news of the sanctioned hit (signed off on by "Joey Doves" Aiuppa) reached Outfit consigliere Tony Accardo, he was infuriated that such a brazen order had been given in the first place.

FBI Agent Tracy Balinao, assigned to the reopened investigation, was a year older than Joe Seifert, who as a four-year-old saw his dead father "lying in the grass" in a pool of blood. Almost thirty years later, in 2003 when the case was reopened, Tracy interviewed Emma and Joe in an effort to piece together the details of the murder.

Lombardo was first tied to Seifert's murder by a government informant and career criminal, Alva Johnson Rodgers, the man who had heard Lombardo's boast at the driving range. Uncle Nick later contributed information as he was being debriefed by Mike Maseth. Since there was no conclusive DNA evidence, nor a definitive eyewitness to identify the masked shooters, it was now up to the FBI OC squad to build a seamless web of evidence that would bring an indictment and a conviction thirty years later.

Tracy Balinao had been with OC1 since 1996, the same year Mike Hartnett joined the squad. Between the 1997 investigative launch and the 2005 indictments, Balinao (in addition to taking three maternity leaves) began working with another tough-minded agent, Chris Williams. As the case approached the indictment stage, Williams exited the squad, leaving Balinao in charge of linking Lombardo to the case.

Balinao was born in Chicago and lived near Wrigley Field before her family moved out to the southwestern suburbs in Oak Forest. Graduating from the University of Illinois in Chicago in 1991, she was recruited by the Bureau and joined the FBI for support and clerical work. After three years of organized crime research, Balinao applied to become an agent around the time of the first Iraq Gulf War. After graduating from Quantico she was transferred back to Chicago, where she worked on the bank robbery detail for about a year and a half before being reassigned to the Organized Crime squad.

Balinao found that police and FBI reports from 1974 about the Seifert murder contained little contact information on the witnesses that was still useful. Women had married and changed their surnames. Other people were deceased. Officers and agents had retired, and witnesses had moved on without leaving Social Security numbers to help trace their current whereabouts.

Nevertheless, many key witnesses were found and came forward. In spite of fear of Outfit reprisal, most agreed to cooperate.

A salesman at the CB Center of America reiterated his sworn statement that Lombardo and Schweihs had dropped in to purchase the police scanners. Another woman reaffirmed that she had seen Fecarotta staking out the premises the week before.

A woman who was hit by Tony Spilotro in his Dodge getaway car on her way to work "reidentified" his picture decades later. At the time, she had taken down Spilotro's license number and picked him out of a lineup, not knowing the person she was pointing out was the infamous hit man.

The rookie policeman who chased the getaway car had become the police chief of Elmhurst, Illinois. One retired FBI agent on the original case flew in from out of state (at his own expense) to supply additional background information. Many other retired policemen and FBI agents cooperated with Balinao in the hope that she could accomplish what so many others couldn't: nail Lombardo.

Perhaps the most interesting witness who revisited the Seifert case was Marvin Lemke. Lemke happened to be doing asphalt work at the Key Pontiac dealership the day of the shooting when he noticed the suspects gathered together. Lemke knew something was going down, because he had committed robberies in the past and had done time. Lemke was the perfect witness, but back in 1974 the investigators thought he was not credible because of his criminal record. But he knew exactly what was going on when he saw all the shooters consolidate into one car.

The dominant piece of evidence that linked Lombardo to Seifert's death was the fingerprint lifted off the application for title of the brown Ford LTD. The original title application, notarized by a secretary in Irwin "Red" Weiner's office and later sent off to the Illinois Secretary of State's office, was later tracked down in Washington, D.C., as part of an organized crime national archives file. The car registration had already been dusted for fingerprints by FBI agent Roy McDaniel and revealed Joe the Clown's full print, proving he had access to the car.

Some of the thirty-year-old case files were missing. But then another agent who was looking at the Michael Cagnoni file called the Two Mikes. "You guys gotta see this," he said. It was a big file on Seifert that they didn't think the Bureau had. That's when they retraced the print that had already been identified as Lombardo's.

Joey later insisted that he must have touched the registration when it was sitting on the secretary's desk at Irv's office, since he was frequently there.

Resurrecting decades-old cases like the Seifert and Ortiz-Morawski murders took tremendous personal tolls on the victims' families. During the Family Secrets investigation, agents like Balinao trod on highly emotional and sensitive family ground. For the Seifert case, the burden was on Tracy and the squad to convince witnesses like Emma and Joe that this time the authorities were building an ironclad case, and had the wherewithal to see it through. It was important that witnesses put their fear aside and testify at the trial. When Tracy would update Joe Seifert with new and pertinent developments regarding the case, he would often ask Balinao to contact his mother herself. This was in an effort to engage her. At first Emma didn't want the FBI anywhere near her; she thought they were bringing up the bad stuff again after she had gotten over it. She was very angry that nothing had been accomplished back then, and now the FBI was telling her she would be safe, after Daniel had cooperated and ended up dead.

The corrosion of organized crime had devastated yet another family. In the decades that passed, Emma Seifert had remarried and moved on with her life, making new friends who may not have known about her tragic past. Meanwhile, Emma's sons Joe and Nick were both deeply traumatized by their father's death. Each, independently of the other, had considered seeking revenge on the man they knew as children as "Uncle Joe."

Agent Chris Mackey encountered a similar situation during the Ortiz-Morawski investigation. When Richard Ortiz's son first heard that his dad had been shot and killed on July 23, 1983, he ran down to the Cicero murder scene the very next day. Later, there was conjecture that the Cicero police were involved. It was hard for Mackey to imagine a young kid having to grow up in Cicero thinking the police might have killed his father, which wasn't true.

When the Cicero Police Department stepped up a fresh inquiry during the Family Secrets investigation, Maseth and Mackey confidentially approached the Cicero police and urged them to back off. The cops were told in so many words that the FBI had a handle on the killers.

During the reopened Vaci investigations, Agent Luigi Mondini spent hours at a restaurant with Emil Vaci's daughters, just listening to them talk about how horrible their life was after their father died.

"What happened to my father? Why was he killed?" they asked.

Suddenly their dad didn't come home. The next day he was found in a ditch, rolled up in a tarp. The Phoenix Police Department investigated for a bit, but nothing came of it. Nobody seemed to care. Now, years later, my uncle Nick would step forward and reveal what really happened.

37.

THE TRIAL STAGE

By the time the Family Secrets defendants went to trial on a sultry Tuesday morning, June 19, 2007, the manner in which FBI agents handled Outfit mobsters had changed dramatically. During the 1960s and 1970s, an FBI agent might have taken a more macho approach. Today, the FBI's strategy is more psychological and less confrontational. With a star witness like my uncle, who had an adversarial relationship with federal agents nearly his whole life, a confrontational approach might not work. There were certain agents he wouldn't speak to. (Some he won't speak to even today.) Cooperation isn't something that is cajoled out of a defendant. Straight talk and earnest negotiating are what brought witnesses like my uncle and me to the table to cooperate. That, and the damaging DNA evidence.

After indictments were served in 2005, the ball was in the court of the three-man prosecution team working closely with the FBI Chicago Organized Crime squad. Because of the amount of local and even national interest in the case, the trial was to be held in downtown Chicago, at the United States district courthouse at 219 South Dearborn, in the large ceremonial courtroom. The court battle was to be presided over by United States District Court judge James Block Zagel.

Zagel, a Chicago native, Harvard Law graduate, and Reagan appointee, had been on the bench since 1987 after serving as the Director of the State Police. Zagel had authored a crime thriller called *Money to Burn,* published by Putnam in 2002. Set in Chicago, the book mixes characters with judicial experience (Judge Paul E. Devine is the story's narrator) with the financial intrigue of the Federal Reserve Bank. The *Wall Street Journal* extolled *Money to Burn* as "a funhouse-mirror morality tale." Later, in April 2009, after the Family Secrets trial, Zagel was selected to preside over another high-profile case: the corruption trial of the disgraced former Illinois governor Rod Blagojevich.

By the time the Family Secrets trial began, the number of defendants had shrunk to five: Frank Calabrese, Sr., James Marcello, Joseph Lombardo, Paul Schiro, and Anthony Doyle. Dropping off along the way by pleading out were Michael Marcello, Nicholas Ferriola, Thomas Johnson, Joseph Venezia, and Dennis Johnson. Frank "Gumba" Saladino had died, as had Mike Ricci. Frank Schweihs, after being diagnosed with cancer, was to be tried separately. Nick, of course, had switched sides. While he had an agreement with the government that he wouldn't have to face the death penalty, he was still on the hook for the crimes he had committed, and his fate would be decided by Zagel at the sentencing phase.

The three-man prosecution team came out of the United States Attorney's Office for the Northern District of Illinois, headed by Patrick Fitzgerald. Fitzgerald had served as the federal prosecutor in charge of the Valerie Plame CIA leak, which led to the prosecution of Vice President Dick Cheney's chief of staff, Lewis "Scooter" Libby. Under Fitzgerald's authority, the Family Secrets prosecution team consisted of three primary chairs: Assistant U.S. Attorneys Mitch Mars, John Scully, and T. Markus Funk. Funk was the last to be added to the team.

Mitch Mars, the lead prosecutor, was a press-shy, low-key prosecutorial genius. He had a youthful bespectacled look and an easygoing style. His office and desk were a legendary mess, with mounds of paperwork stacked everywhere. If an agent had to leave a document in his office, he or she would often tape papers and memos to his chair. As the Chief of the Organized Crime Strike Force, Mars was respected and feared by street soldiers and the Outfit upper echelon.

John Scully, the father figure of the group, had expertise as a mob prosecutor dating back to 1982, when he was with the Department of Justice. In 1990 a merger within the U.S. Attorney's Office resulted in the formation of the local Organized Crime Strike Force units.

In the early 1960s, starting with Attorney General Bobby Kennedy, the federal government pushed the idea of having dedicated people—prosecutors, agents, and representatives of different agencies—to work on the mob in specific cities that had been overrun by organized crime, places like Boston, New York, Pittsburgh, Chicago, Detroit, New Orleans, and Providence.

Scully worked as a federal prosecutor on the case against corrupt cop and former Chicago Police Chief of Detectives William Hanhardt. Our street crew viewed Scully as a dangerous lifelong prosecutor. In our eyes, there were two kinds of prosecutors. One was looking to jump-start his or her career and move on to the private sector. The other was a career prosecutor working for the

G. Mars and Scully were career G-men, and according to my father, you *never* wanted to go up against a career prosecutor.

Prior to signing on to the Operation Family Secrets team, T. Markus Funk had been with the U.S. Attorney's Office since 2000. Before becoming a federal prosecutor, Funk worked as a law professor teaching criminal law at Oxford University in England and later at the University of Chicago and Northwestern University. On loan to the State Department, he spent 2004 through 2006 in Kosovo as the Section Chief for the Department of Justice. In Kosovo, Funk helped the war-torn Muslim majority establish the rule of law and revamp their judicial and prosecutorial systems. In fact, even today Funk's book on Kosovo trial practice remains their most-cited legal source.

When Funk was contacted by the U.S. Attorney's Office in Chicago about a bombshell mob case called Family Secrets, he was immediately intrigued. Though he hadn't worked in the organized crime section, he had gained considerable experience in Kosovo fighting human trafficking and Eastern European organized crime syndicates. When the U.S. Attorney's Office asked if he would be interested in working Family Secrets, Funk, still living on a fortified U.S. base, called his colleagues back in Chicago and asked around about the Family Secrets case. Then he accepted the offer.

The biggest challenge the three prosecutors faced was to keep a complicated case like Family Secrets, spanning nearly four decades, simple. That meant knowing which elements to include and which to leave out. With a one-week burglary or bank robbery trial, a prosecutor could get away with including a few extra facts. But with a long, drawn-out trial like Family Secrets, the jurors could get frustrated if they didn't understand the relevance of certain testimony or were confused by what it meant and how it fit.

Mitch Mars's role as lead prosecutor became crucial. It was important that he put the case together in a streamlined fashion when the time came for me to testify on the stand.

When Family Secrets hit the trial stage there wasn't the traditional sense of FBI agents "handing things off" to the Assistant

U.S. Attorneys. Very few decisions about witnesses or which tapes to play were made without agent input. The FBI and the prosecutors remained a close-knit team throughout the trial, often working eighteen- or even twenty-hour days. Because the schedule was grueling, Maseth often slept in one of Mitch Mars's war room offices, on an inflated air mattress he borrowed from John Scully. Mike Maseth and the team of agents worked with Mars, Scully, and Funk to carefully coordinate the witnesses. Issues and questions arose daily. When would a certain witness be needed? How should they schedule the flights of witnesses? How should they arrange the seating, because one person might be a victim, another, a perpetrator? How could they monitor and keep certain witnesses apart and unaware of each other's role?

The Operation Family Secrets strategy was to cluster five defendants into one solid case, creating a sample spectrum of mob authority. With Frank the German separated, Operation Family Secrets still had a wide-enough range of defendants, a cross section of men from different crews working toward a common end—to advance the interests of the Outfit. Marcello and Lombardo were the boss figures and capos; my father was the dreaded hit man and juice loan crew chief; Schiro and Doyle were loyal soldiers who did the Outfit's bidding. The Assistant U.S. Attorneys and the FBI wanted to make certain they could satisfy the criteria for the RICO charges to a tee. It was the nation's most expansive mob-murder racketeering indictment, and Funk was charged with, among other things, helping establish the homicides. The objective was to collect the homicides, and once it was proven that a defendant had been involved in or had conspired to commit murder, the maximum sentence that defendant faced increased from twenty years to life. The law also states that with any of the co-conspirators, if they all worked together, the act of one represented the acts of all.

I had no communication or contact with the prosecution team during the trial. I spent my days on call in a room downstairs from the courtroom, reliving key moments with my father and mentally preparing myself to go on the stand. I tried to imagine how my father and his defense team might challenge my testimony and integrity in court.

With a case spanning nearly forty years, the question of the statute of limitations was bound to come up. While it's commonly known that the statute of limitations doesn't pertain to murder cases, it was ruled that the Family Secrets prosecution team was allowed a cushion of time regarding the nonmurder aspects of the case.

On the defense team, noted criminal attorney Rick Halprin represented Lombardo. Courtroom tacticians Marc Martin and Thomas Breen repped Jimmy Marcello. Paul "the Indian" Schiro's lawyer was the low-key Paul Wagner. Anthony "Twan" Doyle was represented by Ralph Meczyk. My father chose flashy Joseph "the Shark" Lopez. Lopez is a state-court master at dealing with the press and notorious for his shocking pink socks, shirts, and ties.

Defending my father was never an easy task. In my opinion, the problem is that my father doesn't trust lawyers, and he doesn't believe in telling them the whole story, which puts them at a disadvantage out of the gate. He doesn't like to pay lawyers, either.

There were varying opinions as to whether it was advantageous that Frank Schweihs be tried separately. As anxious as the FBI and Assistant U.S. Attorneys were to nail the German, there was concern that his presence might extend the trial by weeks or even months if he was included in the first round. Schweihs was a psychopath and unlikely to agree to stipulations made among the attorneys designed to speed up the trial process. As the trial date approached it became evident that Schweihs would be severed from the trial because he was too ill with cancer.

I had never met the German, although I knew his daughter Nora. We had mutual friends in Cicero, and she had married and later divorced Michael Talarico. The German was a time bomb who could go off at any moment. Any one of his outbursts could trigger a mistrial. In a criminal career that spanned fifty years, Schweihs had had hundreds of encounters with law enforcement personnel. Prior to sentencing in front of U.S. District Court Judge Ann B. Williams, Schweihs was described by the federal prosecutor as "one of the most violent people to come before this court."

Jury selection for the trial took almost three days, a short period of time considering the complex nature of the case. Prior to the three-month trial, the prosecution team won a ruling to cloak the names of the jurors, which was met with a strenuous objection by the defense. Family Secrets would be tried in front of an anonymous jury.

In preparation for battle, the prosecution team set up three separate war rooms—the smallest for storage, the largest as a strategy room, and the third serving as a general office. On the wall of the large conference room was a calendar and a dry-erase board converted into a three-month calendar constructed with masking tape and marking pens. The prosecution team gradually built a timetable, filling in dates with witness appearances color-coded in yellow, blue, and pink according to which witness was assigned to which prosecutor or agent. Mitch Mars was especially adept at sequencing the prosecution's witness appearances. John Scully, who had history with the most people, was assigned the longest list of witnesses. There would be approximately 130 witnesses, including those for the defense.

Defending the five was going to be a difficult proposition. It's not certain how much of a case a criminal attorney as talented as Rick Halprin had to work with representing the former fugitive Joey Lombardo. The juggernaut the defense team would have the most trouble sinking would be my prison yard tapes. The tapes, coupled with my commentary, represented evidence that would be extremely difficult to refute. How I would fare as a witness would hinge on how effectively I could break my father's gangster code for the jury. Following me on the stand would be my uncle, another star witness with a steel-trap memory and direct testimony as both executioner and participant. It felt strange that after nearly seven years apart, Uncle Nick and I would finally face my father again, though not as blood compatriots but as witnesses for the prosecution in court.

38.

BROKEN CODE

Since all the Family Secrets defendants except for Anthony "Twan" Doyle were in custody, the accused arrived at the federal courthouse accompanied by U.S. marshals via transport bus from the MCC. Before the judge arrived and the jury was ushered in, there was some quiet conversation, but not much, mostly a solemn quiet. Joey Lombardo and Jimmy Marcello talked to each other. Paul Schiro

sat silent. Twan Doyle entered the building flashing, to the delight of the assembled press, his retired badge and police photo ID to security guards. Once inside the courtroom, he acknowledged my father, something the jury did not see—a retired decorated police officer friendly with an Outfit crew chief. The two had a long history as friends and now were co-conspirators.

The government launched its case with Mitch Mars, the seemingly disorganized genius; John Scully, the scholarly patriarch; and T. Markus Funk, the youngest of the trio, and often the feistiest and most aggressive. To the concern of his colleagues, throughout the trial, Mars nursed a nasty cough. The agents kept the war room stocked with cough drops, aspirin, and boxes of Kleenex. Funk would often slip him one of his Ricolas. Mitch would usually dissolve a Life Saver or a cough drop in a glass of water, since he didn't want the jurors—who weren't permitted to eat while in the jury box—to see *him* sitting at the counsel table eating candy or breath mints.

Mars's golden rule was to never piss off the judge, so it was important for anyone associated with the government's case to go out of his or her way to make sure during the discovery process that each defense attorney had been given the necessary copies of scanned government documents.

Every morning my father would put on his smiling face—"Good morning, ladies and gentlemen of the jury. Good morning, your honor, Judge Zagel"—a gesture many saw as disingenuous. His routine attempts to engage in small talk with the prosecution team, seated only three feet away, were rebuffed.

While many of the victims' family members took seats in the gallery, very few members of the defendants' families turned up at the courthouse. Joe Lombardo's son, Joey junior, showed up, but my stepmother, Diane, made herself scarce—perhaps in part because the government characterized her as an unindicted co-conspirator. The prosecution argued to Judge Zagel that my father's conversations with Diane were not subject to husband-wife privilege, because, they charged, she had engaged in criminal conduct and spoken in coded language regarding "recipes" (illegal collections from gambling or juice loans) with my father while he was in prison.

My uncle and I would be permitted to attend the trial only as participants during our testimony on the stand. Outside of a few friends from the street—such as Shorty LaMantia's son Rocky—there was little support for my father. Virtually no one from my family, including aunts, uncles, and my mother, attended the trial.

Kurt was there primarily to witness our father's behavior. Well before the trial, upon hearing about my cooperation with the FBI, my mother, Kurt, and my youngest brother, Nicky, visited my father at FCI Milan. They explained to him that in the interest of the family they would not take sides. My dad agreed. Still, as the group was leaving, my father took Kurt aside and assured him that he could protect him from the wrath of the Outfit brought on by my uncle and me. In return, he asked Kurt to refute our testimony on the witness stand.

"I don't want to get involved," Kurt reiterated.

On the first day of jury selection Kurt called to tell me that a plastic bag containing a digital clock and what appeared to be three sticks of dynamite had been placed on his back door. He wasn't sure what to do about it. A few days prior, he had noticed a prowler dressed in black skulking around the backyard of his house. After he turned on the outdoor lights, the man fled through a hole in the back fence.

Then a spate of threatening notes turned up at Kurt's home. Seeing the acts as desperate, Kurt stood firm. When he discovered the explosive in his yard, he asked me to quietly send the FBI over to determine whether or not the bomb was authentic. (It wasn't.) Once news of the bomb threat hit the media, Kurt was inundated with reporters and cameras at his front door. The FBI offered Kurt and his family witness protection, but citing the media as a bigger problem, he refused and took his family to stay with his in-laws at their family complex in Chinatown.

The Family Secrets jury would be in for a history lesson about the Outfit. James Wagner of the Chicago Crime Commission set the stage by giving the jury a history of the Outfit dating back to Al Capone. Another key witness slated to testify was porn shop owner turned FBI informant William "Red" Wemette, who was being extorted by Joey Lombardo and Frank the German. Scheduled to appear were former burglar Bobby "the Beak" Siegel, Ernie "the Oven" Severino, Sal Romano, and bookmaker Michael Talarico. Another witness, Joel Glickman, was jailed early in the proceedings after refusing to testify. He was to be questioned about a juice loan that my father made back in the late sixties to an insurance executive Glickman worked for. After spending the weekend at the MCC courtesy of Judge Zagel and Markus Funk, Glickman was granted immunity and took the stand. Among the victims and their family members who would testify were Emma Seifert; Joseph Seifert; Dr. Pat Spilotro; and Michael Spilotro's widow, Ann, and her daughter, Michelle.

Once the trial was under way, John Scully presented the prosecution's opening statement, which homed right in on my father, who was accused of carrying out most of the murders. Scully was eager to smudge the mob's romantic appeal by citing the corrosive effects of organized crime on the victims and their families. "This is not *The Sopranos.* This is not *The Godfather.* This case is about real people, real victims."

In building its case, the prosecution would systematically go through each and every murder, beginning with Danny Seifert in 1974 and Michael Albergo in 1970. The remaining sixteen murders would be presented chronologically. Around the trial's midpoint, I would appear as the first star witness.

A few days before I was scheduled to testify, I was so emotionally charged that I could barely sleep. I was constantly on the phone with Lisa, my mother, and my brothers for support. It felt good knowing my family supported me and had my back. When I first agreed to cooperate, one of the conditions I asked of the FBI was to leave my family and my legitimate friends alone. To this day, the FBI has kept its word and has never once talked to my family or bothered any of my hardworking friends.

After going over my testimony with the prosecution team, I

entered the courtroom prepared. The first time I met John Scully, he did a great job of ripping into me during testimony preparation. I told Mr. Scully that I'd go to jail and sit for ten years if it meant taking my father off the streets and keeping him locked up. Not once did I ask for immunity or lie to protect myself. On the contrary, I did my time. I needed Markus Funk, Mitch Mars, and John Scully to pretend they were the best defense team in America, taking turns tearing into me, and they did a great job, much better, actually, than the actual defense attorneys.

The day before I was to testify, I asked Mr. Mars and Mr. Scully if I could go inside and get familiar with the surroundings once everyone had left the courtroom. Escorted by a few FBI agents and U.S. marshals, I spent a few minutes in the courtroom taking it in. I asked where my father would be sitting. After sitting silently on the witness stand for a few moments, I had the strangest feeling. Those moments prepared me for the battle I was about to wage against my father.

When it came time to be sworn in, I was ushered past where the news media were set up and inside the large ceremonial courtroom. Although every major television station and newspaper asked, I didn't grant interviews. It was evident that the victims' families were there to watch me and scrutinize every word I said.

Anticipating my first day on the stand, I was an emotional wreck. Seeing my father for the first time in over six years and knowing that I was beefing on him would be overwhelming. I felt lightheaded, unsteady. The government wasn't sure how effective a witness I would be. For the first day, I was scheduled to take the stand for about thirty minutes. Because of the upcoming Fourth of July holiday, I would then have time to regroup to get my emotions in check.

I walked into the courtroom and there were two tables on one side, three on the other. My dad sat about twenty feet away. There were U.S. marshals and FBI agents present. There was a gallery of news reporters. There were mob fans and groupies trying to find seats.

Then came the moment: me facing my father. As I walked straight toward the judge, I could see my father out of the corner of my eye.

I didn't exactly make a smooth entrance. When I walked into the courtroom and my dad saw me for the first time, my emotions kicked in. Instead of walking up to the box to get sworn in, I stepped up in front of the judge's bench. I thought he would swear me in. With my chin almost up on the judge's bench, I raised my hand. I realized I was more accustomed to sitting at the defendants' table. After the bailiff swore me in and I sat in the witness box, Mr. Scully asked me my name. I spoke with my mouth way too close to the mic. "FRANK CALABRESE." The room appeared to shake. The judge asked me, "Mr. Calabrese, could you please back it up a little?"

Scully asked me to point out my dad. I was told afterward that when I did, it was the first time during the whole trial that my dad didn't stand up and wave and smile to the jury. My father had the same awkward look on his face as I did: two people who were once close and who hadn't seen each other in years. At first he looked sad as the brokenhearted father in disbelief that I was actually doing this. It wasn't easy for me to accept that he was being tried as a mass murderer. I felt a shuddering outpouring of emotion. I wanted to run over and hug and kiss him. I also wanted to beat the life out of him.

I wasn't there to play games or to antagonize anyone. When I walked into the courtroom, I focused straight ahead. Whoever was going to ask me questions, I concentrated on him. During breaks I just sat in my chair, and while everybody else talked and joked around, I didn't talk to anyone. I was there on a mission. When someone asked me to speak, I spoke. When someone asked me to point to my father or Jimmy Marcello, I pointed. My dad was the one mugging, making faces and gestures and rolling his eyes. I believed this would backfire because the jury was watching him the whole time.

The stress of testifying would take a physical toll on me. At MCI Milan I had been diagnosed with multiple sclerosis; now, prior to going on the stand, I was so anxious, scared, and nervous that I needed a cane to walk straight.

When my father saw me walking with a cane, I saw a look in his eyes. It was almost as though he was concerned about me for a brief moment. It was a look I'll never forget and that's hard to describe. It was very affecting. He looked older, but in good physical shape, as strong as ever. Then his Outfit ways seemed to kick in. When I saw him whispering to his lawyer, I knew exactly what he was saying. He was telling Joe Lopez that by walking in with a cane, I was using an old Outfit trick he'd taught me. If the defense tried to challenge my use of the cane, I was ready to pull up my pant-legs and show them how the MS had eaten away the muscles in both legs. While I wasn't challenged in court, there were comments made by my father's team that my use of a cane was just a show. My doctor told me that I needed a cane due to the stress as my MS acted up. I used the cane the whole time I was in Chicago, but once the trial was over, the nervous twitching ended and I didn't need the cane anymore.

The first day, my father sat and listened. But once the tapes rolled and I commented on them, he started with the gestures. I could see him out of the corner of my eye. I could see the manipulative, abusive father back in control.

After the abbreviated first day of testimony, over the July 4 weekend I spent twelve-hour days preparing for my first full day of testimony. I knew that Dad would portray the case as a family dispute to distract attention from the tapes. Yet once I returned to the witness stand it was important for me to be truthful about my past with the crew. Otherwise the defense would rip me apart.

I owned up to the bad I had done. I was a half-assed gangster, collecting money, shaking people down, throwing bricks through windows, burning down a garage. I made it clear that I'd used and sold cocaine, and that I'd stolen from my father. I wanted to be as transparent as possible. What the jury saw was who I was. It wasn't my intention to gloss over my transgressions or my past. I didn't blame anybody else, whether it was my father, my uncle, or the crew. The temptation on the witness stand is to drag other people in and point the finger, but my uncle and I didn't do that. We took responsibility for our acts.

On Monday morning I testified about my tumultuous relationship with my father. I admitted to stealing and recounted how he stuck a gun in my face after he discovered the money was missing. I recounted his infamous words as he held the gun—a snub-nosed .38 revolver stuck inside a black dress sock—to my head.

"I'd rather have you dead than disobey me."

During my days testifying, I recalled making my weekly rounds collecting peep show quarters as a high school student with Uncle Nick. I spoke candidly about my cocaine habit and how I wildly spent and invested portions of my father's money. I described pleading guilty to being part of the crew and being sentenced to fifty-seven months in federal prison. My father wore a slight smirk on his face, scoffing at my testimony. Joseph "the Shark" Lopez explained his client's demeanor to the *Sun-Times* as "always smiling. He's a happy-go-lucky fellow." Yeah, sure.

As a high-profile witness, apart from my awkward entrance, I made few, if any, missteps on the witness stand. Ironically, I believe my strength on the stand was a result of how my dad had schooled me. Don't let people put words in your mouth, he'd said. If, to confuse me or make me look bad, an attorney asked me to say to the exact dollar how much money I had taken, I was honest. If I didn't know the exact amount, I said so. After a while, the judge and the jury got the point: I stole a large amount of money from him. Now let's move on.

I believe what made me valuable as a witness was my commentary on the tapes. I described in detail how the crew operated: collecting street tax, lending out high-interest juice loans, extorting people and businesses, and, at times, killing people. Besides testifying about the killings of William and Charlotte Dauber and Richard Ortiz and Arthur Morawski, I elaborated on the stories my father told on the yard, like the made ceremony. During the playback, Tony Ortiz, Richard Ortiz's son, leaned in and listened intently to my father's words recounting the 1983 murder of *his* father.

Once the heavily coded prison yard tapes were introduced as evidence, they needed to be played, then translated for the jury. As a witness, it was up to me to break the code by interpreting and translating each conversation, no matter how cryptic. It was imperative that the jury understand the gravity of these tapes.

At first a small portion of the tape would be played and stopped, sentence by sentence. Scully questioned me on each portion. Soon it became obvious that the piecemeal process was confusing the jury.

During a break, I suggested a better approach: play an entire section of the tape, and then in my own words I would thoroughly explain the conversation, after which Scully could ask me the questions. When we did this, I could see that the jury understood it better. There were no objections by the defense throughout the playing of the tapes.

Outside, one of the defense attorneys was asked by reporters why they didn't object. It was as if they wanted to stay as far away from the tapes as possible. I noticed that Judge Zagel had a copy of the transcripts and was closely following the conversations. I think he was checking to see if I was making stuff up. By the time I finished decoding the tapes, I was confident that the judge felt I was telling the truth.

The playback of the tapes recorded at Milan between Twan Doyle and my father proved problematic for the prosecution. I wasn't present in the visiting room when the tapes were recorded, so the defense could object to my interpretation and deciphering of the code words used in the conversations. As soon as Scully asked the first question, the defense immediately jumped up and objected. I wasn't present during the conversations, so how could I decode them?

Judge Zagel cleared the courtroom for a sidebar. After I spent a short time in the waiting room, Mitch Mars calmly approached me. He said the judge was going to allow me not only to explain the coded words, but to decode the conversations as I had on the other tapes. That showed the judge's faith in my testimony. Not once did the defense object, because it was obvious I knew what I was talking about.

But on cross-examination, Lopez did challenge me by arguing that during the prison yard conversations, I was "pushing the buttons and pulling the levers" to get my dad to talk, and that his responses were merely empty boasts. Lopez accused me of being an "actor" coached by the FBI. When asked why I didn't walk away from the Outfit life, I responded, "I did. Because I detested the Outfit and didn't like what I saw."

The defense implied that I had coerced my father into saying certain things, but what the jury saw was that you couldn't coerce a man like my father to say or do anything. I got him to open up. I don't know how I did it. I didn't think I could. I still can't believe I did, because my father never talked like that in his entire life.

Despite the prosecution's initial fears, I was turning in convincing testimony on the witness stand. When the defense tried to cross-examine me about pulling the gun out of the sewer with the Orange Peel Grapple and returning it to Uncle Nick, they brought up a discrepancy between my recollection and what was written up in the FBI's 302. Again, I stuck to my original story that I didn't retrieve the gun with the Orange Peel. Rather, I retrieved the gun with my hand and cleaned out the catch basin with the Orange Peel truck. Later I handed the gun over to my uncle. I told the court that I had no control over what an FBI agent wrote in his report. I knew that was the truth, and the jury believed me.

After I finished testifying I was escorted back down to the U.S. Attorney's Office. I had to sit down for a minute. When Luigi saw the look on my face and the tears streaming down, he asked me if I was okay. Of course I *wasn't* okay. Leaving the courtroom, I realized it was the last time I would see my father alive. That was overwhelming.

My uncle followed me on the stand and gave somber, chilling testimony that was also difficult to impeach. Dressed in a long-sleeved prison-issued sweatshirt and sweatpants, my uncle admitted to being a made member of the Outfit. Eclipsing my testimony in terms of drama, Nick gave a vivid account of the murders he had participated in.

As my father sat at the defendants' table, frequently wearing a grin, Nick recounted the murder and torching of Butch Petrocelli, the bombing of Michael Cagnoni, and the killings of Nick D'Andrea, Richard Ortiz, Arthur Morawski, Emil Vaci, John Fecarotta, Michael Albergo, and the Spilotro brothers. He recounted the bombings of a theater, a restaurant, and a trucking company.

"Did you in fact murder John Fecarotta?" Mitch Mars asked my uncle.

"Yes, I did. It was me, my brother Frank, and Johnny Apes. We got the okay from Jimmy LaPietra, who was our capo."

According to Nick's testimony, my father kept about $1.6 million in cash stashed around town, mainly in safety-deposit boxes. He told the story of the time he and my dad buried $250,000 in cash near our Williams Bay, Wisconsin, summer home, only to find out later that the bills reeked.

"Mildew," Nick recalled. "You could never get that smell out. We tried to use cologne but it only made it smell worse."

After four days of testimony for the prosecution, a circumspect Nick sadly referred to himself as "a coward, a chicken, and a rat" for not standing up to his brother and leaving the Outfit. He recalled my father's tendency toward violence, admitting that he feared his older brother should he stray from the Outfit course. On cross-examination, Lopez asked Nick if he really believed his brother would have shot him had he "froze up" on or refused a hit, to which he responded coldly, "My brother would have, yes."

As for the family businesses, when asked by Lopez if my father "put a gun to his [Kurt's] head" to stay with the crew, Uncle Nick shot back, "No, he put a fist in his face."

"And when did the beatings happen?"

"You name the time. The kids went through hell with their father."

"And they gave him hell, didn't they?"

"No, they did not," Nick answered back firmly.

Holding up under pressure, my uncle escaped the lengthy cross-examination unscathed.

"I am a killer," my uncle said sadly before stepping down. "But I am not a serial killer."

Once the defense was finished, the prosecution, eager to get him off the stand, asked only one question on redirect. Had he heard the prison tapes? (He hadn't.) Mars's single question about the tapes restricted the defense to asking only about the tapes. It was a subject the defense sorely wanted to avoid, so Uncle Nick was excused as the attorneys in the room shook their head in disbelief at Mars's shrewdness.

Much to the surprise of the prosecutors, three of the five defendants—Lombardo, my father, and Twan Doyle—took the stand. Who would have thought that the prosecution was going to have multiple chances to cross-examine three of their defendants? In a typical trial, the defendants don't testify; they like to exercise their right not to testify. But this was no typical trial. In a case like Family Secrets, nobody expected the defendants to testify, especially when there were incriminating audiotapes of them.

Twan Doyle had attempted to prepare himself for his time on the witness stand, but the street-smart Doyle, once tendered for cross-examination, had a difficult time explaining away why he said what he said to my father on the tapes. Indeed, his defense attorney seemingly tried to soften what he knew would be an impending blow, ending his direct examination with an odd statement: "I'm going to turn you over to Mr. Funk. He's a very good cross-examiner. . . . Good luck."

And Doyle did indeed have a tough go of it. For example, during Funk's confrontational cross-examination, Doyle visibly struggled when explaining that his prison conversation with my father about shoving an "electric prodder" up my uncle's rectum merely concerned recent psychiatric research Doyle had come across. Doyle claimed that he was only discussing this topic with my dad because this approach might help cure Nick of his "insanity." Funk characterized as "laughable" Doyle's assertions about this form of "shock treatment."

"Anthony Doyle, the Freud of the Chicago Police Department, relaying something he read about in the *Psychiatric Journal*?" Funk asked in response to a defense objection.

Under relentless cross-examination by Markus Funk, Twan Doyle finally lost his carefully monitored cool, angrily rising out of his seat and taking exception to a line of questioning about his physical admiration of my father.

Doyle made the point under direct examination that he was attracted to Frank Calabrese, Sr., when he was a young man because he was strong, worked out a lot, and had big muscles. It was a very strange direct examination. So on cross, Funk inquired about it a little further and Doyle misinterpreted what he was trying to imply, rising out of his chair and asking, "What are you trying to say, Mr. Funk?" Funk did not respond, but instead just looked at him.

Putting Joey Lombardo on the stand was a bold effort to sell the seventy-eight-year-old mobster as neighborly and fatherly. Dressed in a gray jacket and a silver tie, Lombardo flashed his quirky sense of humor when he remarked how cops were lousy tippers back when, as a young shoeshine boy, he gave them five-cent shines. Lombardo grinned and flirted with a blond court reporter. He chatted with the court's sketch artist. He reminisced about his athletic ability as a skater, a golfer, and a handball player as he turned his chair toward the jury while he spoke.

My father's charm on the stand was fleeting, as it didn't take long for his impatience and arrogance to surface. Nor did his snickering and groaning from the defendants' table bolster his cause.

Once a person has testified, the other side can comment on his demeanor. When my dad was audibly giggling while the court was going over a homicide that he had committed, it was fair commentary on his behavior for Funk to stop, point at him, and say, "Is there anything funny here?" Conversely, if the prosecutors had seemed afraid to point at my father or look him in the eye, it would have sent a message to the jury that the defendants were in charge. For a mob trial like Family Secrets, it was important to give the jurors and other people in the room the sense that the prosecution was not afraid of them.

As court-savvy as the defendants were, they were used to being catered to, feared, and treated like bosses. Thus they didn't respond well to being accused, questioned, and second-guessed in public. Inside their world, they'd always been the bosses. No one had ever talked back to my father, other than maybe Angelo or Johnny Apes. Thanks in part to my role in the pretrial preparation, not only was I ready for cross-examination, but the prosecutors, especially T. Markus Funk, really knew how to push my father's buttons by pointing at him, raising their voices, and questioning his authority. He was the boss of the crew, and he was not used to having some pipsqueak or some upstart challenging him, let alone making him look bad. The same went for Lombardo. They didn't take well to someone pointing at them or, in their eyes, mocking them and their testimony.

Taking the stand in his defense, complaining of bad hearing and playing the role of the feeble, elderly man, my father recalled his poverty-stricken childhood and how he grew up eating oatmeal for dinner, and how later, as a working man earning millions, he couldn't possibly have had time to perform the killings of which he was accused. As for his association with the Outfit, he insisted that his mentor, Angelo LaPietra, was not his boss.

"He did never control me—never!" he emphasized on the stand. "Many people feared him. Many people couldn't look him in the eye when they talked to him. I never had that problem."

Although I was not allowed to watch his testimony, my father's primary defense was that my family was conspiring to keep him in jail to steal his money, his jewelry, and the car collection with which he was obsessed. He rambled on about the two million dollars he claimed his family members had stolen from him, even as the prosecution objected. As a result, Judge Zagel removed the jury and threatened my dad with contempt if he continued to talk about it after the prosecution objected and the objection was sustained. My father recounted another bizarre tale about my uncle Nick giving him a sloppy holiday kiss on the lips.

"The kiss he gave for Christmas was a Judas kiss," he exclaimed. "My brother was like Alfredo in *The Godfather.* If he wasn't running things and screwing things up, he wasn't happy."

As for his reaction to my testimony, he could only conclude that I could "make Jesus look like the devil on the cross."

John Scully had delivered the opening statement, and Mitch Mars would handle the summary. Markus Funk was entrusted with the closing argument. As he prepared for his closing PowerPoint presentation, Mitch Mars sat in the back of the war room, reclining on a couple of chairs pushed together. He was shuddering from his unrelenting cold and hacking cough, his coat draped over his body like a blanket. Occasionally he'd shout out directions to Mike Maseth and Funk from the back of the room whenever he felt his team was spinning its wheels. Funk was having a difficult time finding his groove.

Having spent the last few years in the trial-intensive Narcotics unit, Funk was not as comfortable with the OC squad's more "scripted" approach to closing arguments. They did a practice round, but about an hour or so into it, he felt something was not right. Maseth and Funk decided to shelve the scripted approach and go back to delivering a closing like Funk would do in a normal multidefendant conspiracy case, working informally off the PowerPoint and doing it free-form instead of closely following prepared statements.

Having had only a few hours' sleep, Funk disappeared to collect his thoughts. Funk's free-form delivery ran five full hours over the course of two days. During his defendant-by-defendant, murder-by-murder, count-by-count survey of the prior months' evidence, Funk repeatedly and directly challenged my father's claims of innocence, taking my father to task for what he had done in life and how he had tried to use his time on the witness stand to distance himself from that conduct.

My father did not appreciate the attention. While discussing one particularly gruesome homicide, Funk caught my father smirking and chuckling to himself. He wheeled around, pointed at my father, and said to the jury, "See this man laughing? There is nothing funny here. There is simply nothing to laugh about in this case!" My father's smile vanished.

Mitch Mars continued the onslaught during his powerful rebuttal closing argument. In response to Mars's charge that my father had "left a trail of bodies in his wake," my dad blurted out a line that will go down in Family Secrets infamy.

"Dem are lies!"

The jury was not sequestered and was out for three days. On the fourth day, it delivered the verdict. On September 10, 2007, the five defendants were found guilty of racketeering and conspiracy, which included charges of loan-sharking, extortion, and illegal gambling. Over the objections of the defense, the jury took a weeklong break, during which time Judge Zagel revoked Twan Doyle's bail. The jury reconvened to deliberate a breakdown of who they felt was responsible for which murders. On September 27, which marked the thirty-third anniversary of the killing of Daniel Seifert, my father, the Clown, and Little Jimmy were convicted of murder.

My father was found "responsible" for the most killings: seven—those of Michael Albergo, William and Charlotte Dauber, Michael Cagnoni, Arthur Morawski and Richard Ortiz, and John Fecarotta. The jury was deadlocked on his responsibility for six of the deaths: those of Paul Haggerty, Henry Cosentino, John Mendell, Donald Renno, Vincent Moretti, and Butch Petrocelli. (At the time of sentencing, however, in determining if there were "aggravating circumstances," Judge Zagel would agree with Funk and also hold my father and his co-defendants legally responsible for those additional murders.)

James Marcello was found responsible for the murders of Anthony and Michael Spilotro. Joseph Lombardo was responsible for the murder of Daniel Seifert. The jury was deadlocked on Paul

Schiro's responsibility for the death of Emil Vaci. (At sentencing, Judge Zagel found Schiro did in fact participate in the Vaci homicide.)

The verdicts proved to be controversial to the victims' family members, who became very vocal about the outcome. Some had waited decades for justice and closure. Upon hearing the verdicts, Charlene Moravecek, the widow of Paul Haggerty, whose murder remained unaccounted for, cried out, "I've waited thirty-one and a half years for this?"

"I'm feeling pretty crappy," admitted Bob D'Andrea, after the jury deadlocked on whether Jimmy Marcello beat his father to death. "Deadlock might as well be innocent." Zagel later agreed with Funk that Marcello participated.

After my father was found responsible for shotgunning Richard Ortiz to death, his son, Tony Ortiz, reveled in the conviction. "Finally, it's over. It's closure! We've been waiting for this for a very long time. He won't be smirking any longer."

Once all five defendants were found guilty, a seventeen-month pause preceded sentencing. My uncle received immunity and a small amount of money deposited in his prison commissary account, allowing him to buy toiletries and small food items. His fate, along with the fates of the five defendants, would be decided by Judge Zagel in February 2009, when everyone—the defendants, the legal teams, and the victims' family members—reunited for sentencing. Two key players would be missing from this emotional event, with Funk remaining as the sole member of the trial team still in the employ of the G.

39.

THE ROAD TO JUSTICE

When Mitch Mars approached the witness stand to cross-examine Joe Lombardo, he leaned in and eyeballed the Clown for a few seconds. Lombardo, no stranger to lawyerly intimidation, leaned in and imitated Mars's penetrating stare.

"Mitch was the best lawyer I'd ever seen in my life, bar none," Mike Maseth once told me. "He was fast on his feet and he knew how to deal with witnesses and other lawyers. He knew how to deal with the judge. Nobody could get anything past him."

While Lombardo took the stand in his defense and denied his role as an Outfit gangster, Mars designated him as a capo of the Grand Avenue crew. He was not, Mars asserted, financier Allen Dorfman's errand boy, and he did more than conduct illegal dice games. The Clown, also known as Lumpy, embezzled and brokered multimillion-dollar deals with Dorfman. Mars wondered aloud how an ex–shoeshine boy lackey would score $2 million on a Dorfman-orchestrated transaction that cost Lombardo out of pocket $43,000.

Mars hammered away at Lombardo's involvement in the Seifert slaying, the prosecution's most challenging aspect of Operation Family Secrets. During closing arguments he presented seventeen reasons why Lombardo was guilty of murder. (When discussing the Spilotro case, Mitch gave the jury 240,000 reasons why Marcello was guilty of Tony and Michael's slayings—that would be the $240,000 that Marcello paid Uncle Nick to keep his mouth shut. Mars argued that someone would not pay that kind of money unless he had good reason to—like covering up a murder.)

Mars cross-examined Joey Lombardo and carved him up, according to court observers. It's not that he screamed or yelled—Mitch was only five foot seven and he was not flashy. Markus Funk, despite his years spent in the hallowed halls of academia, was more your prototypical prosecutor, an imposing six-foot-four blond opponent.

Yet every one of those mobsters knew Mitch because he had been the Chief of the Organized Crime Section of the U.S. Attorney's Office for the past fifteen years and had tried the most significant organized crime cases in the country. Honest to a fault and a man of unimpeachable integrity, Mitch usually credited his trial partners, FBI agents, and those who made contributions to the prosecution of a successful case.

During the trial Mitch had a persistent cough and was told by his colleagues to get to the doctor. If he had any other serious health problems during the trial, he didn't let on to his associates. Wanting to see it through to the verdicts, Mitch didn't visit the doctor until early October of 2007. He never returned to his beloved office.

Everybody assumed he had a cold. Right after the trial, he finally went to the doctor to get some tests. After Mike Maseth called up Mars and asked how the tests were going, Mars told Mike he couldn't get them done because his oxygen levels were too low. "What do you mean your oxygen levels are too low?" The doctors took an X-ray and found that he had a liter and a half of fluid in his lungs. They removed the fluid and did a CAT scan, and two days later the doctors diagnosed cancer in both lungs.

After hearing the news that he had lung cancer, Mars, a nonsmoker, quietly arranged for a leave of absence. Four months later, on Tuesday night, February 19, 2008, Mitch Mars died at age fifty-five.

The next morning Patrick Fitzgerald sent out a personal e-mail to his staff. "We lost a very dear friend and a treasured colleague today," wrote Fitzgerald. He praised Mars's long career of public service.

Mars first joined the U.S. government in 1977 as a staff lawyer for the House of Representatives, having served on the House investigation of the John F. Kennedy and Martin Luther King, Jr., assassinations. In 1980 Mars joined the Organized Crime Strike Force in Chicago, and in 1990 his office merged with the U.S. Attorney's Office. In 1992 Mars became the Organized Crime supervisor, a position he held until 2007, along with the title of Assistant U.S. Attorney.

Mitch Mars came from the South Side of Chicago, and like many of his Outfit adversaries, he rooted for the White Sox rather than the Chicago Cubs. In addition to convicting my father, James Marcello, and Joe Lombardo, Mars successfully prosecuted Albert "Caesar" Tocco, Ernest Rocco "Rocky" Infelise, Harry Aleman, Salvatore "Solly" DeLaurentis, cocaine dealer John Cappas, former Cicero mayor Betty Loren-Maltese, and former Cicero assessor Frank Maltese.

Mike Hartnett had done the Betty Loren-Maltese Cicero

case with Mitch Mars and recalled how the trial lasted thirteen pressure-packed weeks. Hartnett agreed that Mars was the best in a courtroom. Great directs, spectacular cross-examinations. He could tear someone apart, but he had such a great personality, he didn't come off as cocky or egotistical.

According to his colleagues, Mars became a prosecutor for just the right reason: to put criminals in jail. He didn't use it as a stepping-stone to go into the lucrative private sector. He treated federal agents and courthouse staff with respect. If Mitch was trying the case, the Feds knew they weren't going to lose. They didn't care which defense attorneys were on the other side. Mars would smoke them.

Another of Mars's contemporaries recalled Mitch's intuitive ability to zero in on a potentially hot case. Back in 1982 one of the suspects Mars was looking at was Paul "Peanuts" Panczko, a notorious robber and burglar who spent twenty-three years in and out of prison. Panczko had been involved in staking out a place. He and his cohorts got stopped by some Chicago cops (one of them being Dennis Farina, the future actor). Peanuts had a gun with him. Since he was a convicted felon, this was illegal.

When the case was brought in—you had to get an indictment approved by the U.S. Attorney—the government initially wasn't going to prosecute the case. But Mitch decided, "Let's go after him for this gun. He probably knows a lot and we need to keep him off the street."

Consequently, Peanuts Panczko cooperated and went into the Witness Protection Program, but not before he wore a wire against other mobsters, including James "Dukey" Basile. Mars's move created a chain reaction, and after he was busted, Dukey wore a wire against Jerry Scarpelli, another mob killer involved with the Wild Bunch.

Unlike many lawyers who sit in their spacious offices and have a hard time relating to the average person, Mitch *was* the average person. If he went to meet somebody, he would drive his own car and run out into the rain with the hood of his jacket up. He wasn't the almighty guy. Although he was smarter than many, it wasn't always about doing things his way. He listened intently, and that was why he was able to prosecute our case so flawlessly.

Mars had a bottom-line way of getting to the facts. For example, during the Family Secrets trial, Uncle Nick testified about the number of bosses who were at the Bensenville house for the ambush and murder of the Spilotros. Many were skeptical that so many mob higher-ups would actually be there. Jimmy Marcello's lawyer, Marc Martin, called Nick a liar and questioned his testimony about the killers wearing gloves. Why wouldn't the streetwise Spilotro brothers, Martin asked, flee after seeing a bunch of mobsters waiting for them wearing gloves?

"They [the Spilotros] weren't going to get out of the house no matter what they thought," Mars replied. "[The mobsters] could have worn T-shirts that said, 'We're Here to Kill the Spilotros.' It didn't matter. They weren't getting out of there."

On February 23, 2008—almost a year before sentences were handed down—funeral services were held for Mitchell Mars in a village named, appropriately, Justice, Illinois. The road to Justice was closed as the motorcade drove west from Chicago—which would have irritated Mars for the inconvenience it might have caused the average citizen.

Beside each on-ramp to the expressway, people waved. Later, an honor guard presided over his viewing at the Damar Kaminski Funeral Home in Justice. Three thousand people showed up between 3 p.m. and 9 p.m. on a workday. People who had never met Mars waited in a line for two and a half hours to pay their respects and view the casket.

One person who came through the line said to Mitch's mom, "I never met your son but I just wanted to come and say thank you. You raised a great son. He did great things for this community. We need more people like him."

John Scully delivered the eulogy at a private Catholic service at St. Cletus Cathedral in LaGrange the following day. Later that week, a memorial ceremony was held at the Dirksen Federal

Building. The ceremonial courtroom was filled with six hundred fellow professionals, and Mike Maseth spoke to the crowd.

Was Family Secrets Mars's greatest case? Who knows? But I think it is fair to say that Family Secrets was the culmination of his career. He'd done a lot of mob cases, more than any other person in the history of Chicago. Make no mistake, Mitch was a thorn in the Outfit's side.

"Criminal cases are about accountability and justice," said Mitch Mars during the closing arguments of the trial, "not only for the defendants, but also justice for our system, justice for our society, and justice for the victims. Our system works. It is the greatest system in the world. But it only works when those who should be held accountable are held accountable."

40.

I KEEP THINKING THIS IS A DREAM

Five weeks after the guilty verdicts were announced, Mitch Mars sent a letter to my father's lawyer, Joe Lopez, stating that prosecutors Mars and Funk had met with an anonymous jury member regarding an

alleged threat that my dad had directed to U.S. Attorney Funk during the trial's contentious closing arguments. According to the letter, a copy of which was sent to Judge Zagel, the juror "partly heard and partly read" my father's lips saying to Funk, "You're a fucking dead man." According to the letter, during deliberations, three other jurors "confirmed the juror's observations and heard Mr. Calabrese say the same thing."

Lopez dismissed the threat as "nonsense," the figment of "an overactive imagination." But the accusation set off alarms among the co-defendants. Rick Halprin, Lombardo's attorney, stated, "I have grave concerns about this. This is, to say the least, novel. You would assume it impacted their [the jury's] thought process. We know from the letter that one-third of them talked about it."

Marc Martin, representing Jimmy Marcello, claimed that from the start of the trial, Marcello had been angling for a severance from my father, his grumbling and snickering co-defendant. "Marcello has been complaining about this since day one and this just adds more fuel to the fire," Martin told the press, and he vowed to raise the issue during posttrial motions. He questioned whether the prosecutors broke the rules by meeting with the juror without the court's permission.

"My client has more brains than that," Lopez responded. "We were surrounded by FBI agents and U.S. Attorneys and spectators and nobody heard anything, and now a month later? Why wasn't something said immediately?"

During trial testimony regarding my dad, Joey Lombardo was overheard saying, "Man, I'm tied to the bumper of the car this guy's driving and he's dragging me over the cliff with him."

Judge Zagel called for an unusual closed-door hearing to "establish the details surrounding the alleged remarks." While the defense attorneys requested a retrial once the jurors were called back and questioned, Judge Zagel declined such action, opting to call in the juror who had originally stepped forward. During the hearing, the juror was asked questions and Funk was put under oath and cross-examined by defense counsel. Judge

Zagel, having heard all the evidence he needed, ruled that my father had in fact uttered the threat. Another set of facts had been resolved against my dad.

Three months later, on June 11, 2008, it was time for Frank Schweihs to face the music. Schweihs was as treacherous on the streets as my father. Potential witnesses were hoping that the German would die before his trial date so that they wouldn't have to take the stand. Ailing from cancer and emaciated, he was confined to a wheelchair, which didn't rob the German of any of his trademark charm. During the criminal hearing, the seventy-eight-year-old Schweihs struggled out of his wheelchair and gazed over at Funk, who was to first-chair (lead) the prosecution, and called him out. "You making eyes at me? Yeah, you . . . you making eyes at me?"

Funk did not respond verbally, but the look he shot Schweihs spoke for itself.

Seated near Schweihs was another federal prosecutor, Amarjeet Bhachu. Bhachu, a Sikh, wore a turban, which further irritated the irascible gangster.

"Where are we, in a foreign country?"

Schweihs's trial was scheduled to start in October 2008, with Funk leading the team, and prosecutors Bhachu and Marny Zimmer backing him up, but the German wouldn't make it—lung cancer and a brain tumor claimed him six weeks later. His funeral was marred when the body was delivered late to the mortuary. His family, already upset that Schweihs had passed away without any family members present, was more distressed when his funeral was delayed after the Cook County medical examiner, by regulation, demanded that the body be examined because Schweihs had died in custody. "Mobster's Late for His Own Funeral," the *Sun-Times* headline smirked, highlighting that the German was someone only a mother or a close family member could love. This is the same Schweihs that mob boss Jimmy Marcello referred to as "Hitler," as in "Give it to Hitler," the order to murder someone. An anonymous "mourner" showed up at the funeral parlor and was asked why he attended. He replied, "I just wanted to make sure he was dead."

By September of 2008, with Frank Schweihs dead and buried, Judge Zagel quashed the notion of a Family Secrets retrial for four of the defendants, clearing the way for final sentencing. But prior to his sentencing, my father would pull one more stunt that would land him deeper in federal solitary confinement. As a result of a bizarre eighteen-page letter that was smuggled out, typed up, and e-mailed to Frank Coconate, a Chicago political activist and longtime friend of both me and my dad, the letter and additional information emerged indicating that my father intended to make good on his threat to kill Funk. He was then transferred to the MCC's toughest lockdown.

Coconate and I had a long history dating back to when we both worked for the city of Chicago. My dad took an instant liking to Coconate, one of my closest friends and running buddies, a brash personality with a history of taking on local Chicago politicians and city officials. Coconate was one of the few among my friends who hung out socially with my father and Diane in Florida, where the Calabrese family vacationed.

A gadfly, Coconate, after receiving the text via e-mail, surrendered the contents of the note to local ABC newsman Chuck Goudie. Whether or not the opening sentence, "Hi to my friend how are you and your family doing?" is a veiled threat to Coconate's family, most of the stream-of-consciousness writing is directed at trying to enlist Coconate to take to the streets and investigate the dangling factors involving my father's case. Part of the text is fixated (to the point of obsession) on the "disappearance" of a stable of antique cars that my dad had stashed in Huntley, Illinois.

Throughout the trial, my father maintained that I had stolen his automobiles. The topic persisted until Judge Zagel, with the jury removed, dealt with the subject by calling witnesses and trying to get to the bottom of his accusations. Failing to find any relevance to the case or to my father's culpability, the subject of his missing antique cars was set aside.

The Coconate letter itself is a fascinating study. On one level, it's the ramblings of a maniac. On another, it's a mad manipulator at work. He sets up the letter by baiting Coconate, an extremely jealous man involving anything to do with his wife, whom I dated in high school.

> While I was away at Milan, with my son, he told me some ridiulas [*sic*] lies about you and your wife. . . . I would like to tell you what he said, but I would rather tell you in person about you and your wife. You will not be happy.

Throughout the letter are a series of questions and reminiscences put to Coconate.

> Do you remember when you would come by the house, with my son, and your wife, [did you] ever see me mistreating my boys or their wives?
>
> Question. You remember how Jr. was so humble, and kind to me when we were at Miland [*sic*]? Did you not see him hug and kiss me, and tell me that he loved me?
>
> Question. Tell me everything you can in regards to Frankie telling you how he wanted to set me up. . . .
>
> Again please think hard. I want you to please tell me anything you can about my son Kurt or his brother Frank. If they were involved in buisness(es) [*sic*] . . .
>
> Do you know if Jr. has been spending a lot of money? And where has he been spending it at?

Toward the end of his frantic screed, my father goes on a religious rant that twists his interpretation of Christianity and the Bible (paraphrasing Mark 13:12) to fit his circumstances. This from the man who referred to the Apostles' Creed as "Apollo Creed." He goes on in part,

> Did you ever read the Bible? If you read it you would understand how smart those people 2,000 years ago were. I started reading it because a could [good friend] of mine sent it to me a month after I was locked up. It's amazing, how the Bible tells you

> things about what's happening in our lifes [*sic*] today, that was happening then. It also tells you in the Bible that the son will betray father, father will betray son, brother will betray brother, along with other family members. All because of money and earthly material things.

Now in solitary confinement in an environment reserved for terrorists and enemies of the state, and because of his veiled threats to us and his extraordinary direct death threat to a federal prosecutor, my dad is now closely monitored and restricted to one visitor and one fifteen-minute phone call every couple of weeks.

With prosecutor John Scully retired and prosecutor Mitch Mars deceased, it was left to Markus Funk to handle all of the Operation Family Secrets sentencing and other posttrial litigation. My father wasn't the first of the Operation Family Secrets defendants to be sentenced. Preceding him was Dennis Johnson, described as a "bit player" and the one bright spot among the eleven indicted co-defendants. He received six months in federal prison for his part in converting video poker games into barroom gambling devices while working for Jimmy Marcello's M&M Amusement. Johnson was remorseful and vowed to change his ways.

"Take a chance on me," he pleaded with Judge Zagel. "I'm a great person, a good person. I help people whenever I get a chance." While the judge took that chance, Johnson's partners weren't as fortunate. His brother Thomas Johnson and Joseph "Family Man" Venezia received thirty and forty months respectively.

Mickey Marcello received eight and a half years for his part in gathering information for his imprisoned half brother, including his help in instituting four thousand dollars in monthly hush money payments to my uncle's family. Nick Ferriola, one of my father's street crew errand boys, received three years. Although the jury was deadlocked on Paul "the Indian" Schiro's role in killing his friend Emil Vaci, he was sentenced to twenty years. Anthony "Twan" Doyle was sentenced to twelve years. His annual police pension of thirty thousand dollars was revoked.

The combined restitution and forfeiture amount for the Family Secrets defendants totaled over twenty million dollars. In addition, the prosecution made the novel request that the estates of the non-career-criminal victims be reimbursed for the lost wages resulting from the homicides. Judge Zagel agreed with Funk's legal maneuver, and held the defendants additionally responsible for an additional seven-million-dollar restitution award.

On Wednesday afternoon, January 28, 2009, at 2:40 p.m., my father was ushered into Judge Zagel's courtroom, dressed in an orange prison jumpsuit with his glasses strangely tied around the back of his head with a torn strip from a white undershirt. Prior to sentencing him on the three counts—the RICO, the extortion of Connie's Pizza, and the bookmaking charges—the judge scheduled the victim impact statements to be heard. Such statements are designed to give crime victims the opportunity to use the criminal justice system as a public forum to describe the personal effect a defendant's crimes had on them and their families. After the victims' families, prosecutor Funk would have his say, and then my father would address the court, after which he would immediately be sentenced.

First up was Charlene Moravecek, one of the most emotional speakers representing the victims' families. It was charged that my father had slit the throat of her husband, Paul Haggerty. (The jury deadlocked in assigning my dad responsibility for Haggerty's death, but Judge Zagel agreed with Funk, holding my father legally—and financially—responsible for the cold-blooded execution.)

Moravecek had waited over thirty years to face my dad. After addressing the judge, Moravecek turned around to my father and asked rhetorically, "Where was God thirty-two years ago when you slit his throat?

"You broke my heart, but you'll never take away my dignity," she added.

"God bless you," my dad answered.

"Don't even try," Moravecek shot back, staring my father

down. She was escorted out of the courtroom by the victim-witness advocate seated at the prosecution table.

The most potent statement came from Tony Ortiz, whose father, Richard Ortiz, was shotgunned to death by my uncle and Jimmy DiForti while my dad watched from the car. Tony, who was twelve years old at the time, came from a family of ten children. He described to the court how he quit high school to help support his family after they lost their house, and how, without his father to cheer him on, he gave up his one true passion, playing baseball. He described Richard Ortiz as a good father and said that in spite of his tragic death, something good came out of it. Tony became a devoted husband and father to four children, not letting a day go by without expressing his love to his wife and kids.

As the victims addressed the court, my father barely seemed to be paying attention; he had his head down and scribbled notes on a pad of paper. The overall theme of many of the family members' outrage was my father's snickering and laughter during the trial. Seated among the victims waiting to speak were my brothers, Kurt and Nicky.

Right up to the last minute that morning, Kurt didn't know whether he should appear. He decided he needed to air his feelings, to get them out. He and Nicky ended up sitting with the victims. Nobody knew Nicky because he had kept a low profile at the trial. When Kurt got up, he was nervous and apprehensive about whether the victims' family members felt he belonged. Security was tight, with my dad surrounded by three U.S. marshals. As Kurt got up to speak, attorney Lopez raised an objection. Kurt hardly qualified as a victim.

"Not on the same level as these people," Kurt declared, "but I am definitely a victim of my father."

Kurt went on to speak about the verbal and physical abuse he and his brothers took. The beatings. The thrown objects. At the end of his statement, Kurt had one final demand.

"I would like you to apologize for never being a father to me. You were an enforcer, not a father, who forced me to become something I never wanted to be. I had no choice."

Dad defiantly shouted back, accusing his "worthless" son of lying and stealing. "I never hit you. I never abused you. All the neighbors will tell you that."

Joe Lopez stood up and voiced disapproval to the judge, arguing that the proceedings had devolved into a media circus, insinuating that the victims' statements were "a dog and pony show." After his comment, an air of disgust and disbelief hung briefly over the courtroom. Kurt was taken aback, especially when my father looked like he was going to come after him. He couldn't understand why the judge didn't stop him from yelling out. That threw Kurt a little.

After Kurt's statement, the defense presented a series of arguments, some of which dealt with the sentencing reports, the combination of murder charges and RICO, and an argument about the viability of a conspiracy. There was an argument regarding the relevance of including the Nick Sarillo bombing, that Jimmy Marcello was not my dad's boss, and that my father shouldn't have to pay restitution to the victims of crimes committed prior to certain restitution laws being enacted. Judge Zagel overruled everything, citing the restitution question as a civil matter.

During allocution, my father launched into a chaotic cascade of accusations and denials, at one point even turning away from the lectern and apologizing directly to Funk for the death threat the jurors "thought" they had heard my father make and for the "inconvenience" this had caused Funk and his family. He was sorry that Kurt was threatened during the trial, but he maintained that he had had no part in it. He was not laughing at the victims (which the judge granted him), but at the false testimony that came from his family members. He wasn't a part of the Outfit, nor did anybody from that organization give him money. He didn't attend their dinners. He was an individual, which was why he was respected. He didn't beat or hurt anyone for money. It was his policy to never put hands on anyone who couldn't pay. He charged 2 percent for legal business loans. He had already done his time for loan-sharking. He'd paid his debt to society. Why was he a part of this trial?

My father bounced from one subject to another in a shaky voice, sometimes without finishing a previous thought, already on to the next. Which family member stole $3 million from him? Who stole $240,000 in equity from the home of his mother, Sophie Calabrese? His son Frankie stole from him, putting junk up his nose and stealing his cars. His son Kurt stole from him. He bemoaned his health problems. He wore a pacemaker. He was dealing with heart and pituitary problems, not to mention high blood pressure.

"There's no reason for me to be living in that hellhole," he repeated over and over, referring to his solitary confinement.

He didn't deserve the treatment he was getting. He demanded to be strapped to a lie detector and tested. He had killed no one, nor was he a party to any murders. He urged his people to quit bookmaking and make an honest living. The threats against Kurt were orchestrated to poison the jury's minds against him.

"I would be glad to sit with all the jurors, though I don't know their names, have a talk, and they would see a different man than the one they were afraid of, and they would know that I was not guilty."

My dad spoke for forty-five minutes. He had proof that I had stolen his antique automobiles. He only "held" money for Johnny Apes. God was his master. He wasn't anywhere near any of the crime scenes. He said that I had seen every gangster movie ever made, and all I wanted was to be a gangster. He told me I had no business running around "with those kinds of people." He had never done business with Jimmy Marcello. The papers were full of lies. The jury was tainted.

"I keep thinking this is a dream. This isn't reality."

In a bizarre gesture, he referred to the late Mitch Mars: "I'm sorry to hear about Mr. Mars. I heard several people crying for him. Sounds like terrible death. I hope I don't die of cancer."

Then he called for a minute of silent prayer. The judge gazed at him incredulously. Some in the courtroom interpreted my dad's behavior as showing he was nervous and frightened while addressing the court. Although I wasn't there, I must respectfully disagree. My father was not scared. After they removed the tumor close to his pituitary gland, his memory slipped a bit. He's on a lot of medication. The shaking and the nerves, forgetting things, skipping over subjects—those were not fear, but his illness and his rage coming out simultaneously. He always had difficulty controlling his words, his emotions, and his thoughts when the terrible rage took over.

As for his sitting in a room with twelve jurors and convincing them he's the nicest guy in the world, you know what? He could! I've seen him do it many times with me and my family, with counselors in jail. Even U.S. marshals assigned to watch him and his co-defendants, perhaps because they were to some extent "starstruck" or otherwise fell under his spell, treated him noticeably better than the "average criminal," laughing at his jokes and making small talk with him before Judge Zagel assumed the bench. Watch him go in and out of different personalities. His bottom jaw juts out. His teeth clench. His eyes get glassy.

Almost every adversity in my father's life was dealt with and decided by a sit-down. In a mob sit-down, you can sway people into believing certain things by avoiding the main points of contention. He's the master of the sit-down. But a trial is different. At a trial, the judge keeps things on point, and the prosecutors, not operating in awe or fear of any defendant, know that you, as a defendant, are now on their "turf." You can't stray from the central issues or from the truth. And that's what sank my father. The emergence of truth.

At 4:55 p.m., Judge Zagel had the final say.

Responding to a letter written on my father's behalf, Judge Zagel found it reprehensible that my father categorized many of his victims as drug dealers and criminals deserving of their fates, and that society had in some cases actually benefited financially from their deaths. Zagel was openly disgusted with my father's denial and his greed, and especially with the callousness of his laughing at certain testimony that seemed funny to him. What Judge Zagel found extraordinary was the testimony of my uncle and me against our own blood. It was felt we were credible witnesses, and it was his family that ultimately buried him and sealed his fate.

"Perhaps you do not have a loving family," Judge Zagel surmised.

On the RICO charge, my father was sentenced to separate sentences of life in prison for each of the homicides the jury tagged him with. For the second count of extortion, he received 240 months. For his bookmaking activities, he got another 60 months. In the event that an appeals court throws out one or more counts, the time will keep running on the remaining convictions.

"Your crimes are unspeakable and my sentence is shut," Zagel continued. "If for any reason you are released from prison, you will go to a custodial center."

Judge Zagel threw the book at my dad. He received multiple sentences of natural life, plus twenty-five years. I would have liked to have been there, standing next to and supporting my brothers. But I didn't need to stand in front of my father and point a finger and challenge him with dirty or mean looks.

I had no idea what kind of circus he and his lawyers would put on. On the other hand, had I gone and watched him come out as an old man who was remorseful, that would have bothered me. You're looking at two people inside one body. One is this vicious man who could take your life in a second. Then there's the other man, a loving father that I'd want to care for.

In the weeks that followed, Judge Zagel finished sentencing the remaining Family Secrets defendants. Joey "the Clown" Lombardo was sentenced after Judge Zagel remarked, "In the end, we are judged by our actions, not by our wit or our smiles. In cases like this, we are judged by the worst things we have done, and the worst things you have done are terrible."

The Clown would be sentenced to life in prison, primarily for the murder of his once-close friend, Daniel Seifert. Lombardo had this to say to Seifert's wife and two sons: "First, I want to say to Emma Seifert, Joe Seifert, and Nicky Seifert, I was sorry for the loss then, I'm sorry for the loss now. I want the court and the Seifert family to know I did not kill Danny Seifert and had nothing to do with it, before, during or after. . . . Where is the evidence, Funk? Where is the evidence?"

Leaving the courthouse three decades after her husband's murder, Emma Seifert admitted, "I'll never feel safe."

As for James "Jimmy Light" Marcello, in a far less dramatic atmosphere than the sentencing of my father or Lombardo, Judge Zagel handed down a sentence of life in prison. Little Jimmy was found responsible for the murders of Tony and Michael Spilotro. In a strange twist of irony that had become the trademark of Operation Family Secrets, during the time leading up to the trial, investigators discovered that Marcello and his brother had received information concerning the fact of, and nature of, my uncle's cooperation with the Feds. They had secretly obtained this information from none other than decorated Deputy U.S. Marshal John Ambrose, who was on two of Nick's top-secret witness security details. Following Ambrose's 2009 trial, which was handled by prosecutor Funk, Judge John F. Grady sentenced Ambrose to hard time in a Texas federal penitentiary for endangering my uncle's life and for besmirching his badge and the trust of his colleagues.

When it came time for James Marcello's own sentencing, he showed no emotion, barely nodding his head. He was clad in a sport coat and slacks instead of prison orange.

"I regret you didn't live a better life," Zagel said to Marcello, "but you will have to pay for your crimes."

The final Family Secrets tally of sentences went like this:

Frank Calabrese, Sr.: Multiple life sentences, plus 300 months
Joey "the Clown" Lombardo: Life
James "Little Jimmy" Marcello: Multiple life sentences
Paul "the Indian" Schiro: 20 years
Anthony "Twan" Doyle: 12 years
Michael "Mickey" Marcello: 8.5 years
Nick Ferriola: 3 years
Joseph "Family Man" Venezia: 40 months

Thomas Johnson: 30 months
Dennis Johnson: 6 months

That left my uncle, Nick Calabrese. What would be his fate? How would the judge take into account his participation in fourteen murders while factoring in his cooperation and testimony in putting away the primary players and leaders of the Chicago Outfit?

In anticipation of my uncle's sentencing, once again I put pen to paper.

41.

THE UMBRELLA EFFECT

In 1995, before the Calabrese clan was herded off to prison, Uncle Nick took it upon himself to see Johnny Apes, the Outfit underboss to whom he reported. Nick complained to Johnny that his brother had involved his sons in his legal problems and wasn't doing anything to keep us from going to jail.

"What do you want me to do?" Johnny Apes asked Nick.

"I'm just telling you. You're the boss."

Johnny Apes handed my uncle a pistol. "This is the best I can do."

A few months later, I sat with Uncle Nick. By then, we were both estranged from my dad.

I said, "I don't know what to do. I'm on the run from my father and I know you're not talking to him, either."

Uncle Nick offered me the pistol that Johnny Apes gave him.

Prior to his death in 1999, Angelo LaPietra made a comment to his granddaughter Angela that my father should never have brought Kurt and me into his business, and that it was a cardinal sin that should have been dealt with by the bosses.

In January 2001, six years before the Family Secrets trial, I left Chicago and moved to a rural Cary, Illinois, town house and reunited with Lisa and my two children. A year later, we decided to leave the Midwest. The family was getting along well. During that time, I gradually shared bits of information with Lisa about my ongoing cooperation with the FBI OC squad and Agent Mike Maseth. Once the indictments fell, a major Mafia trial was now on the horizon. After Lisa and I received threatening calls that we suspected came from one of my father's surrogates, I realized it would be best if my family left Illinois to start a new life elsewhere.

Wanting to go someplace warm, at first I looked into relocating to Florida, but I didn't find anything affordable. A trip west to Nevada didn't pan out either. After a pit stop in Arizona, I lined up an appointment with a local real-estate agent. I phoned Lisa with the news. I had put in a lowball bid on a modest single-family home in a cul-de-sac. Arizona wasn't only a haven for retired golfers and ex-gangsters. The schools were good, and there were plenty of children in the neighborhood. Arizona's dry climate was less likely to aggravate my MS symptoms than were the humidity and cold of Chicago.

At the beginning of June 2002, I loaded up my family for the long drive to the Southwest. The government provided me with a modest stipend to relocate. The sum, dispensed monthly, was markedly less than what a company in the private sector might pay an employee to move cross-country. We were Arizona-bound.

The Witness Security Program was never an option. Had my family and I gone into WITSEC, I would have become a man with no history or past, which I felt would permanently limit me to low-paying jobs. Being in WITSEC would have meant giving up contact with family and friends, something I wasn't willing to do. I also felt it would do grave harm to my children if they had to conceal their real identities.

Besides, I'm not one to run and hide. It's not how my dad raised me.

Arriving in Arizona, I opened up a West Coast office of a skin care company of which I had part ownership. After a couple of years of successfully building the business, I was offered a buyout and decided it was time to do what I loved the most: go into the restaurant business and make pizzas.

Lisa and I opened a boutique pizza parlor in an unassuming strip mall. The bistro served quality Chicago thin-crust pizza along with some of the same Italian entrées I whipped up during my days working at Armand's in Elmwood Park. Lisa became the salad queen of the eatery, and as we built the business, I worked seven days a week to make it a success. Settling into new surroundings, I sat with Lisa and the kids to explain what I had been through during the past decade. Back with my family, I would put the lessons of my relationship with my father to work on my own children. I vowed that together we would have a loving, team-driven family unit.

By the summer of 2007, when CNN began broadcasting coverage of the Family Secrets trial, my dad's face filled the television screen. Friends from Chicago and neighbors who knew the Calabrese name began asking questions. Then some of the kids' friends at school discovered on the Internet the murderous ways of "Grandpa Poppi." Amazingly, the kids and I learned how nonjudgmental Arizona residents could be. ("A few of the kids at school thought we were cool," my daughter, Kelly Calabrese, recalled.) The Family Secrets trial added another Arizona angle when Anthony Doyle, who had retired and settled in the small desert town of Wickenburg, Arizona, was returned to Chicago to stand trial.

While the children adapted to their new home, Lisa was concerned about their safety. During the trial, journalists and news vans flocked to our pizza joint, much to the displeasure of the strip's landlord. When the hair salon next door alerted me that reporters were asking questions about their new neighbor's past, something had to give.

Lisa became frightened by unsavory-looking characters that showed up in the mall. With increased trial publicity, she worried that if I continued to make myself accessible around the restaurant and someone from the Outfit tried to kill me, it could jeopardize the safety of our children, our employees, and our patrons.

Luigi Mondini, my handling agent, and Assistant U.S. Attorney John Scully flew into Arizona to reassure Lisa. I was undaunted and ready to complete my mission. About that time, the U.S. Attorney's Office and the FBI worked with me on my pending testimony. Before I was flown back to Chicago, for security purposes, I was holed up in a secret location in preparation for my appearance on the stand.

Responding to Lisa's fears, Luigi secured a place in a gated compound residence in Tucson for me to prep the next five weeks. Lisa and I decided to close the restaurant for the summer, with hopes of reopening in the fall after the trial. We decided that if word circulated that I was temporarily in protective custody, the rest of the family would be safe. Although there was no evidence that I or the family had been stalked by members of the Outfit, there was speculation that my father had hired private detectives to locate me. An alarming moment occurred when a man in a Jeep with Illinois license plates sped up to the front of our house and screeched his tires loudly. It turned out to be a friend of a neighbor, who, ironically, was an ex–New York City cop.

After the Operation Family Secrets convictions and sentencing, life for my family in Arizona returned to a semblance of normality. Although my father currently serves his prison sentence in solitary confinement apart from the general population at the U.S. Medical Center for Federal Prisoners (MCFP) in Springfield, Missouri, his presence still lingers miles away in the Southwest.

Lisa calls it the Umbrella Effect. The fear of him doesn't stop simply because he's locked up. To this day, Lisa has nightmares about the man. His aura penetrates prison walls. A guy like Frank Calabrese, Sr., doesn't just affect one person. He looms over us like a large umbrella—from me to my wife and her immediate family, to my kids, and to the friends of my children. Not once did my father seem to realize how his actions affected those around him.

As for my personal safety, I'm pragmatic. If people can kill presidents, they can kill me. Nobody is invincible and completely safe in today's world.

After the publicity surrounding the trial, the verdicts, and the subsequent sentencing, Lisa and I reluctantly closed down our pizza parlor. When I joined a new company I met with my manager to explain my past.

I gave my boss the heads-up. We talked man-to-man. Some of the people who now worked with me were people I had known at the restaurant, so I figured it was only a matter of time before the word got out. Besides, I didn't want to blindside my boss. I told him about my past and that I would be glad to answer any questions. If there was a problem, I would rather walk away than make him fire me.

He told me it was admirable that I had taken a bad situation and turned it into a positive. Not having walked in my shoes, after learning my story, he felt fortunate that *he* had grown up in a hardworking family with a father who was kind to him. He hoped that I would stick around.

On December 1, 2008, ten years after my fateful letter to Special Agent Tom Bourgeois, I sent another letter, this time to Judge Zagel concerning the fate of Uncle Nick, who was to be sentenced on March 26, 2009, for his role in Operation Family Secrets.

The letter read in part:

> I want the court to know that while my uncle did some terrible things, he is a good man. By testifying, he was trying to do the right thing. While it isn't my intention to justify anything he has done, I know in my heart that he is ready to spend the rest of his life as a productive member of society.
>
> It was extremely difficult to testify against my uncle and take him away from his family. He was there for everybody; putting their needs first. . . . I believe in my heart that if my uncle received a second chance, he would be a model citizen and family man. I would put my freedom on the line to guarantee it.

Uncle Nick cooperated in January 2002, and after completing his racketeering sentence in November 2002, he remained in custody, working with Mike Maseth and the other FBI agents. As he testified, "I let fear control my life, and beneath that fear was a coward who didn't walk away from that life."

My uncle was sentenced to twelve years and four months for his part in the fourteen Family Secrets murders he committed with my father. His sentence came out to less than one year per killing.

In explaining the logic behind his sentencing, Judge Zagel stated that, unlike defendants Joe Lombardo and my father, Nick showed remorse and shame for his crimes. Zagel noted that Nick had committed fourteen grisly murders and that the sentence was bound to resonate negatively with the general public and more so with the victims' family members and survivors.

Charlene Moravecek looked over at my uncle and pronounced, "He is the devil." She left the sentencing in tears and fainted outside the courtroom.

Tony Ortiz was crushed that Zagel didn't give Nick more time. He wasn't buying my uncle's professions of remorse. "He shot my dad in the head with a shotgun nine times," Ortiz later told the press. "Did he once apologize to any of the families? No, he did not."

But Zagel, ordinarily viewed as a law-and-order judge,

explained that without revealing firsthand testimony from criminals like my uncle, how could families in the future gain closure by seeing *their* loved ones' killers brought to justice? Zagel reminded the court that Nick, once released, would forever be looking over his shoulder, and he reminded Nick that the Outfit "will not forgive or relent in their pursuit of you."

While a good number of people seethed that Zagel "went easy" on Uncle Nick, I and members of my family had hoped that his time served between 2002 and 2009 would be sufficient to free him. Instead, with a few months shaved off for good behavior, he could be a free man in 2013.

My uncle entered an "open-end" arrangement, which placed his destiny in the hands of Judge Zagel. Part of that agreement was that the states could not prosecute him for any of the murder charges. Otherwise, there was no deal. Zagel could have sentenced him to life, or Nick could have walked away. He got twelve years, seven more years than Sammy "the Bull" Gravano got for cooperating, and the Bull admitted to being involved in killing nineteen people.

It is clear that without our testimony, Operation Family Secrets wouldn't have developed. Yet I'm sure it was extremely difficult for Assistant U.S. Attorney Funk to plead my uncle's case for leniency. He had to have anticipated the unpopular reaction to Uncle Nick's sentence. Yet my uncle's contribution to the case was essential in gaining the convictions of the Outfit's upper echelon, and sent a message that the Outfit would no longer be tolerated.

Prosecutors don't win popularity contests with family, friends, and neighbors by advocating shorter sentences for convicted murderers who cooperate with the Feds. I'm sure Funk struggled with the whole process of speaking on behalf of my uncle. But the public doesn't realize that future defendants need to know that if they come forward and cooperate, there's something in it for them if they're truthful. A deal was a deal, and now it was the government's turn to hold up its end of the bargain. And Funk did not renege on the deal. He told Judge Zagel that the Nicholas Calabrese with whom Funk had many interactions was impossible to square with the cold-blooded and methodical executioner Nick admitted to having once been: my uncle, in short, presented a "walking, talking, breathing paradox."

In the final analysis, I'm happy that I came forward and named my uncle as John Fecarotta's killer. By doing so, I ultimately saved both of our lives. It enabled Nick to atone for his sins and step away from my father and the mob. I and a lot of working-class citizens of Illinois are now free of Frank Calabrese, Sr.'s grasp and of the Outfit. The price of liberty is eternal vigilance. If society is to be free of organized crime and the Outfit, we can't have enablers—politicians, the business community, corrupt cops, and ordinary citizens—who make it possible for organized crime to exist.

With the success of Operation Family Secrets in the history books, Mike Maseth was asked to make a special presentation about the case that would be available for various government functions, conventions, and FBI and law enforcement gatherings. When the FBI held one of its national conferences in 2008, Mike and his colleagues from the Chicago OC squad were invited to give a PowerPoint presentation outlining the entire investigation. To Maseth's surprise, his hard-boiled, seen-it-all audience of law enforcement peers gave an enthusiastic thumbs-up response. When Mike told me about the positive reaction he had received from the presentations, he invited me to be a participant in future sessions. I was intrigued.

My initial reaction was that nobody would be interested in my story. What if people thought I was just a guy who beefed on his father? I wanted to get on with my life. But when Mike called me about a law enforcement conference in California, I decided to give it a try. I sat down with Mike and Luigi and went over the highlights. We put together a tight presentation. At first I was nervous telling my personal story to a roomful of strangers. But then I couldn't believe the response and the empathy we received, especially during the question-and-answer period afterward. It was remarkable. My family and a few of my friends also urged me to tell my story. They felt it was a moving family tale and a story of courage. Yet I didn't feel what I did was courageous. I did it only because it was the right thing to do.

Lisa said something that made a lot of sense. I needed to tell my story because there are people in similar situations, trapped inside their own family secrets. There are people out there who are afraid to stand up and speak up against abusive family situations. They feel as if they're locked in a cage of secrecy, and there's no way out. I believe my story shows there *is* a way out. What is important is that it doesn't have to be the wrong way out.

With my father safely behind bars, I live with both the relief and the regret. Turning against him is something I will live with for the rest of my life. I've never felt good about cooperating. To this day I carry his picture in my wallet. I look at it wishing things could have been different.

It will never be over between us. I know that one day he'll be waiting for me at the gates of heaven or hell, hoping to finish this. And if he becomes a ghost, an angry ghost, he'll be on my doorstep haunting me forever. But at least now he isn't in a position to hurt anyone else or bring any more misery to my family. It's like he said one day in court: "My son, he don't scare easy."

Epilogue

BEHIND THE PICTURE FRAME

On Tuesday, March 23, 2010, thirteen months after my father was sentenced to life plus twenty-five years, a team of U.S. Marshals, FBI agents including Mike Maseth, and a locksmith dropped in for a surprise search at my father's former residence at 14 Meadowood Drive in Oak Brook, catching his wife, Diane Cimino, completely off guard. The warrant prepared by Funk

was served by the marshals. They were looking for hidden compartments containing cash or other valuables.

During the time leading up to the raid, I kept in touch with Mike. I worked with the FBI to help them find my dad's hidden money. The three of us—my brother Kurt, Uncle Nick, and I—independently cooperated. Our reason for wanting to help stemmed from the trial. My dad's defense was that Uncle Nick, Kurt, and I had set him up and conspired to keep him locked up for life so that we could steal his money. We took this seriously and wanted to prove that he was lying.

I received a call from Mike Maseth the day of the search of the Oak Brook home. I told Mike that since the entire basement of the house was paneled, he should pay attention to any pegboard or drywall screws next to a wine rack or behind a framed picture. As the marshals searched the basement, Mike concentrated on other parts of the house. While searching the garage and checking out the cars, he received a text message from one of the marshals who was in the basement.

"Mike, you need to come down here."

When Mike failed to respond immediately, another text arrived from the marshal.

"No. You really need to come downstairs now."

As Mike entered the basement, he saw an X-Box 360 set up in the TV area where my father's kids played their video games. To the left of the television, a framed piece hung on the wall containing approximately half a dozen family photos. After the marshals popped the drywall screws behind the framed piece, they struck pay dirt.

Behind the picture frame was a hollowed-out storage compartment. Inside was a box filled with envelopes containing hundreds of thousands of dollars in cash. In addition, black velvet bags of jewelry and loose diamonds were retrieved. There were guns, one of which was clean and ready-wrapped in cloth. (Whenever we stored guns, we always made sure they were clean so as to be free of any tell-tale fingerprints.) They were what we called "throwaways," 2- and 5-shot pistols, easily concealable in the palm of your hand, that fired .22 long ammo. There were also microcassette recordings my father made. (According to my sources, some politicians were nervous about what was on the tapes.) Ironically, my father had secretly taped his unsuspecting partners whenever he wasn't around to witness firsthand what business was being transacted.

While Mike searched the premises, we kept in touch by cell phone. Hearing about the cash find made sense to me. It reminded me of the times Grandma Sophie used to tell me that whenever Diane needed money, she'd head downstairs to the basement. The money she brought upstairs smelled moldy—or *muffah*—as Sophie would say.

The stash included twenty-seven $1,000 bills dating back to 1928. These bills were last printed in 1945, and while the Federal Reserve stopped circulating them in 1969, they remain legal tender. Since no Federal Reserve Notes have ever been declared invalid, if you had one, technically you could still spend it, which would be foolish because now they are worth between $1,100 to over $2,000 to collectors. (In 1969 President Nixon signed an executive order suspending distribution of high-denomination notes as a way of fighting organized crime, by making it harder to move large amounts of currency.)

After discovering the basement stash, Mike moved upstairs with a marshal to Diane's bedroom, where they encountered a locked rolltop desk, which the locksmith had to open. They found approximately $26,000 in cash in a drawer. This brought the cash total recovered on 14 Meadowood Drive to $728,481. Later that day, the marshal's search uncovered another $110,000 in United States Savings Bonds.

While my father's cash haul was quite dramatic, it didn't match the value of the nearly one thousand pieces of jewelry and diamonds hidden behind the picture frame in the basement. Most of it still had inventory tags. There were expensive watches and fourteen signet and diamond rings, some worth between $30,000 and $50,000. Much of the jewelry was believed to have been purchased by my father or collected as collateral for juice loans. It's doubtful that he was involved in a jewelry heist.

The search for my father's assets marked the first time in Illinois history that restitution had ever been sought for homicide victims. Until now, restitution generally applied to white collar crimes and bank fraud cases.

By the time Operation Family Secrets went to court in the summer of 2007, my father claimed he was penniless and that his sons had stolen vast amounts of his money—totaling millions. Since he declared himself a pauper, the taxpayers footed the bill for his defense. He wasn't the only Family Secrets defendant to plead poverty. Paul Schiro and Twan Doyle did as well.

My father's cry of indigence was not his first time. He played that card during our case in 1997 when he, Uncle Nick, my brother Kurt, and I (in addition to other crew members) pled out. As part of my father's plea, he set up an agreement with Mitch Mars's office wherein my grandmother Sophie would cover his $750,000 fine by signing over her property. The problem was, my father deceived the U.S. Attorney's Office and the taxpayers when they failed to obtain my grandmother's co-signature before my father finalized his deal by pleading guilty and accepting a ten-year federal sentence. According to my father, my grandmother had changed her mind. Still penniless on paper, Mitch Mars and the government collected very little toward my father's fine. Outside of a few dollars collected toward the court costs of our RICO, my father avoided paying his $750,000 fine.

After burning the government previously, my dad was ordered in 2007 to pay restitution based on any assets that could be legally forfeited. The government was able to grab houses and property no matter whose names they were under. My father learned that merely changing the names on deeds and titles wasn't enough to hide his wealth.

Under Judge Zagel's ruling, the families of the defendant's murder victims were entitled to compensation based on the loss of earnings from the family provider. By estimating each victims' earnings potential, the court came up with a figure—$4.5 million—that my father (along with the other defendants) were now required to pay in the form of restitution. However, restitution obligations wouldn't stop there. Once the initial $4.5 million was paid out to the victims' families, the American taxpayers were *next* in line for an *additional* $20 million. No longer was my father viewed as a pauper. All the Family Secrets defendants were now jointly responsible to pay for the murder and mayhem they had participated in over the past thirty-five years.

I understand that people make mistakes. Some choose a life of crime the same way some choose to play sports: as a means to escape poverty, using money to measure and validate their success. I wish my father wasn't one of those people. I often fantasized about sitting with him, watching sports, sharing a pizza, or planning a fishing trip with my brothers Kurt and Nicky, four men out on a "guy" trip together. I know my brothers had a similar wish. Too bad my dad didn't.

In the past, my lifestyle was very different and distorted. Everything revolved around my father and money. Stay in the fast lane. Make money at anyone's expense. Play mind games by getting inside peoples' heads using scare tactics, threats, and coercion. Those days are gone. Instead, I remind myself each day to think differently. Stay on the straight and narrow, do the right thing, and be grateful by accepting life's small victories. Today I am relieved I don't have to put up with my father's intimidation and violence. The control he had over me is no more.

News of the March 2010 raid on my father's hidden stash created a stir within the media. Sixteen days later, three career criminals were arrested outside the Bridgeport, Illinois, compound formerly owned by Angelo "the Hook." Angelo was known as one of the few bosses who lived in the same turf that he controlled.

The three suspects included Jerry Scalise, who had reportedly been at the scene of the 1980 murders of William and Charlotte Dauber. Scalise was arrested on the evening of April 8, 2010, with two other accomplices, Arthur "the Genius" Rachel and Robert "Bobby" Pullia. Scalise and Rachel had previously served twelve years in a U.K. penitentiary for the 1980 heist of 1.5 million English pounds worth of jewelry from Graff's, a ritzy jeweler in the Knightsbridge section of London. Their haul included the fabled Marlborough Diamond, a 26-karat stone that was never recovered.

The recent press made light of the ages of the three: Scalise, 73, Rachel, 71, and Pullia, 69. Dubbed "aging mobsters" and "senior citizens," they wrote flippantly of the arrests with headlines like "Pensioners Arrested for Planning Chicago Bank Robbery." The Feds viewed their intentions in a far more serious light. In the words of the government, "this case involves three career criminals with virtually no legitimate work history who were plotting to use guns and violence to rob armored car personnel and to flee using a van specifically modified so that the men had the ability [to] shoot at anyone approaching." The van's modifications included peep holes drilled for viewing as well as for shooting at police. After their arrests, the three were charged in a 2007 bank robbery in suburban La Grange that netted $120,000. By bugging the trio's van months earlier, the FBI had collected hours of recordings of the men "discussing their violent criminal intentions," which included killing an unnamed Family Secrets witness. (First-chair prosecutor on the Scalise, Rachel, and Pullia caper was Family Secrets prosecutor T. Markus Funk.)

It is not clear what Scalise and his gang's intentions were. It could have been inspired by the FBI's million-dollar haul taken from my father's place two weeks prior, or possibly they were looking for the lost Marlborough diamond inside Angelo's house. Angelo had died in 1999, shortly after serving his sixteen-year sentence in Leavenworth federal penitentiary for the famous $2 million Las Vegas skim uncovered by Operation Strawman during the late 1970s and early 1980s.

Living at Angelo's fortress-like house was his daughter Joann, my brother Kurt's mother-in-law. Once the FBI suspected that the three men were casing the place and were poised to invade the home and endanger its occupants, agents set up twenty-four-hour surveillance outside. Undoubtedly they saw my brother Kurt visit the house many times.

The FBI's fears that the three suspects were planning a home invasion weren't unfounded. A few days before, the FBI watched Scalise and his accomplices, dressed in black clothing, drilling holes outside one of the compound's windows. On Easter Sunday, my mother, who was visiting Joann, noticed a folded newspaper placed on the back lawn outside the window. Leaving a newspaper or a magazine behind at a potential crime scene is an old Outfit trick. Had my mother picked it up, the perpetrators would have known that the scene might have been corrupted, and that the operation needed to be called off. However, my mother disregarded the newspaper, and it remained on the lawn.

The attempted invasion of the LaPietra compound brought up a serious issue for any gangsters still operating within the ailing Outfit, not to mention those currently incarcerated. How safe *are* their families if guys like Scalise and his crew are confident enough to loot the home of a boss and endanger his family while he's sitting in jail or, worse, after his death? You have to wonder, after the FBI foiled Scalise's alleged plans, what Little Jimmy Marcello, Joey "the Clown" Lombardo, or my father were thinking. Has the Outfit lost that much respect that they are now vulnerable to any third-rate shakedown? Worse, are they no longer feared and are mobsters' families now vulnerable to ordinary criminals? While I'm not one to pine for the old days of the Outfit, times sure have changed.

ACKNOWLEDGMENTS

I want to thank my family for understanding why this happened and especially thank my mother and brothers Kurt and Nicky for all that I put them through. I hope they can get on with their lives. I want to thank my ex-wife Lisa for believing in me, and my daughter Kelly Ann and son Anthony for their love and understanding. I love you both with all my heart, and I am thankful to be part of your lives. I want to thank my close friends, who prefer to stay anonymous, for taking the time to be interviewed and provide an insight into the relationship my father and I had. Thank you for verifying what really happened.

The authors are indebted to a number of people that helped make this book possible, starting with the cooperation and support from the dedicated men and women of the FBI, Director Robert S. Mueller; Special Agent in Charge of the Chicago FBI office, Robert D. Grant; FBI agents Royden R. Rice, Michael W. Maseth, John M. Malul, Luigi Mondini, Tracy L. Balinao, Michael B. Hartnett, Christopher J. Mackey, and Neal S. Schiff. We are grateful to an extraordinary group of public servants from the United States Attorney's Office, Northern District of Illinois, led by Patrick J. Fitzgerald, the late Mitch Mars, T. Markus Funk, and former Assistant U.S. Attorney John J. Scully (recently appointed to the Circuit Court of Lake County), who was most helpful in clarifying procedural issues.

We are grateful for the counsel and input received from Professor G. Robert Blakey, University of Notre Dame School of Law, in helping us understand Title IX, USC, 1961–1968 of the RICO laws. Professor Blakey created the RICO legislation that is used by the Department of Justice in the fight against organized crime.

Joining us along the way were former Superintendent of the

Chicago Police Department Joseph DiLeonardi; former Chief of Patrol of the Chicago Police Department James A. Maurer; Tactical Officer James Gochee and his wife, Marge; Detective James Jack (Ret.); John "Bulldog" Drummond; attorneys Marc H. Schwartz, Patrick A. Tuite, Rick Halprin, Harry Slavis, Michael R. Kien, and the late Robert Maheu; and journalists Jim McCough, Dan Moldea, and Michael Robinson. Former gangster Frank Cullotta gave a perspective from the "other side," and thanks also to Robert Cooley.

We owe a debt of gratitude to Ryan Fischer-Harbage, our agent, who gave us direction, passion, and enthusiasm; to Peter Meyer for his calm, steady hand; to Joel Glickman and Jaron Summers; and to retired FBI agents James Wagner, Tom Bourgeois, and Zack Shelton (formerly with the Chicago Organized Crime Squad, who provided history and context).

A tip of the hat goes to the late Frank "Lefty" Rosenthal. The irascible "Lefty" was extremely generous, and we are saddened that he won't be on the journey with us. To the writer extraordinaire Nick Pileggi for his input and guidance, we remain grateful.

A book of this nature could not exist without the cooperation of the many sources who gave interviews on background only. We appreciate your trust. We are beholden to the Random House/Broadway Books team of Diane Salvatore, Charles Conrad, Jenna Ciongoli, Dyana Messina, and David Drake for their passion, their integrity, and their faith in a difficult project.

Paul Pompian would like to thank his wife, Polly Pompian, for her support and love. A heartfelt thanks to a special group whose generosity and friendship won't be forgotten: Roger Golden, attorney and friend who has been there every step of the way; long-time pal David B. Dahl, CPA, who is without peer in his understanding of financial crimes; the courageous Frank Calabrese, Jr.; Ronald J. Lewis, Esq., and his wife, Superior Court Judge Maureen Duffy-Lewis; the David T. Busch and Betty Busch families; the Richard C. and Rita Busch families; Neil and Myra Pompian; Richard Pompian; Mike Ditka, Tom Kenny, Robin McKay, George Laftsidis, and the kind staff at Ditka's Restaurant; the Grotto

Oakbrook Restaurant; Gibson's Restaurant and John Colletti and Steve Lombardo, Joe DeMondo, JC, RD, Esther R. Felsenfeld Brandon, William P. Jacobson, Esq., and John and Nan Burrows, Yilen Pan, P.G. Sturges, Andrew Rigrod, Esq., Chris Andrews, David Bugliari, Michael Vogler, Philip J. Hacker, Dr. Paul Geller, Dr. Jordan Geller, Dr. Barry Neidorf, Dr. Leon Bender, Dr. Lawrence Rivkin, Dr. Saul Rosoff, Dr. Parsa Zadeh, Dr. Myles Zakheim, Al and Lauren Salerno, Robert Fraade, John Herzfeld, Sonjia Brandon, Lois Kaesler, Charmaine Leonetti, Mike and Claudia Uretz, Craig Braun, Robert "Bob" Magee (retired homicide detective), Neil Tardio, Scott Metcalf, John Stecenko, Cherelle George, Jack Gilardi, Michael and Toni Melon, Michael Miller, Jerry and Arlene Jacobius, the late Jacob Applebaum, and my late father and mother, George and Lillian Pompian.

Keith Zimmerman expresses his sincere appreciation to Gladys Zimmerman and to Gladys Phillips, Doris Zimmerman, Steven Rybicki, future writers Callum, Alistair, and Iona Beaton, and to the memory of Joe Zimmerman, Alex Phillips, Oren Harari, and Kinky.

Kent Zimmerman would like to thank family, friends, and colleagues: Deborah Zimmerman, Nitin John Abraham, Doris Zimmerman, Edward Preciado, Lloyd and Tam Senzaki, Naveen and Viniti Abraham, John and Tara Abraham, the Rybickis, Paul Pompian, Scott Waxman, Danny Alberga at Bella Luna, Frank Coconate, and especially Frank "the Man" Calabrese, Jr. (there, now you finally have a nickname!), Lisa Swan, and Kelly Calabrese. A shout-out to all the guys in and around San Quentin's H-Unit, past, present, and future, Laura Bowman Salzsieder, Jill Brown, Paul McNabb, Jack Boulware, Jane Ganahl, and all the writers at Litquake. And to Michael Tolkin, Ron Lantz, John Cappas, Paul and Karen Slavit, Scott and Jan Kokjer, Logan and Noah Miller (twin power), Leslie, Jordan, and Dylan Harari, and Alan Black, too. I miss Jeannie Preciado, Oren Harari, and especially Joe Zimmerman.

About the Authors

Frank Calabrese, Jr., lived in his native Chicago for thirty-nine years. Mentored by his father and brought into the Chicago Outfit at age eighteen, Frank Jr. became a key member of the notorious 26th Street/Chinatown crew led by Angelo "The Hook" LaPietra and his father, Frank Calabrese, Sr. After going to prison, Frank Jr. turned his life around, and through his testimony in the landmark 2007 Family Secrets trial helped the FBI and the U.S. Attorneys bring down his father and the Chicago Outfit. He now resides in Arizona with his ex-wife and two children.

Keith and Kent Zimmerman have co-authored *New York Times* and *London Times* best sellers. They've written books with pop-culture icons like John Lydon of the Sex Pistols, Sonny Barger of the Hells Angels, Alice Cooper, country singing star Trace Adkins, the *American Chopper* Teutul family, *Mythbusters,* and the Monterey Jazz Festival. They also co-wrote the biography of Black Panther Party leader Huey P. Newton and penned two pulp thrillers.

Paul Pompian was born and raised on the South Side of Chicago and came by his interest in the Outfit naturally. Mr. Pompian has produced over fifty motion pictures and television programs. His awards include "The Christopher," the Venice Palm, the Emmy, and the Governors Media award. He's a graduate of Loyola University, Chicago, and The New College School of Law, San Francisco, and lives in Los Angeles with his wife, Polly, and dog, Boss.